Chuck B

make me a
Legend

The
Dream of a Better
Tomorrow

DESTINY IMAGE₀ PUBLISHERS, INC.

P.O. Box 310, Shippensburg, PA 17257-0310

"Speaking to the Purposes of God for This Generation and for the Generations to Come."

This book and all other Destiny Image, Revival Press, MercyPlace, Fresh Bread, Destiny Image Fiction, and Treasure House books are available at Christian bookstores and distributors worldwide.

For a U.S. bookstore nearest you, call 1-800-722-6774.

For more information on foreign distributors, call 717-532-3040.

Reach us on the Internet: www.destinyimage.com.

ISBN 13 TP: 978-0-7684-3985-4

ISBN 13 Ebook: 978-0-7684-8929-3

For Worldwide Distribution, Printed in the U.S.A.

2 3 4 5 6 7 8 9 / 16 15 14 13 12

My Four Leaf Clover

This book is dedicated to my four leaf clover: Mom, Emily, Coree, and Heaven.

Mom, I still miss you every day, and I'm doing my best to value other people, just like you did. My mercy gift, people skills, and work ethic—they came from you, Mom! I've taken the unbearable pain of losing you and have channeled it into my obsession for building a better tomorrow. In discouraging moments, when I feel like I can't take another step, I always hear you cheering me on. Just as I said when I preached your funeral, "I am a prince only because my mom was a queen."

Emily, the wife of my youth, the love of my life, and my best friend of all time. If we didn't have such a high, heavenly calling, I am positive I would run away with you to a secret mountain cottage—the kind of place where people come out only for food once a month. Every time I smile, it's because there is a piece of you beaming from my happy heart. God was brilliant for giving us to each other. You are always beautiful, industrious, faithful, forgiving, perfectly happy, and so many other great things! I have definitely gotten the better end of this deal so far. Thank you for giving me twenty "fairy tale" years. Let's plan on living at least fifty more hilarious, adventurous years of building tomorrow's better world together; raising our children, grandchildren, and great-grandchildren; and doing every amazing activity on our huge bucket list! Thank you for believing in me a million more times than I ever believed in myself.

Coree and Heaven, our greatest achievements of all time. Nothing your mom and I ever do with our lives will come close to comparing with the amazement we feel every time we think about you two!

The way you've sacrificed, and even thrived, in the ever-changing environment you have known since you came into this world—you two inspire us every day! We have always tried so hard not to take your selfless hearts for granted, as you have always amazed us by lending Mom and Dad to everyone else, without hesitation—and neither of you ever complained about it, not even one time. Thank you!

You have had way too much exposure to disgusting church politics, witnessed your mom and dad being hacked to pieces with words by heartless, angry mobs, and you have grown up highly visible to the world, in this all-glass house of ours. Yet somehow, you still love Jesus and His Church with all your hearts! You still care about helping hurting people. I can't wait to see the adults you both have become twenty years from today!

Acknowledgements

My Great Cloud of Witnesses

"Therefore, since we are surrounded by such a great cloud of witnesses, let us throw off everything that hinders and the sin that so easily entangles. And let us run with perseverance the race marked out for us." —Hebrews 12:1 NIV

My life is a result—a sum of many great influences, multiplied with God's grace—and my submission to His great will. Every experience and every relationship, from early childhood to this priceless moment, is worthy of mention. But for the sake of a few trees, some ink, and your time, here are the highlights.

I want to thank my *legendary* mentors, past and present, for blazing a very clear path ahead of me! You have always challenged me, always served me just like Jesus served His disciples, and even now, make me feel like a much bigger champion than I am! Since I've mentioned most of your names throughout the book, and you certainly know who you are, I will save my readers the redundancy of another long list.

Dear Kent Henry, it was on that unforgettable hyper car ride to Stony Creek, in your exceptional prophetic manner; you mined this book from my heart when I didn't even know it was there. You have a rare gift for creating the future in people through your casual words!

To my dear *legendary* business coach, Mike Ferry—you taught me so many foundational principles for success in life and business. The $1,000 a month I paid for your advice was the greatest business investment of my life so far!

I want to thank my *legendary* peers—to all of my pastor, and ministry pals, to the beautiful people of your cheery congregations, and especially to the greatest church family on earth, my very best friends—the *legendary* people of *Destiny Family Center!*

To my past and current leadership teams, and to all of the beautiful people from my fairy tale home community! Especially to those who stood with us during the great divide of 2009. I will never forget you—and neither will God. May He favor you for the rest of your lives—because of your love and loyalty to us. It's really easy to write about *legends*, when I'm surrounded with so many of them. I'm so honored when you call me your pastor and *friend*. Your pronounced hunger for the next great awakening makes you all the living specimens of this project!

In the beginning of everything great, there isn't much of a tangible reward. Here, I want to say thank you to the financial forerunners, who gave to little more than a dream. You gave your hard earned incomes, your luxuries and retirements, and your blood, sweat, and tears—and you stood with us before there was something to gain from our partnership. May God bless you in this life and in the life to come!

To my *legendary* prayer team leader Mary Ferrell, and to the rest of my beloved prayer team—if there is anywhere I want to have favor, it's with people who pray like you pray! This book is the answer to your prayers and mine. In the five years it took me to write it, you created an impenetrable force field of blessing around my life. Sometimes, when I get quiet enough, I can see and hear you praying for me in real-time visions. You make the difference; I owe you my life—thank you!

Thank you Rob Michon, for lifting me back to my feet two years ago, after I had thrown in the towel! I will never forget the exact place I was standing on my patio when you inspired my second wind! Thank you Jonathan Woodard for telling me to write a daily blog—what a difference it's made to so many people—especially to me! Thank you Achim Zahren for cheering so loudly—even though we disagree politically, you are one of my most frenzied fans of all time—and I am yours! Thank you Aswan North, for blazing a pure trail from obscurity to celebrity—right in front of my face! I've learned so much from watching you succeed without violating your spiritual compass. Thank you, Pam Myers, for desiring this book more than any other person; you are the biggest MMAL enthusiast so far.

Thank you, Marcus Maranto, for showing me how to use Microsoft Word like a best-selling author—and for being honest with me about the pathetic-ness of that original first chapter. After I finished crying, I got up and transformed that vague introduction into three very impressive opening chapters!

Thank you Ben Scott for inspiring the world with your astonishing photography and digital artwork! Your highly creative images inspired some of my greatest lines. Thank you Gail Strother for treating me like a fellow author before I was one—your journey inspires me. Thank you Megan Doyle, Marcus Maranto, Kristin Via, Melanie Thomas, Kayla Folsom, and Destiny Image for helping with this historical first edit. You guys polished my manuscript like a team of old-fashioned shoe shiners. I still cannot believe how perfectly every paragraph, line, and word is placed in this book. Your expert touch transformed my passionate message into a classic work of art!

Thank you Kristin Via—for laying your whole life down to serve God as my personal assistant. You have loved my family so extravagantly; it actually makes me feel uncomfortable sometimes. You are the greatest servant I've ever known!

To my rapidly expanding blog and social networking tribe. *Woooo!* You make every second of every day feel just like Christmas morning. I bounce from bed so much earlier than I should, just to read your newest comments. Then, they keep coming to me all day long. I feel like I know every one of you in a "bff" kind of way. One of my favorite things to do in life is write my daily blog, knowing how much it means to so many people! Sometimes, you guys are so over the top with your cheers; I have to wonder if Kristin is paying you to encourage me!

For all those who grew weary on this very long journey, and lost your confidence in us, even though some of you walked away in a time when we really needed your support, I still thank God for the good times we once shared. Hopefully this book will help explain some of the reasoning behind my apparent madness. Maybe it'll even work a few miracles. God bless you for taking part of this journey with us!

To my loving family—I can't imagine how this heavenly calling of mine has been so hard to understand at times. I've done my best to balance my schedule, so that you will always know how special you are to me. To my nephews, nieces, and cousins—you inspire me every day! To my spiritual sons and daughters, too many to list—your love has changed my life forever.

To my dad Chuck, brother Jason, cousin Helen, aunts, uncles, and grandparents still living—you're all the blood I have left and I love you so much!

To my remarkable in-laws—I've thanked God that I married into your family at least several thousand times! To Merle and Millie—thanks for showing me what patience is all about. Hopefully the investment of love and mercy you gave me in those early days has paid off well. I love your daughter, because she is so much like the two of you. Merle, I loved you as a son loves his father and I miss you something terrible—you are the man I want my son to become!

To my departed *legends*—Mom, Hon, Momma, Tuff, Merle, Glenden, and Rocky. I talked to each of you about this book, and I so wanted you to read it. I tried to finish before you died! And now five years later, you have all gone to Heaven. It was my highest honor to lead six of you to Jesus. I can hear you cheering for me all the time. Your little Chucky authored his first book—and this is only the start of a million great things I am going to do with my life. I will run my race as well as I can run it—then I will rest with you someday soon!

Finally, one more time, to my dearest Emily, Coree, Heaven, Abby Codrea, and Cole Moore. I didn't write this book alone—we wrote it together! We lived way below our potential means these past five years, and you guys never once made me feel like doing something more immediately rewarding. Emily, thank you handing me the best thoughts of this book on our daily distance runs! You are a million times more brilliant then I am!

Wow, this took longer than I promised. But this is my first book, and I really wanted to thank quite a few people. There are so many others I would love to mention here, but if I started listing names, you'd be reading for another 50 pages! So please be thankful I kept it general and please remember my friends in your prayers. Ask God to bless them forever, as well as those I could not mention here. God bless you all!

Endorsements

There is something inside each of us that yearns to make a difference. Yet day after day, year after year, we find ourselves settled into mediocrity. Chuck Balsamo skillfully dissects the forces that keep us where we are, then stirs our hearts to become the legends we were created to be. *Make Me A Legend* is full of profound revelation, inspiration, and motivation. Finally, a book that will not only challenge you to soar, but will give you the tools for the journey as well. *Make Me A Legend* is an absolute must-read for all that have thought, *Is this really all there is?*

GAIL L. STROTHER
Author of *Appoint Us A King*
www.appointusaking.com

Mind blowing! In one minute I was holding my side and laughing my head off, and then I was on my knees praying for the next great awakening! A perfect mixture of humor and high persuasion.

RICHARD HOLMES, Lead Pastor
Trinity Harvest Church
Pikeville, Kentucky

This is God's NOW message, parachuted from the heavens. Pick it up!

REN JONES
The Ren Jones Coaching Group
www.Coachren.com
Cincinnati, Ohio

Make Me A Legend is a once in a lifetime book that will ignite deep hope in every reader. This hope will fuel your desire for seeing and believing in destiny again. You'll realize that there really is time to yet fulfill it.

These pages are so personal and passionate; it will move you to new and higher places of change and caring. From the very first chapter **Beauty is Sleeping** . . . an awakening begins to happen. In the chapter **Get A Dream** . . . fresh vision will sweep over you that it's never to late to begin. And then a new understanding of your value and importance will unfold as you read **Untame Yourself**.

It is rare that a book could overcome so much of the negative in our lives, while at the same time setting a new course for **Tomorrow's Great Hope**.

This book will be good for your heart and illuminating to your mind. Don't delay, don't over think it, just pick it up, and take it in and go to new horizons today.

KENT HENRY, Worship Leader

Kent Henry Ministries

Chesterfield, Missouri

Make Me A Legend is a manifesto to the soul. Empowering, encouraging, engaging and challenging—from the creative, inspirational spirit of a true leader. Read it and LIVE!

DAVID FRECH, Founding Pastor

Church of the Harvest

Olathe, Kansas

Chuck Balsamo won't stop praying, preaching and writing until an epic spiritual tsunami engulfs the world. As you read this book, watch out—the tsunami may start with you!

JIM BUCHAN, Senior Staff Writer

Inspiration Ministries (INSP Channel)

Charlotte, North Carolina

Make Me A Legend is a prophetic message that carries the potential to shatter the religious norms that have confined the body of Christ to a small-minded existence and a diminishing impact in our world! As one of Chuck's mentors, I have witnessed his exodus from obscurity to legendary, knowing the day would come when his voice would be released to the nations. Chuck Balsamo writes with a raw passion, spiritual insight, and humble transparency that will make him one of the leading voices for the supernatural move that

God has begun in these days. If you are ready to be awakened to the legendary potential that's been lying dormant within you, then what you hold in your hands is the wake up call for which your spirit has been crying out! *Make Me A Legend* is not just a book; it's the beginning of a movement!"

MARION DALTON, Founding Pastor & Visionary Leader
Bethel Harvest Church
Lexington, Kentucky

Chuck Balsamo is one of the most passionate men of God I know and I believe his book, *Make Me A Legend* is an eye opening revelation. The Prophet Joel declared, 'your young men shall see visions.' I know Chuck Balsamo has seen a vision that is attached to practical keys that will release legendary results. For the last forty years I have been in full time ministry and the prophetic has been the office and gifting that God has honored me to be used by the Holy Ghost in. This book has that corporate prophetic anointing on it that will cause radical changes in individuals, churches and communities. I encourage the strong in heart to take the time to read *Make Me A Legend*!

DR. TIM BAGWELL, Senior Pastor
Word of Life Christian Center
Lone Tree, Colorado

Make Me A Legend by my friend Chuck Balsamo is loaded with insight! An inspiration for anyone who has ever 'Hit the wall' in their walk with God.

DR. DOUGLAS J. WINGATE, President and Founder
Life Christian University
Tampa, Florida

This book is the next spiritual shot-heard-around-the-world! Masterfully written, highly provocative—a must read for all who long for a better tomorrow.

CHRISTOPHER L. WHETZEL, Founding Pastor
Believers Victory Center
Moorefield, West Virginia

Contents

Preface by Coree Balsamo 15

Foreword by Heaven Balsamo. 17

Introduction   Tomorrow's Better World 19

Chapter 1   Beauty Is Sleeping. 21

Chapter 2   My Greatest Spiritual Fantasy. 31

Chapter 3   The Legend Begins. 45

Chapter 4   Tomorrow's Great Hope 61

Chapter 5   Exposed to the Bigger Cause. 73

Chapter 6   Hurry Up and Find Rock Bottom! 89

Chapter 7   Earn Your Keep 103

Chapter 8   Get a Dream 119

Chapter 9   Build an Extravagant Foundation: *Why?*. 133

Chapter 10   Build an Extravagant Foundation: *How?*. 145

Chapter 11   Celebrate Your Progress 167

Chapter 12   Stop Being So Human 185

Chapter 13   Put on Your Legends Cloak. 197

Chapter 14   Get Connected: Mentors, Peers, and Apprentices 213

Chapter 15   Bow Lower as You Climb Higher. 233

Chapter 16   Take Your Heart Up With You 249

Chapter 17   Untame Yourself 271

Preface

Hello, I'm Coree Balsamo, the son of an amazing dad—Chuck Balsamo, author of this book. Just for the record, I'm also the son of an amazing mom—Emily Balsamo, dad's wife of 20 years and my best friend of all time. I'm writing to you from Washington DC, where I'm attending the Art Institute for web design and interactive media. In the next 5 years I hope to receive my college degree, launch a very successful Web Design Company, purchase (or build) a country house, and be happily married—possibly with children.

I know this sounds like a high goal with a short deadline, but I'm not pulling it out of the air. My dad has made me an expert at seeing God's dream, setting achievable checkpoints, overcoming obstacles, and turning today's plans into tomorrow's realities. He has always taught me that no star is too high to reach.

In a society of parents and leaders who say, "Do what I say, but not what I do," I thank God for a true role model like my father. Especially over the past few years, I have come to realize how privileged I am to be raised by the man who's inspiring the rest of the world. I know this sounds crazy, but some people act like my dad is part of the royal family. While they appreciate the fortune of short visits and special moments, I appreciate a lifetime of being his son. While his teachings are rare and priceless, his example is even more rare. Just like the eagle learns to soar through the process of imprinting, I have learned to soar by soaring with my father.

One thing that I admire the most about Chuck Balsamo is how dedicated he is to his work while still making time to spend with his family. He is the master of balancing a picture perfect life. I can't believe how much he loves my mom, my sister, and me. Because of this, I know how to be a good husband, father, and provider when I begin the journey of having my own family.

Through my dad I've learned so much about God. My spiritual foundation is unshakable. He's taught me to never resort to the negative things in life. He's taught me to never let my own problems keep me from reaching out to other people. He has always been there for anyone who has needed his help. I can't tell you the amount of times I've woken up in the mornings to the sight of my dad pouring out his life to a confused, suffering person. Again and again, I've watched him give away money he doesn't have. He has inspired me, to one day be, the "Legend" that he is.

Chuck Balsamo has always been there for my friends—and they love him for it! His influence in their lives is really hard to believe. So many people consider *my* dad *their* spiritual father and best friend. They say he's the coolest dad in the universe because of his spastic attitude and sense of adventure—and because he's fanatically interested in what they are doing. When they go through hard times, they always come to him for advice and he always lifts them back to their feet. He has taught all of us to dream big. The bigger the better! He applauds our achievements and oftentimes makes a huge deal over very little things. Even when we know that he's exaggerating our greatness, we still love it when he cheers for us and joins our dreams—as if you would think they were dreams of his own.

If it seems like I'm exaggerating, please know that every word is coming 100% from my heart. My dad isn't perfect, but he's never been a hypocrite. What people see in public is exactly who he is in private. When he makes mistakes, he apologizes to us in humility. This frees the rest of us to live boldly without the fear of failure. Whenever I've made stubborn, wrong choices, he's always navigated me back onto the right path for my life. No matter what I've chosen to do with my future he has always supported me. My dad is merciful. He's never shut me out. He's never let me down.

If my dad's writings have even a slight chance at giving you the heart he's given me, then this book is worth a hundred million dollars! Over the past five years, I have watched him pour his heart and soul into this project. He's prayed many times over every word in this book. I believe that *Make Me A Legend* comes from God, through my dad, to the world. As cliché as it might sound, this book will change your life forever!

—COREE JOHNATHAN BALSAMO, son of a *legend*

Foreword

Hello world changer! My name is Heaven Balsamo and I am the luckiest girl alive because my father and best friend is Chuck Balsamo. I am currently 19 years old and attending the Art Institute of Washington, DC for my degree in baking and pastry. Cooking and making cakes, have been passions of mine ever since I was a child. I hope one day to have my own bakery and make amazing cakes for people. This passion for high achievement came from my dad, Chuck Balsamo, author of this great book!

If there is one thing I could say about my dad, it is that he cares more about people than any other person I have met. In every decision I have ever made in my life, my dad has been on the front row as my BIGGEST fan. He is the person who has taught me to set worthwhile goals, to trust God, and to fearlessly reach for the best opportunities to succeed in everything I do. (I wish I could tell you about my mom too, because she is the greatest woman I've ever known—straight from Proverbs 31, with the heart and character of Ruth.)

In May of 2011, I was nominated to compete in the Capital One Bank's Sweet Eats Challenge hosted by the Washington National Zoo. The judges for this competition were famous Chefs from Hell's Kitchen and Top Chef. My team won second place that night! At the event, there was gourmet food to sample from 100 great Washington restaurants—more food than any one person could eat in ten years time! As you can imagine, the entry tickets were very expensive, so I didn't think anyone would be there to support me.

Then, the day before the competition, Dad called to say that mom had surprised him with a ticket and then he surprised her back—and they were both coming! Of course, I asked him not to spend that kind of money, and he insisted that he knew how much it meant to me, and that he and mom would do anything to be there. I had amazing confidence during the entire competition because I saw that, instead of enjoying all the sights and flavors, my dad chose to stay right there and watch me make my cake—once again, as my biggest fan!

Dad's love for everyone is amazing! I could write a book twice the size of the one you're holding, filled with stories about all the great and selfless things my father has done to help people succeed. From the way he ran his business, to the way he leads our church, to the things he writes in his inspirational daily blogs, to all of the encouraging messages he sends to people in his social network, to actually letting other teenagers and young adults live with us—Dad wakes up every morning not thinking about himself, but about how he can help everyone else.

Are you getting a picture of how big his heart is for YOU? This is why he *had* to write *Make Me A Legend*. He has a beautiful dream about a better tomorrow! Because of his brilliant teachings, his dream is an achievable dream. His dream gives *so much* new hope to my friends and me! Through his guidance and because of his book, we feel very optimistic about the future. It seems like Chuck Balsamo might be starting a movement with this dream! And for his sake and ours, I hope it happens.

For the past five years, I have watched my dad set every word and every sentence perfectly in its spot—with so much prayer. There were times when we all wondered if he would finish in this lifetime. It's releasing now, at the perfect time—when our world needs it most! I believe this book is definitely creating the legends of today and tomorrow! It's going to make a difference far greater than anything my dad has ever hoped for.

Chuck Balsamo has given me the tools to be the greatest I can be. Now, through *Make Me A Legend*, he is doing the same for you! It is easy to fail when you don't know where you are going, but your dreams are very possible when you learn the godly principles sited here. I want to thank my dad for being my biggest frenzied fan and my greatest cheerleader! I want to thank my dad also for pouring out the last several years of his life, turning *Make Me A Legend* into a reality. I invite you to read my dad's book and really let it change your life in the same way my dad has changed mine. God bless you all.

—HEAVEN ASHLEE BALSAMO, daughter of a *legend*

Tomorrow's Better World

I have a son and a daughter, both teenagers, both high school graduates, both off to college—at the same time. These are terrible, wonderful days for my wife and me. On the one hand, we wallow in the grief of losing our two best friends; and on the other hand, we are excited as they leap from our safe nest and into the air—with confidence, character, and faith!

Sometimes I wonder, *What if my life ended next week in unexpected tragedy? What if I had just seven more days with the children of my legacy? How would they get through future crises if I wasn't there to hold them when they cried? What if I wasn't there to guide them out of confusion, or make them smile and laugh—or rave their names on life's big days?*

If I did know my life was almost over, I would draft a farewell—but what would I say to them? I would study their dreams and predict their biggest obstacles, and seal my imperative lessons in a book. Then I would fly away with a smile, knowing that my dear Coree and Heaven would always dream big, live bold, and make a difference—and that their *legendary* lives would echo in eternity!

Even though I plan to stay here as long as I can, I have written my departure letter—you are holding it. A loving father's legend manifesto for his young adult children. It's my billionaire's inheritance—my cherished values, and my God-sized dream! *Make Me a Legend* presents the unmitigated truth about this modern civilization—wandering in confusion and mourning in the shadows of a post-Christian era. It predicts an emergent *legend* tribe of epic proportions—men and women who will lay everything on the line for the greatest ambition of all time!

For my international friends, you will notice that a few very specific messages are written about my homeland, the United States of America. That's because I know our condition far better than I know the condition of other countries. So as you read my plea to fellow Americans, I hope you will feel compelled to pray for us as you care and pray for your own people. Every nation needs the kind of immediate, widespread, positive change this book suggests!

My desire is that this hyper message of hope will possess the hearts and minds of my children, family, and friends, and millions of others, especially you—so that perhaps, a hundred years from today, we will be remembered as the *legends* of a millennia, and creators of *tomorrow's better world.*

Chapter 1

Beauty Is Sleeping

How can you see into my eyes like open doors? Leading you down into my core where I've become so numb. Without a soul my spirit's sleeping somewhere cold, until you find it there and lead it back home.

—AMY LEE of the band Evanescence

ACCORDING TO THE WORLD ATLAS...

There are currently 193 countries[1] housing 6.9 billion[2] humans on this earth. With more than 6,900 known languages[3] and an infinite range of cultural variations, we are remarkably different. Despite this vast diversity, there is a common and growing restlessness tying us together as one unified species. I am alluding to our profound, universal desperation for some sort of awakening. We're not sure how it happened, but this human race of ours is all screwed up right now. With our accumulated intelligence, we have distorted the pure experience of life. Thinking ourselves to be wise, we are becoming fools—until life for so many people today is pointless and empty. God, really—save this planet!

More and more of us gather in private around this imperative theme. We rendezvous in coffee houses and office break rooms, on cell phones and over the Internet; we cannot seem to sufficiently curb our widespread craving. From nearly every city worldwide and throughout the countrysides, there is a rising band of restless souls sniffing for a roadway back—all the way back to the bygone simplicities of yesteryear. Even though we can't seem to agree about which path will lead us out, we all want something or someone from this world or another to break our curse and wake us up!

BEAUTY *IS* SLEEPING

Everyone knows the Disney classic *Sleeping Beauty* and how the king and queen's beautiful daughter, Aurora, pricked her finger on the spindle of a spinning wheel and fell into a deep sleep because of a curse. The slumber fell on Aurora's sixteenth birthday just as the evil witch Maleficent pronounced it. The only way to break the spell was for Aurora to receive her first true love's kiss.

There were three good fairies in this story: mistress Flora, mistress Fauna, and mistress Merryweather. To prevent heartbreak in the King and Queen, the three fairies flew around the kingdom, putting everyone to sleep until Aurora could be cured—everyone but a prince.

There was a promising young prince who was supposed to marry the princess someday, but the princess fell asleep before this could happen. The Prince's name was Philip.

Immediately following Aurora's slumber, Maleficent captured Philip and hurried him to the forbidden mountains before he could break the spell with a first true love's kiss.

With the help of the three good fairies, Prince Phillip escaped from the witch's evil tower. He used his magical sword to cut through a mystical growth of thick, thorny bushes (caused by a spell) and defeated Maleficent, who had transformed herself into a dragon.

Philip ran all the way to the castle of Aurora, approached the fair princess, bent down, and kissed her. Aurora opened her eyes, the curse was broken— Prince Phillip had awakened his princess! Everyone in the kingdom also awoke, and Princess Aurora and Prince Phillip appeared together, walking down the stairs in the castle. And the storybook closes with the perfect words of every good fairy tale, "And they lived happily ever after."

FAIRY TALE CLASSIC OR SPOT-ON PROPHECY?

You and I know many real-life sleeping beauties, just like the young princess from this fairy tale classic—potential legends now lying motionless as under a devilish curse. Sometime around our sixteenth birthday, if we are not guarded, it happens to everyone. The curse whispers to us and woos us from the shadows until we cannot refuse it a second longer; just one slight touch, and *the slumber rushes in!* Our curious little fingers prick against that spinning wheel. And then we sleep—for years, decades, or even a lifetime!

In *Sleeping Beauty*, I see the great love story between God and humans. In that first darkest moment of all eternity, as Adam (the first created human) recklessly pressed his teeth down into that enchanting, forbidden fruit—just one taste from that tree of the knowledge of good and evil—humankind was severed from righteousness, left hopelessly barricaded from everything warm and good. The creature was cut from the lifeline of its Creator; the child was orphaned from the Father. From that maleficent day forward, every human soul came into the earth smothered in a cloak of darkness. Each new generation took its turn groaning and thrashing, dreaming of a day when the Prince would come!

All the ancient prophets promised us a great Prince. One by one, they stretched out their surrendered arms and pointed their daring fingers deep into their paled horizons to a day they described as "the fullness of time," when God would come to us as a Prince. Line upon line, precept upon precept, here a little, there a little, the prophets meticulously depicted how the mightiest One of all would kneel before us, and in one unsurpassable act of humility—with the greatest kiss of all time—He would bring us back to life!

Just as predicted, that moment opened like the blossoming of a rare flower. Every living thing from first creation to last infinity pulsed in chorus with that central act of Love! It was 2,000 years ago when the Prince made His move. He walked away from all the splendors of His highest Heaven. He braved His way down into the decrepit regions of this dying earth, cloaked Himself with perfect humility, and lived the necessary sinless life. The Prince suffered for His princess, paying her ransom—His life for hers. All by Himself, He absorbed the curse of her fallen nature. He gave a love without bounds—it transcended time. He is the Prince who rescued His princess and every (willing) hopeless person before Him, with Him, and after Him—with a first true love's kiss!

In his world famous worship song "How He Loves," John Mark McMillian sings,

He is jealous for me,
Loves like a hurricane, I am a tree,
Bending beneath the weight of his wind and mercy.

When all of a sudden,
I am unaware of these afflictions eclipsed by glory,
And I realize just how beautiful You are,
And how great Your affections are for me.

And oh, how He loves us so,
Oh, how He loves us,
How He loves us all...

We are His portion and He is our prize,
Drawn to redemption by the grace in His eyes,
If grace is an ocean, we're all sinking.
So Heaven meets earth like a sloppy wet kiss,
And my heart turns violently inside of my chest,
I don't have time to maintain these regrets,
When I think about, the way...

He loves us,
Whoa! how He loves us,
Whoa! how He loves us,
Oh how He loves.
Yeah, He loves us,
Whoa! how He loves us,
Whoa! how He loves us,
Whoa! how He loves.[4]

I'm positive that *Sleeping Beauty* is so much more than a pleasant bedtime story for the kids. It is a prophecy of surprising precision coming true! Look around, there's no movement. Listen, there's no sound. The whole world is sleeping—the zombies are everywhere waiting for resuscitation! So I pray day and night, really I do—that God will send His Prince to every sleeping person, that He will send you and me in the Spirit of His Prince, that *we should kiss the sleepers and wake them!*

A SONG FOR THIS GENERATION

Alternative rock band, Evanescence, sings about a sleeping generation in their hit song "Bring Me to Life." The words of the song evoke a deep cry that makes me wonder, *Did singer-songwriter Amy Lee know she wasn't just ruling the music charts and selling lots of albums? Did she ever whisper to God in the middle of the night, wondering over the prophetic likelihood of that song?* I'd love to know! *Did she ever feel that she was sensing something—a desperate cry from the souls of people to the ears of God?* Every time I hear the song, it's as if I'm taken on a dreamlike adventure. In 3 minutes and 56 seconds of listening, a muscular hand rips me from the surface of my habitation into the orbit above my head. For a few of the most concentrated heartbeats of my life, I look upon the human race with a God's-eye view!

Every time I hear Amy Lee sing her prophecy, I spread my wings as wide as they will stretch; and from a few hundred miles up, I look down, lean in, shut my eyes, and plummet to the ground with the blazing wake of a giant comet. At just the moment it seems that I am doomed to a certain terminal impact, the wind inflates my wings, turning me at just thirty feet from the ground! And I fly at warp speeds across the face of the earth—all 197 million square miles of it—through every street, house, park, court, and square of every city and nation. Somehow I'm able to see them all; I burn straight through their eyes and into the sleepy, soulish centers of 6.9 billion humans! What a rush!

But when the music fades, I am left alone, my heart bleeding—beauty is sleeping and, *O God, she won't wake up!* After you read the following lyrics, please download the live video version of this Evanescence hit from the Internet, close your eyes (or keep them open) and listen with your heart, as Amy Lee wails out a message—up from the entranced heart of sleeping Aurora to the hopeful ears of her loving prince! Perhaps as you do this, it will happen— that you too will be taken on this same adventure.

BRING ME TO LIFE[5]

How can you see into my eyes like open doors?
Leading you down into my core where I've become so numb.
Without a soul, my spirit's sleeping somewhere cold
Until you find it there and lead it back home.

(Wake me up.) Wake me up inside.
(I can't wake up.) Wake me up inside.

(Save me.) Call my name and save me from the dark.
(Wake me up.) Bid my blood to run,
(I can't wake up.) Before I come undone.
(Save me.) Save me from the nothing I've become.

Now that I know what I'm without, you can't just leave me.
Breathe into me and make me real.
Bring me to life.

Bring me to life.
(I've been living a lie. There's nothing inside.)
Bring me to life.

Frozen inside without your touch, without your love, darling.
Only you are the life among the dead.

(All of this time I can't believe I couldn't see,
Kept in the dark, but you were there in front of me.)
I've been sleeping a thousand years, it seems,
I've got to open my eyes to everything.
(Without a thought, without a voice, without a soul,
don't let me die here. There must be something more.)
Bring me to life.

Bring me to life.
(I've been living a lie. There's nothing inside.)
Bring me to life.[6]

CAN THESE BONES LIVE AGAIN?

Once upon a time, thousands of years ago, there lived a man—a prophet. He was no ordinary man, not even an ordinary prophet. He had an astonishing gift for seeing visions of the future. Today, we might put this kind of man away in a mental institution for the better part of his life!

They called him Ezekiel. He was a loner who spent an outrageous number of hours meditating on the Law of Moses and praying to God. Sometimes when this prophet opened his eyes, he could not tell if he was standing on the physical earth or if he had been translated into another dimension. He time-traveled in prayer onto the landscapes of a future horizon and, therefore, spoke some of the most riveting messages in the entire Bible. His prophecies always happened exactly as he said they would.

Ezekiel gave a few very bizarre prophetic illustrations. One time he lay on his left side for 390 days as a sign of bearing the sins of the Northern Kingdom of Israel (see Ezek. 4:8-10), then another forty days as a sign of bearing the sins of the Southern Kingdom of Judah. And for the entire 430 days, he ate food cooked over a fire fueled by dried cow dung—he did all of this under the direct command of God, to predict the impending scarcity of provision, fuel, and every necessity of life, which the Jews would experience during a siege of Jerusalem (see Ezek. 11-16). History verifies how every detail of this prophecy turned out just as Ezekiel said it would.

It happened one day in the not so ordinary life of this not so ordinary prophet that perhaps Ezekiel was worshiping the Lord or he was meditating on the Law of Moses or he was praying for God to come and awaken his nation. Ezekiel doesn't really mention what he was doing that morning or where he was doing it. Maybe that's because everything else happening in his life at that moment now seemed miniscule in comparison with what came next. It's been kept preserved for almost 2,600 years in the holy words of the hallowed prophet, one of the most famous open visions of all time. I now present to you straight from the pages of the Holy Bible—Ezekiel's Dry Bones Valley!

The Lord took hold of me [Ezekiel], and I was carried away by the Spirit of the Lord to a valley filled with bones. He led me all around among the bones that covered the valley floor. They were scattered everywhere across the ground and were completely dried out. Then He asked me, "Son of man, can these bones become living people again?"

"O Sovereign Lord," I replied, "You alone know the answer to that."

Then He said to me, "Speak a prophetic message to these bones and say, 'Dry bones, listen to the word of the Lord! This is what the Sovereign Lord says: Look! I am going to put breath into you and make you live again! I will put flesh and muscles on you and cover you with skin. I will put breath into you, and you will come to life. Then you will know that I am the Lord.'"

So I spoke this message, just as He told me. Suddenly as I spoke, there was a rattling noise all across the valley. The bones of each body came together and attached themselves as complete skeletons. Then as I watched, muscles and flesh formed over the bones. Then skin formed to cover their bodies, but they still had no breath in them.

Then He said to me, "Speak a prophetic message to the winds, son of man. Speak a prophetic message and say, 'This is what the Sovereign Lord says: Come, O breath, from the four winds! Breathe into these dead bodies so they may live again.'"

So I spoke the message as He commanded me, and breath came into their bodies. They all came to life and stood up on their feet—a great army.

Then He said to me, "Son of man, these bones represent the people of Israel. They are saying, 'We have become old, dry bones—all hope is gone. Our nation is finished.' Therefore, prophesy to them and say, 'This is what the Sovereign Lord says: O my people, I will open your graves of exile and cause you to rise again. Then I will bring you back to the land of Israel. When this happens, O my people, you will know that I am the Lord. I will put my Spirit in you, and you will live again and return home to your own land. Then you will know that I, the Lord, have spoken, and I have done what I said. Yes, the Lord has spoken!'" (Ezekiel 37:1-14)

RAISE YOUR HAND

Do you ever wonder if God is flying around the planet looking for His next Ezekiel? If He is, my hand is up! I hope yours is too. I'm serious! I want the Lord to *take hold of me* again and again! More than anyone can know, I want Him to *carry me away by the Spirit of the Lord to a valley filled with bones.*

I want Him to fly me all around the bones covering the valley floors of my generation! I want Him to show me the real condition of these bones as they are right now scattered everywhere across the ground and completely dried out. And I want to hear Him ask me, just like He asked Ezekiel, *"Son of man, can these bones become living people again?"*

I want to respond to Him, just as Ezekiel did, "O Sovereign Lord, You alone know the answer to that!" Then I will say, "O Your Majesty, I am here for You—I'll fly over the deadest places, and prophesy to the driest bones; I will awaken Your winds from the four corners of the earth; and *we* will awaken the legends together!"

Then maybe His Majesty will say to me, "Go ahead, Chuck Balsamo! Speak to these dry bones; tell them about the next great awakening. Prophesy to them saying, 'Dry people, *listen* to the word of the Lord! This is what the Sovereign Lord says: Look! I am going to put breath into you and make you live again! I will put flesh and muscles on you and cover you with skin. I will put breath into you, and you will come to life. Then you will know that I am the Lord.'"

Then, without a second's hesitation, I will pack my lungs tight with His creative powers, tilt back my head, open my mouth as wide as possible, and breathe out His passion like the winds of Heaven! Just as it happened when Ezekiel spoke, I too will hear a thunderous rattling noise over my family, friends, and people from around the world I have never met before; sometimes so loudly I may not be able to hear myself speak!

Against all odds, the spiritual bones of a multitude of people will connect together all at once until they are standing perfectly upright before their Creator—a vast sea of bare skeletons. As I watch, I will see great, hulking muscles and fleshy tissue forming over each of them. Finally, God will cover them entirely, as skin covers the human body!

And after all this, I want to hear God say to me, "Don't stop now, little guy; keep giving the message! Speak it again! Shout out to the winds, son of man! Tell the winds, 'This is what the Sovereign Lord says: Come, O breath, from the four winds! Breathe into these dead bodies so they may live again.'"

As I speak every message just as He commands me, I want to hear and feel the sound and force of *ruach* blowing across my eager audiences. *Ruach* is the Hebrew word used to describe the divine wind—the Spirit-wind of God that imparts divine, living properties to everything it blows over.

Dear God, I want to see millions of us breathing in Your divine wind until we are bouncing up and down on our feet—the most legendary army of all time! My hand is raised, so I know that I'm going to see all of this and more, "*For the eyes of the Lord range throughout the earth to strengthen those whose hearts are fully committed to Him...*" (2 Chron. 16:9 NIV).

Dear reader, is your hand raised yet? Come on, hurry up! Get both hands up in the air; wave to the heavens like you're flagging down a rescue plane from a stranded island! Really do this, right now—wherever you are sitting at this moment. Close your eyes and raise your hands. Now hold them up for a minute or two. Don't hesitate! If you're lying down, roll over to your knees and then stand to your feet, scale the nearest high mountain ridge, get up on your tiptoes, and wave like there's no tomorrow! *"Hey, God, over here—pick me!"*

I am absolutely certain about this; life is so much bigger than a search for the next *American Idol!* His Majesty, the Ruler of the everlasting universe, is right now searching for a volunteer—one hungry heart, one wild and adventurous soul! Now is the time for His followers to stop being so timid about the future—it's time to stop kicking cans and looking down on ourselves. I believe more than anything that God is waiting to hear something from you. So come on, even if you don't fully mean it yet, say it once just for fun and see what happens—just a simple, opening prayer, *"Dear God, make me a legend!"*

Coming Up

So far, I've given you a spot-on picture of today's spiritually slumbering world. Maybe my words are nothing more than an artistic rendering of the things you've already perceived. That's the goal—to give you the message you're already looking for! Hopefully, now you're soaring with the wonder of what all of this means to you, and how you might become a pioneer for tomorrow's better world!

I offer you the surprise of what can be, the marvel of a brighter day. Maybe, even if it was only for a blink or two, you actually saw the entire world sedated under a spell, lovesick for a Prince. I've hinted at the possibility of a worldwide spiritual awakening. In Chapter 2, I'm going to tell you all about my one great spiritual fantasy—the greatest awakening of all time!

Chapter 2

My Greatest Spiritual Fantasy

"Is there a chance? Obviously there's a chance. You never want to eliminate the chance. But it's a long shot."
—JIM McCROSSIN, professional ice hockey coach[1]

LET'S DREAM A DREAM TOGETHER

Let's gaze forward with great eagerness into the not too distant future and behold together the limitless potential of what can be. Let's fantasize about you and me living to see *the greatest spiritual awakening of all time!*

This is my one great spiritual fantasy. But it's more than a fantasy! I'm positive this dream is perfectly within our reach. Perhaps it has already begun, is just now beginning, or it is just about to begin! In a time when it seems like family values, the effectiveness of the church, the pure worship of God, and character, standards, and morals are all things of the past, we must keep reminding ourselves, *"where sin abounded, grace did much more abound"* (Rom. 5:20b KJV).

On April 11, 1988, David Wilkerson, the dear departed pastor of Times Square Church in New York, opened his Sunday morning sermon with these commanding words:

> The New Testament church was born in a blaze of glory. The Holy Ghost came down upon it with fire, and the first Christians spoke with tongues and prophesied. They experienced smiting conviction, and multitudes were converted. They broke out on the right and on the left and were greatly enlarged. The

fear of God fell upon them and upon all who saw them. There were signs, wonders, and miracles. The dead were raised. Fearless evangelists went everywhere preaching the Word. Jails could not hold them. Storms could not drown them. When their possessions were seized, they continued to rejoice. When they were stoned, hanged, burned, or crucified, they went out singing and praising God. It was a triumphant church, unafraid of Satan, irreverent toward idols, unmoved by plagues or persecution. It was a blood-washed church, living and dying in victory.

What is the last-hour church going to be like? How will the church go out in its final hour? Will it go out as a fat, prosperous, self-seeking church, counting heads, getting out the vote? Will it be just a handful of true believers holding on, watching death and apostasy eat away at it like a cancer? Will the last-day church live in dread and fear as AIDS and other plagues ravage the masses? Will fewer and fewer overcome the world? Will coldness and apostasy leave it weak, mocked, and powerless? Will the church go out of this age full of hypocrisy, with great praise, worship, and prayer meetings where unclean hands and impure hearts offer strange fire?

To be sure, there is going to be a great falling away or apostasy. There will be spiritual harlotry on all sides. Because sin abounds, the love of many will grow cold. There will come deceivers, teaching doctrines of demons. People will have itching ears and will flock to hear soft preaching. Deceptions will get so bad that even the elect will be tested severely.

But the church of Jesus Christ is not going out with a whimper or a limp. It is going out victorious, with joy unspeakable, riding a river of peace. It is going out in freedom from all bondage, with its foot on Satan's neck. And every member of this true church will live and die without fear. The tempter's power will be broken. Christians will be holy and will tear down idols. They will be just as strong in the Lord as the first Christians.[2]

LIGHT ALWAYS SHINES IN THE DARK

Sure, some of David Wilkerson's language is dated, especially since we're reading this message more than 20 years after he preached it. It's a bit preachy for some, but it was jolting on the morning it thundered within the walls of that prime, moving New York City church. Even if you don't fully appreciate the excessiveness of Wilkerson's passion, there's no denying the solid truth presented in his message.

There is always time for one last great awakening! Sometimes, when you and I consider the gross darkness blanketing this current world without looking back into the brightness of our history, we may lose all hope for a better tomorrow. Our history, however, shows us a different story. No society is ever too far beyond God's reach. Darkness is no match for God's light and love. When God is requested, He always surges into the darkness. The darker the world, the greater the need—and the more ambitious God is about flashing onto the scene! If the blazing sulfur has not yet fallen, then there is still hope! God comes to us when things cannot get any worse because that's when we usually reach for Him. It's when we cannot do a single thing to fix ourselves, when the darkness is dreadful, and we are brought to our senses in hopeless exhaustion—He rushes in!

Now let me show you what I mean. I have to warn you that the next seven pages are loaded with information. It's not easy condensing 200 years of history into such a short space. I was very tempted to cut this section out of the book, knowing how much some people dislike history lessons. Hopefully, you will appreciate what I've done and you will be greatly inspired as you learn about the first and second great awakenings and the great prayer revival of 1857-1858. As you read through these inspirational accounts, recognize the obvious parallels between the past and present. Dare to believe that you and I are the catalysts of another great awakening!

THE FIRST GREAT AWAKENING[3]

Just a few decades prior to the First Great Awakening, there was just a faint pulse beating in the Christian Church. Spiritual fires burned low in colonial America, England, and Western Europe. The only real enthusiasm for Christ in England flashed out through the Puritans. At that time, the state-approved church had Parliament pass the "Act of Uniformity," which forbade nearly 2,000 Puritan ministers from preaching on the streets and even in their churches. All who would not submit were ejected from their churches. The famous Puritan John Bunyan preached anyway, until he was imprisoned for his faith—not once, but repeatedly! Always upon his release, Bunyan went back to preaching, even though he was aware of the prohibitions. "Many, like Bunyon, were imprisoned, hundreds suffered and some died."[4]

"This was the age of Voltaire and Volney, an age of skepticism, deism, profanity, drunkenness, gambling, hatred of real Christianity, and immorality."[5] In his article, *The First Great Awakening—Jonathan Edwards*, John Cauchi writes:

> The "Half Way Covenant" of 1662 had opened the way for unconverted people to become members of the church and soon unconverted ministers were allowed into pulpits across the land. Secret apostasies and flagrant sins corrupted and weakened the churches. Jonathan Dickinson of New Jersey described the state of the church there: "Religion was in a very low state, professors generally dead and lifeless, and the body of our people careless, carnal and secure." In Pennsylvania Rev. Samuel Blair stated, "Religion lay as it were dying, and ready to expire its last breath of life in this part of the visible church." The same conditions obtained everywhere throughout all the Colonies, from New England to the far South. It was a hopeless situation but "man's extremity was God's opportunity."[6]

During this time, it seemed to everyone that evil would prevail over good and God's great light would never shine again. But in 1727, in Saxony, Germany, a fire sparked and then blazed to dazzle the earth for more than thirty years! Maybe you've heard of the legendary Count Nikolaus Ludwig Von Zinzendorf. He is arguably the greatest prayer movement facilitator of all time. Zinzendorf's rare passion for prayer attracted a *legendary* group of men and women to his German estate. His place became known as *Herrnhut*, which in German means, "the Lord's watchful care."[7] His group of radicals was chiseled into history as the Moravian intercessors who kindled the First Great Awakening.

According to David Legge:

> The very first building that was ever built in Herrnhut, in this estate of this great German man [Count Von Zinzendorf], they inscribed upon it Psalm 84 verse 3. Psalm 84 was their favourite Psalm, and they put verse 3 on this building: "Yea, the sparrow hath found an house, and the swallow a nest for herself, where she may lay her young, even thine altars, O Lord of hosts, my King, and my God." It was under that verse and in that place called "Herrnhut," that the Moravians learnt to pray.[8]

After many great sessions of prayer, a spiritual fire had fallen on these Moravians not unlike the outpouring in the Book of Acts. One day, after reading, *"The fire shall ever be burning upon the altar; it shall never go out"* (Lev. 6:13 KJV), the Moravians covenanted together that they would start a fire of prayer at Zinzendorf's Herrnhut altar, and each person (children included) took turns praying in one-hour increments 24 hours a day—not just for a week or two. These *legends* prayed like this for 100 years!

> The Moravian revival swept through the world effecting people in all classes of society, from the poorest to the richest and the highest of the ranks of society. Nations such as America, England, India, Scotland, Africa, Western Europe and many other lands were ultimately set ablaze from the fire bands of this revival. Great men of God such Jonathon Edwards, John Wesley and Charles Wesley, George Whitefield, Lady Huntington, John Erskine, David Brainerd and Peter Bohler were among those raised as bright stars of glory from this revival.[9]

Jonathan Edwards migrated west and organized a prayer movement that changed the moral climate of America. Benjamin Franklin spoke of the awakening when he said, "From being thoughtless and indifferent about religion, it seemed as if all the world were growing religious, so that one could not walk through Philadelphia in the evening without hearing Psalms sung in different families of every street."[10]

Jonathan Edwards, who is generally assigned the highest rank among American theologians, died in 1764. Northampton, Massachusetts, where he pastored his church, was at the center of the First Great Awakening. With Edwards' passing, "the spiritual state of the church plunged. Again, the 'salt of the earth lost its savor.' Terrible problems began to plague America."[11] Whether some people like it or not, God always sends His awakenings through chosen people—some to start the fires, others to keep them burning. And when these people are gone, the fires are gone with them—unless the next generation has truly caught the flame.

THE SECOND GREAT AWAKENING[12]

The United States experienced another spiritual slump following the American Revolution from 1775-1783.

> Drunkenness became epidemic. Out of a population of five million, 300,000 were confirmed drunkards; Profanity was of the most shocking kind. For the first time in the history of the American settlement, women were afraid to go out at night for fear of assault. Bank robberies were a daily occurrence.[13]

> A poll taken at Harvard had discovered not one believer in the whole student body. They took a poll at Princeton, a much more evangelical place, where they discovered only two believers in the student body, and only five that did not belong to the filthy speech movement of that day. Students rioted. They held a mock communion at Williams College, and they put on anti-Christian plays at Dartmouth. They burned down the Nassau Hall at Princeton. They forced the resignation of the president of Harvard. They took a Bible out of a local Presbyterian church in New Jersey, and they burnt it in a public bonfire. Christians were so few on campus in the 1790s that they met in secret, like a communist cell, and kept their minutes in code so that no one would know.[14]

Secular society had given up on the Christian Church. "The Chief Justice of the United States, John Marshall, wrote to the Bishop of Virginia, James Madison, that the Church 'was too far gone ever to be redeemed.'"[15] Well-known atheist François-Marie Arouet (Voltaire) predicted, "Christianity will be forgotten in 30 years' time."[16] So little did these silly people know of God's unlimited love and power!

> In 1794, conditions had reached their worst. Of course, dire cir-
> cumstances never open the illimitable resources of heaven, but
> prayer does. A Baptist minister, Isaac Backus, known as much
> for his praying as for his exhorting, had an encounter with the
> Holy Spirit. The impression left upon him was: *There's only one*
> *power on earth that commands the power of heaven—prayer.* He
> wrote "Plea for Prayer for Revival of Religion" and mailed it to
> ministers of every denomination in the United States, pleading
> each pastor to set aside the first Monday of each month as a time
> to open his church all day in order to conduct extraordinary
> prayer for revival.[17]

By 1798, a tremendous spiritual fire had started—a fire so white hot that the churches could not accommodate those inquiring about salvation! Inspired by what was happening, Presbyterian James McGready left his comfortable life in Pennsylvania to lead three small churches in Logan County, Kentucky. At that time, Logan County was overrunning with "murderers, robbers, horse thieves, highway robbers, and counterfeiters"[18]—the most unlikely place to launch a spiritual awakening. (Logan County was the modern-day Camden, NJ, and even worse than Camden—a territory where outlaws were the majority!)

In addition to Isaac Backus's first Monday prayer initiative, Pastor McGready also insisted his followers spend time each Saturday at sunset and Sunday at sunrise praying for revival. Then he started up an annual four-day community-wide communion service. And in June of 1800, a multitude came to the small Red River Presbyterian Church for one of these communion events. Methodist preacher John McGee was asked to preach at the event, and as he did, people began shouting all over the room.

McGee attempted to quiet the room:

> I exhorted them to let the Lord Omnipotent reign in their
> hearts and submit to Him, and their souls should live. Many
> broke silence. The woman in the east end of the house shouted
> tremendously. I left the pulpit to go to her.... Several spoke to

me: "You know these people. Presbyterians are much for order, they will not bear this confusion, go back and be quiet.' I turned to go back, and was near falling, the power of God was strong upon me. I turned again and losing sight of the fear of man, I went through the house exhorting with all possible ecstasy and energy. [And in a matter of moments,] the floor was covered with the slain; their screams for mercy pierced the heavens![19]

John McGee, confident this was a genuine visitation from God, convinced Pastor McGready to call for a second observance of the Lord's Supper one month later at another one of McGready's churches, Gasper River Presbyterian. It was in July of 1800 when large numbers of people began arriving. "A multitude estimated at 11,000 flocked to this camp meeting."[20] To put this into perspective, consider that Lexington, the largest city in Kentucky at that time, only had a population of 1,800 people.

The first camp meeting was born, and outdoor services were convened. People came in wagons and camped with tents, bedrolls, and bare necessities. In the words of McGready himself:

> No person seemed to wish to go home—hunger and sleep seems to affect nobody—eternal things were the vast concern. Here awakenings and converting work was to be found in every part of the multitude. Sober professors, who had been communicants for many years, now lying prostrate on the ground, crying out in such language as this: "Oh! How I would have despised any person a few days ago, who would have acted as I am doing now! But I cannot help it!" Persons of every description, white and black, were to be found in every part of the multitude...crying out for mercy in the most extreme distress.[21]

Those "pleas for prayer for revival of religion" were being answered. The Second Great Awakening was very much the realization of that prayer movement. The fires that were first sparked in those humble prayer gatherings were now spreading into every village of the nation!

Barton Stone, another pastor who visited the camp meetings, was seriously moved by what he saw. In August 1801, he published his own camp meeting invitation, and "to the utter astonishment of all, over 20,000 people arrived for the six-day camp meeting!"[22] Masses of humanity could be seen for miles. The roads were covered with wagons, carriages, horses, and footmen moving toward the camp. People were sectioned off into manageable groups, and ministers of all denominations were drafted into service. From trees, stumps, and wagons, preachers exhorted continuously, day and night, twenty-four hours a day! Thousands were converted during that historic event, remembered today as the legendary *Cane Ridge Revival*.

According to John F. Thornbury:

> There is certainly enough evidence to convince anyone that during the awakening era God worked supernaturally both in Great Britain and in America. During these glorious days the realities of the eternal world were keenly felt. Sinners were brought under powerful conviction for sin and were converted by the thousands. The saints of God rejoiced. Churches doubled, tripled, and quadrupled overnight. An impartial observer had to be impressed with the moral and spiritual changes, which were taking place. George Baxter, president of Washington Academy (now Washington and Lee University), visited Kentucky during the height of the Second Great Awakening and wrote to Archibald Alexander, "I found Kentucky the most moral place I had ever been in...a religious awe seemed to pervade the country" During the awakenings infidel clubs closed down, houses of prostitution were boarded up, and other vexatious social problems were, at least temporarily, solved.[23]

THE GREAT PRAYER AWAKENING OF 1857-1858[24]

The Second Great Awakening didn't last forever. "By 1857, churches were sliding downhill again. Thousands of Americans were disillusioned with Christianity. William Miller, a New England farmer, had captured nationwide attention with his prediction that Christ would return on October 22, 1844. When nothing happened, many abandoned their faith."[25] But not for long! According to revival historian Winkie Pratney, "a near socio-economic collapse jolted America away from her apathy into a national cry for spiritual reality."[26]

In 1856, Methodist William Arthur published a book of fiery sermons that closed with a prayer pleading with God to "Crown this nineteenth century with a revival of pure and undefiled religion—greater than any demonstration of the Spirit ever vouchsafed to man." His prayer was answered when the greatest revival in American history began the very next year.[27]

The awakening really ignited when:

Jeremiah Lanphier, a concerned layman, started a noon prayer meeting for New York businessmen. Only six people came to the first prayer meeting on September 23, 1857, on the third floor of the Consistory of the Old Dutch Reformed Church on Fulton Street. By spring, daily prayer meetings sprang up in many locations and daily attendance had grown to 10,000. America's greatest Spiritual awakening was under way. It was called the Layman's Prayer Revival because laymen led it.[28]

FROM THE BRINK OF ANNIHILATION

Once again, in a dark moral and spiritual hour, everything changed in a very short period of time! Prayer meetings began spreading all over the country. According to J. Edwin Orr:

The prayer movement crossed the Alleghenies, and soon crowded halls and churches all the way to Omaha. In Ohio, two hundred towns reported 12,000 converts in a couple of months; in Indiana, 150 towns announced 4500 converts; in Michigan, early morning prayer meetings were crowded by businessmen of all denominations; in Illinois as well a hundred and fifty towns reported up to 4000 converts; in Iowa, unprecedented interest in religion was reported; in St. Louis and Missouri towns the prayer meetings were all crowded out, the churched filled; similar reports came from Wisconsin, Minnesota and Nebraska. In Chicago, population 100,000, two thousand men met a noon for prayer, while churches were conducting two or three or four meetings a day.[29]

In his article, *Prayer and Revival,* Orr writes:

> Trinity Episcopal Church in Chicago had a hundred and twenty-one members in 1857; fourteen hundred in 1860. That was typical of the churches. More than a million people were converted to God in one year out of a population of thirty million. Then that same revival jumped the Atlantic, appeared in Ulster, Scotland and Wales, then England, parts of Europe, South Africa and South India anywhere there was an evangelical cause. It sent mission pioneers to many countries. Effects were felt for forty years. Having begun in a movement of prayer, it was sustained by a movement of prayer.[30]

Can you imagine this kind of spiritual fire blazing through today's Christian church? Based on our current population, that would mean 20 million awakened Americans loving and serving Christ just like the early church. And it would rise fast—in three years' time! Such a *happy* thought.

I could go on with revival stories until tears are streaming down your face for several hours or more. *Revival: Principles to Change the World* by Winkie Pratney is the best book I've read on this subject. Get your hands on this revival classic, read it once a year for the next 20 years (just as I have) and watch what happens to your spiritual passion!

Over and over again, in biblical and secular history, God has been able to move society from the brink of spiritual annihilation to the intermittent moments we now refer to as the Great Awakenings. Every time it seems like the world is too far gone—like evil has taken over our civilization—good rose up to challenge evil one more time!

THE BREATH OF A PRINCE

This book, *Make Me a Legend,* comes to earth out of a profound chain of prayer sessions. During the five years it took me to create this message, I prayed and wrote, and then prayed over everything that I wrote until I felt like every chapter, paragraph, and line perfectly (or very closely) represented God's heart to us right now.

I'm definitely not claiming a replacement to the Bible—just a prayerfully inspired, spiritual message for this modern world. My aim was not to write from my *mind*, but from my *spirit*. So go ahead and breathe! Because I'm positive this is one of those *ruach* moments I talked about in Chapter 1! Remember *ruach*? It's the Hebrew word used to describe the divine wind— the Spirit-wind of God that imparts divine living properties to everything it blows over. I'm positive that the essence of this message comes to us straight from the lungs of our Great Prince!

I'm surely not the only person saying some of these things, and I certainly won't be the last one to say them. At least I hope not! I feel like my message is one of many similar messages blowing through God's prophetic pipeline— an urgent series of *ruach* messages coming from numerous national voices— to perhaps fan into existence the greatest spiritual awakening of all time!

THE BIGGEST LONG SHOT

I know the spiritual fantasy I'm describing here must seem like the biggest long shot you've ever tried to wrap your mind around. If you've stimulated your imagination and freed yourself to fantasize with me about being part of this great spiritual awakening, then you've felt energized for a minute or two! I'm hopeful that you are still wiping away a few tears and feeling a few lingering goose pimples. This is the kind of dream we wait all our lives to hear!

When you first saw *Make Me a Legend,* something about this intriguing title triggered your curiosity. Maybe you've felt that your world needed a *legend,* and maybe even recently you've been thinking, *Hey, why not me? Maybe I can still do something to save the world!* Am I right? Everywhere I go, people are seriously frustrated with the current state of their lives. Even some of the most successful people in today's world feel like something big is missing—modern life is hollow! So many of us carry a great dream of saving our world, and yet here we are making it so much worse every day we fail to act! In the words attributed to Edmund Burke, "All that is necessary for the triumph of evil is that good men do nothing."[31]

Some people never act on a God-sized dream, mostly because they lack the special tools and masterful techniques necessary to make it happen! This book is your very own Craftsman toolbox! It's your comprehensive *legend* manual! I've loaded you up with all the tools and techniques you'll need to achieve at the highest level! If your dream mechanism is shot, I'll shock it back to life! Then, I'll filter your fresh new dreams through a God paradigm, make all the necessary adjustments, and we'll get on with building tomorrow's better world—you and me, just like Meriwether Lewis and William Clark, or Orville and Wilbur Wright. With just a few new *legends* at a time, everything will start to change. Sounds like a whole lot of fun, doesn't it?

Just as with most things, *legends* are not born—they are created! *Legends* are not accidents—they are accomplishments. *Legends* don't usually enter this world with a silver spoon in their mouth or some other kind of "unfair" advantage. Legendary people are gradually forged in the fires of challenge and experience. They leverage everything and make the most of seasons and moments, extracting wisdom and a skill from every good and bad happenstance. You'll never find *legends* burning up their days grumbling over how life is happening to them. No way! *Legends* harness greatness for the perfect causes in the perfect moments, to create large and lasting change for many.

There is a great need for legends! It is true that this world is very sleepy, but it is not even close to being outside of God's reach. You and I can wake it up again! From the ranks of a growing dissent, more and more of us have seen too much to watch and wait any longer. Our dreams are substantial, our resolve is unrelenting—there is no doubt about it, we are the *legends* of a better tomorrow!

COMING UP

You are a chosen one—in the next chapter, we start the great adventure!

Chapter 3

The Legend Begins

It's said that the West was built on legends. And that legends are a way of understanding things greater than ourselves. Forces that shape our lives, events that defy explanation. Individuals whose lives soar to the heavens or fall to the earth. This is how legends are born.

—Caretaker (Sam Elliott), Ghost Rider

He Was a Good Man...

Perfect in all his ways! So perfect, in fact, that there was only one like him in the *whole, wide world*. Oh yes, his story is truly beyond the expanse of human expression. While he was alive, the planet was a far better place. He was so selfless—giving the shirt right off his back to every helpless person he ever met. Wait a minute! This kindly fellow was so benevolent that he gave away everything he had, right on down to his socks and underpants! His compassion was even beyond the likes of Blessed Teresa of Calcutta. *Yeah, that's right!*

As far as work ethic goes, he was the hardest worker you would ever meet. Somehow he managed on just two hours of sleep a night, never allowing himself rest because he was always laying down his dear life for everyone else. Let me tell you, he was the nicest man to ever grace the earth; he always spoke with such gentle words. He was like a superhero, really. Oh, the stories we will tell today, for he is gone now, and right here at this funeral service, his legend begins!

Have you ever heard a highly embellished fable like this one? Have you ever started one or helped to spread one around? I'll bet you have. We've all done it a time or two. Why do we do this? Because at funerals, we lose ourselves in the misfortune of the moment. We get caught up in an emotional frenzy and we *saint* even the vilest of people. All it takes is one sobering glance into an occupied casket, and every unpleasant notion we ever had about the person vanishes.

We all feel badly for people when they pass on, don't we? And out of respect for both them and their survivors, we sympathetically amend all our unfavorable recollections. Sympathy has a way of beautifying our memories of people. We involuntarily rewrite history at every place our life intersected with that of the deceased. If we were angry about something, we finally let it go. If we were at odds with the person, we kick ourselves really hard for not working things out while they were still alive. The more we think about them, the more we want to honor them. We get swept away in a spirit of compassionate exaggeration. Before we know it, we have thrown together our amended recollections and created a very believable *fairy tale*.

I think it makes us feel good to help the world remember a better version of our departed acquaintances. After all, our enhanced version of some people is so much more motivating than the unimpressive, easily forgotten, *factual* version! What scares me is when the exaggeration is so far off the charts that family members start looking at each other and thinking, *What the heck is that preacher talking about? He's definitely not talking about our Bob. I appreciate what he's trying to do, but come on now, let's be honest.*

I run and hide when I am asked to speak at the funeral of a deceased villain. Fortunately, this has only happened a handful of times, but it goes the same every time. I start out feeling so badly for the old grouch, and as hard as I try to steer clear of giving an opinion either way, I always end up recruited as the guy who tells the tall tale first. God forgive me!

No matter how hard we concentrate, all we're able to see beyond the funeral is the legend we have created. Within weeks of the burial, the legend is so well-established in our hearts that we are not able to remember even one tiny fragment of reality. Even though the person only did one kind deed in an entire lifetime, that's the deed we've showcased. Every time it comes up, we stretch the facts a little more. Oh, how easily we con ourselves into believing tales when we very much need to believe them!

INSPIRATION DEPRIVATION

What if funerals are not the only time we do this? What if we're all fabricating these make-believe legends for our own selfish reasons? We all want something to believe in so badly that we just can't help ourselves! In a world wasting away from dreamlessness and underachievement, it's awkward dreaming God-sized dreams, isn't it? It's just far too easy for us to blend in and be bland in a tasteless society. We need inspiration a hundred times more than any of us are comfortable owning up to! We love to be inspired. We want to be inspired. We *need* to be inspired!

I wonder if we're all suffering from a really bad case of *inspiration deprivation*. Maybe we're aiming so low because we can't seem to justify the risk of going where none of our peers are brave enough to go themselves. Sure, deep down in our bellies, we know that the slight possibility for legendary achievement exists, but without living, breathing models, we are left questioning the actual probability. So as an instinct of survival, we are driven of necessity again and again to suit up in black and head for the nearest funeral with pen, paper, and a very desperate imagination!

Oh, that someone in this current era would raise the bar for you and me. Oh, for a contemporary or two! We need kindred spirits to race ahead with the blazing torch of a worthwhile mission! Give us a real-time story, based in straight truth, that brings us to our feet. Kick down our emotional floodgates! Send water pouring from our eyes and a thousand goose bumps up and down our slouching spines. Show us a prototype! Give us a pioneer! We long for a daring trailblazer! The whole world waits for a living *legend* to challenge the humdrum routine of life. Someone. *Anyone!*

Maybe it's just me, but it seems that most are running out of exaggerations. I'm worn out from painting pretty faces on putrid people. I'm crushed to the core every time another one of our "role models" turns out to be a fraud. I'm not hard to please and I'm not demanding graceless perfection. I just want someone to inspire me with a pure race from start to finish. That's all!

> *As for me, my life has already been poured out as an offering to God. The **time of my death is near.** I have fought the good fight, **I have finished the race,** and **I have remained faithful. And now***

the prize awaits me—the crown of righteousness, which the Lord, the righteous Judge, will give me on the day of His return. And the prize is not just for me but for all who eagerly look forward to His appearing (2 Timothy 4:6-8).

Where can we find these people in today's world? Every time we spot new ones riding on the heights, they crash and burn just as quickly as they rise to fly. Even the ones who start out with good character and humble aspirations all buckle under the weighty temptations that come with great success. Regrettably, they end up doing the things they vowed never to do; then, in front of an unforgiving Church and world, they collapse and are devoured! And since today's merciless society knows so little about restoring our fallen, the greats of yesterday are seldom the greats of tomorrow. This leaves myriads of aspiring young apprentices swerving on and off their own paths to greatness without a guide.

WHAT IS A *LEGEND*?

The word legend comes from the Latin adjective *legenda*, which means "for reading, or to be read."[1] Originally, *legenda* referred only to written stories, not to traditional stories transmitted orally from generation to generation. This restriction also applied to the English word *legend* when it was first used in the late 14th century. A legend first referred only to the written accounts of saints' lives.

To hear the term passed around in today's popular culture, it's easy to see that a *legend* is more than a traditional story handed down from earlier times. We now also use the word *legend* when referring to a person or achievement worthy of inspiring such a story. A *legend* is *anyone or anything whose fame promises to be enduring.* Thus we speak of the *legendary* accomplishments of a major league baseball star or the *legendary* voice of a famous opera singer.

We see a legend or we read about one and we wonder if we're being far too ordinary in our approach to life. While some settle for commonplace achievement, legends break from the restrictions of their humanity. They compose history with the rhythmic pounding of their unrelenting hearts! Legends challenge the undersized ambitions of everyday people.

Even knowing that most legends contain a mix of fact and fiction, we are helpless to hush the dreams they unleash within us. It is through the legends we are confronted with a difficult reality—that we are big fish only because of our small tanks. Perhaps eventually, the inspiration will come! Perhaps then, more people will rage against the boredom that comes with being average and yearn for bigger waters and boundless frontiers.

THE DESIRE TO INSPIRE

I have an outrageous desire to inspire people! Every morning I roll over and smack my gorgeous wife with a great big kiss on her sexy little nose, and I parachute confidently from our high-rise bed. In the still dark hours of each new day, I speed into my prayer room with electrifying levels of passion and creativity!

Without even a drop of caffeine in my hyped-up body, my fingers shake at the knuckles every time they charge onto the platform of my MacBook Pro. As I splash messages onto the pages of my daily blog (and for years this book), I see visions of all those restless people scattered across the earth waiting to be motivated. I feel them grabbing for my ankles from the dark places, so I press on vigorously against the ever-revolving wheels of time to inspire them with what I believe God wants me to share.

I wish you could borrow my eyes and live in my visions for just a day or two. You would burst into flames with me. And the longer we continue on this epic quest together, the hotter you will burn. These kinds of truths are highly flammable! If this sounds too radical, you may be tempted to turn away and run. Before you do, tell me, how many more promising years are you willing to let pass you by as you wait for someone or something to wake you from the slumber that has overtaken the world and much of the modern-day Church? The truths within this book can wake up any sleeper—right here, right now! I'm positive about this.

Years ago when I first started seeing my vision of a better tomorrow, I also saw that there were not very many legends in the race yet. Have you noticed this? Maybe it's because you and I are just now pioneering tomorrow's better world! Think about this. The future was waiting for both of us. You don't really think we just happened into each other, do you? *No way.*

I'm guessing you have the heart of a forerunner, just like me. Just think of all we can do together! This connection between us was destined! All my prayer friends and I commissioned this book to search for you. This is the golden ticket to your greatest adventure. If you're interested, we can inspire the world together!

WAITING TO BE FREED

Michelangelo's legendary sculpture, La Pieta, took two years to sculpt from one piece of marble. In fine detail it depicts the Virgin Mary holding her dead son, Jesus, across her lap. It is said that a few days after Michelangelo finished the sculpture, he overheard a visitor saying that someone else produced this work. Michelangelo then signed his name to his masterpiece. It was the only work that he signed. Michelangelo viewed sculpture as a release of the figure that was trapped inside the marble.[2] He is quoted as saying, "I saw the angel in the marble and carved until I set him free."[3]

We are all magnificent little God-creations caged in stone blocks waiting to be freed! Even though some are far more naturally gifted than others, we are exceedingly comparable. Yet, despite our similarities, some feed drugs and death to a city of junkies, while others supply life-giving humanitarian aid to dying children in ravaged third world countries.

Each of us has to take a long, hard, honest look in the mirror. Take a look right now. What do you see? Instead of an angel in dazzling armor, is there a destructive little demon looking back at you? You might see yourself as an aimless, shapeless figure waiting to be chiseled into a magnificent masterpiece. Even if you don't know how your life may turn out, smile! The work has begun! The chiseling is well underway, and with every turn of these pages, you're another strike of the hammer closer to becoming the best person you've ever been!

ORDINARY REQUIRES NOTHING

You may feel like protesting all this pressure to become legendary. After reading these first few chapters, you may ask, "Hey, Chuck Balsamo, what if I was born for *ordinary*? What if you're just putting pressure on me to become something that I will never be?" My only logical response for you is: Why did you pick up a book with the title, *Make Me a Legend?*

Ordinary, by definition, means common and unremarkable. Ordinary is the human default. Ordinary is the natural end and consequence of an uninspired life. There is no need for a book to show people how to be average—just stay away from writings like this one and from motivators like me, and ordinary will happen all by itself, I promise!

CREATURES OF DISTINCTION

The following are stories of 15 ordinary stone blocks, meticulously chiseled into 15 highly-recognizable creatures of distinction. *If they could become great, then we also can become great.* In reading their stories, you and I can start to imagine our limitless potential! I've included website addresses as endnotes so you can read more about these legends at your leisure.

- *Neil Armstrong:* On July 21, 1969, Neil Armstrong became the very first human to set his boots onto the surface of our moon. He inspired a global audience when he said, "That's one small step for man, one giant leap for mankind."[4]

- *George Washington:* "As commander of the Continental army, Washington led an assembly of citizen soldiers he described as, 'Sometimes half-starved; always in rags, without pay and experiencing, at times, every species of distress which human nature is capable of undergoing.' With this ragtag army and his political ability to appease civilian commanders and gain support from other countries, Washington defeated one of the world's foremost armies and brought independence to the United States of America!"[5]

- *Alexander Fleming:* Sir Alexander Fleming was the inventor of penicillin, which has healed millions, and he was the recipient of the Nobel Prize in Medicine.[6]

- *Alexander Graham Bell:* Inventor of the telephone and many other inventions.[7]

- *Louis Pasteur:* Contributor to the development of the first vaccines. Pasteur is best known for the process of *pasteurization,* which stops milk from going sour.[8]

- *Florence Nightingale*: She felt a call from God at the age of 17, "to do something toward lifting the load of suffering from the helpless and miserable." Florence Nightingale was the founder of modern nursing and made outstanding contributions to the knowledge and improvement of public health.[9]

- *Thomas Jefferson*: Horticulturist, statesman, architect, archaeologist, inventor, founder of the University of Virginia, third President of the United States, and principal author of the Declaration of Independence.[10]

- *Thomas Edison*: He invented many devices that greatly influenced life around the world, including the light bulb, the phonograph, and movies. Edison tried over 2,000 different experiments before the first incandescent light bulb worked. When asked how it felt to fail so many times he replied, "I never failed once. It just happened to be a 2,000-step process.'"[11]

- *Wilbur and Orville Wright*: They invented and built the world's first successful engined airplane, and made the first controlled, powered, and sustained human flight![12]

- *Saint Frances Xavier Cabrini*: As a nun in the Catholic Church, she founded schools, hospitals, and orphanages in England, France, Spain, South America, and the United States. In 1946 she became the first American citizen to be canonized, when she was elevated to sainthood by Pope Pius XII. She is the patron saint of immigrants.[13]

- *Ludwig Van Beethoven*: Despite ultimately becoming completely deaf, Beethoven continues to astonish the world as one of the most influential composers of all time.[14]

- *Henry Ford*: 800 million of his brilliant machines cover the earth today, more than 100 years after he invented them. Henry Ford gave us the automobile.[15]

- *Michael Jordan*: The greatest basketball player of all time, scoring 32,292 points, snatching 6,672 rebounds, and making 5,633 assists. He won 5 NBA championships with the Chicago Bulls, earned 5 NBA MVP awards, had 14 NBA All-Star invitations, and will likely remain as the greatest basketball player for many years.[16]

- *Coonetis Spurgintoo*: His legend dates all the way back to the dinosaurs. When still very young, Coonetis lost his beloved father during a violent Tyrannosaurus Rex attack. On July 1, 4,017 B.C., while searching for a way to protect his family against further attacks, this kid invented fire. (Just kidding; I made this one up for affect!)

- *Jesus Christ*: Jesus came to earth by miraculous conception and was the first and only Person ever to live a sinless life. He performed miracles unequalled in history and founded the world's largest religious movement when He died a sacrificial death and miraculously came to life again. He is the great hope of humankind and the greatest inspiration of all time![17]

What do all these men and women have in common? Even though each one started out just like the rest of us, these *legends* refused to live and die as ordinary people. In every case (except Jesus Christ), we see a tiny pod shoved out into the world with little more than the slightest promise of greatness. They grew up strong, conceived God-sized dreams, dismissed all logic, outlasted their critics, and galloped valiantly onto the pages of history. Take away any one of these legends and this world becomes less than it is right now. Each one did something that had never been done before. They sought out the world's biggest challenges and they overcame those challenges in remarkable conquest! This is why we continue to acknowledge their accomplishments decades, centuries, and even millennia after their passing.

HALT, AND PROVE IDENTITY

When I was a kid, I loved to watch wrestling with my friends Brian, Jeff, and John, my brother Jason, and my uncle "Tuff." I can still recite from memory that mouthy exchange between Ric Flair and Lex Luger during their notorious interview with Gordon Solie. It was just before their 1988 world title matchup, and Flair was fired up! Luger was a mountain of *steel*; Flair was a mountain of *attitude*. This was sure to be the contest of the decade, the clash between a vicious *legend* and his very eligible, up-and-rising challenger!

I remember wrestler Ric Flair glaring into the camera, sending goose bumps over the wrestling nation as he arrogantly taunted his gargantuan opponent with these legendary words that I share here to the best of my recollection:

Flair: "Well, Gordon Solie, when your name is Ric Flair and you have been king of this sport for *ten years—six times—*you learn to fear no man, and listen to no one else's opinions except your own!" [Turning to his valet women] "Now, woman, you tell Gordon Solie and the rest of the World Wrestling Federation what you think about Lex Luger!"

Woman: "I just think he needs to get his engines started."

Flair: "That's right! Because the one and only—Whoa! World Heavyweight Champion—is gonna walk that aisle, and Luger—*Gear up, big man!* [Smacking his left hand on his flexed right arm] Because Ric Flair is *coming—your—way!* Whoa!" [Both fists clinched and both arms popping big, fat veins for ten seconds of sheer, booming intimidation!]

What is a contest without two bona fide contenders? Back in his day, Ric Flair was a fierce contender, remembered for often saying things like: "To be the man, you have to beat the man! And I am that man! Whoa!"

According to Mr. Flair, the only way to become a champion is to climb into a ring and slap down a champion. I agree with him! There is no other way up! Contending with chumps will never get you anywhere in life. Let's face it; nobody's going to take any of us seriously if, at thirty, forty, or sixty years of age, we're still bragging about smacking around some scrawny little *diaper demon!*

People go crazy over championship contests. Extremely large hordes of obsessive followers stampede their way into the world's largest venues every time a little guy demonstrates the guts to face a giant. We root loudly for the little guy. We worship the underdog who, against insurmountable odds, brings the giant down. The bigger the challenge, the more we are intrigued. Show us a plot set in epic impossibility, and we are all ears. We relate so well because real life is heaving with challenges—many of them far beyond any easy conquest.

Challenge is defined as "a stimulating task or problem," "a calling to account or into question," "an order to *halt* and *prove* identity."[18] Without a real challenge, we lack the opportunity to *halt* and outwardly exhibit our innermost greatness. Challenge pinpoints our very worst and stirs up our very best. I believe there is something legendary lying dormant inside of every person, and unless we are challenged, we will never know just how amazing we could have been.

Whatever fails to kill us makes us better and stronger.[19] Adversity isn't supposed to be the end of us; it is merely the backdrop of our defining moments. When we face challenges, our smoldering greatness has a chance to flash out for all to see. So guess what, my friend? Those excruciating challenges you've been protesting all this time are *not* going to kill you! In fact, they have been sent to showcase your greatness! Just hold on and you'll see. Everything is really working out to your advantage, and after God gets finished turning the current hellish trial into your next big win, the devil will wish he had never laid eyes on you. If he had only known how you would come through this fiery furnace with a hefty promotion, he would have never thrown you down into the flames! This is exactly what the apostle Paul was trying to say in the following verses:

> *That is why we never give up. Though our bodies are dying, our spirits are being renewed every day. For our present troubles are* **small** *and won't last very long.* **Yet they produce for us a glory** *that vastly outweighs them and will last forever! So we don't look at the troubles we can see now; rather,* **we fix our gaze on things that cannot be seen.** *For the things we see now will soon be gone, but the things we cannot see will last forever* (2 Corinthians 4:16-18).

> *No, the wisdom we speak of is the mystery of God—His plan that was previously hidden, even though He made it for our ultimate glory before the world began. But the rulers of this world* **have not understood it;** *if they had,* **they would not have crucified** *our glorious Lord* (1 Corinthians 2:7-8).

BORN FOR A CRISIS

You may just now be climbing up onto the threshold of your great destiny. Your temporary physical life may look like a chaotic disaster, stacked high in unbearable layers of crisis. You may feel like no one in the entire world sympathizes with you about this unfair hand you have been dealt. I say, on the contrary, that there is nothing unfair happening to you. If there is no crisis—no conflict, no real threat, nothing to be lost and nothing to be gained—then there is no need for you to move beyond ordinary.

God has made up His mind; He has come to take you higher. Everything is perfect for your sudden rise from obscurity. You've grown so much over the years and *this is it*—your time to show the world that you are anything but ordinary!

Hurry up and tackle the little things, because just beyond your personal tribulations is a world gone to pot, one that's longing to experience everything you have to offer. You and I have come onto this scene at this exact time because we were born for these advanced levels of crisis. The national and global threats of today and tomorrow are far too real. This era is threatened with the probability of a full-scale nuclear war. Tiny countries face annihilation at the hands of demon-powered, tyrannical leaders. Daily, we're anguishing with countless horrendous accidents, incurable diseases, natural disasters, and global starvation. And the greatest tragedy—the *billions of living souls who will never find the path of peace and salvation without the legends!*

Would you like to aim for something huge? This world needs a few hundred thousand prophets, apostles, evangelists, pastors, and teachers to reignite the Christian Church—now! We need a few hundred thousand politicians, professors, humanitarians, and other key influencers to *rise now*, willing to leverage their powers for the greater good of our sickly and sleeping civilization.

Millions of hopeless, innocent souls wait for a *legend* to step up and face every one of these 21st century threats, or more blood will spill and more good people will die. If not you, who? If not now, when? This world needs a new order of physicians who are in the profession of healing for the life they can bring instead of the luxuries they can take away. We need a new order of politicians who aim for public service instead of personal renown. We need a new order of attorneys and judges with ancient values and a sober cry for justice, and a new order of millionaires and billionaires with a saintly revelation of stewardship and a pleasure for funding great causes. We all need to become a far better kind of people, doing the right and best and difficult things, and for far nobler reasons. Then we need to infuse this into our children and grand-children—far more intentionally than has been done over the past 100 years.

LIVES POURED OUT

If you are not nose to nose with a serious challenge right now, then I have to ask you, are you hiding away in the apparent safety of a low-risk, low-challenge life? Be honest. Is your life embarrassingly easy these days? If so, what should we do about this? Do you have the guts to pray for a challenge so big it cannot be accomplished without a hundred billion dollars and a super-hero suit?

Instead of shuffling down the easiest paths, I believe we should go after the biggest adventures with the highest risks! We should prove ourselves faithful with the lesser assignments, until God promotes us to the greater assignments. And then we should keep proving ourselves faithful and capable as we rise to the crest!

Instead of shrinking back from life's big challenges and shoveling our unique talents under the fear of what may happen along the way, we should express a bigger faith. Instead of shoving our unique commissions off to some other more responsible soul, we should be responsible. Instead of covering our eyes and ears and hoping someone else will step up, we should search for the biggest challenges of our day, and ask God for a chance at solving them. We should keep asking, until He finally turns and says to us, "Go ahead! Go change the world! Go make history. Do what's in your heart, for I am working with you!"

Legends have a ferocious degree of resolve. Legends are always peti-tioning God for something bold and dangerous! If you're going to live like a *legend*, you're going to have to *want* the big assignments, *commit* to the big assignments, and determine to *finish* the big assignments, no matter what that means! Consider Paul's ferocious resolve:

And now I am bound by the Spirit to go to Jerusalem. I don't know what awaits me, except that the Holy Spirit tells me in city *after city that jail and suffering lie ahead. **But my life is worth nothing to me unless I use it for finishing the work assigned me** by the Lord Jesus—the work of telling others the Good News about the wonderful grace of God* (Acts 20:22-24).

All this talk about daring challenges makes me want to beat my chest like Tarzan, smack my left hand on my flexed right arm, climb into some championship ring, and call out a hundred giant challengers all at once! I feel bound by God's Spirit, just like Paul did. I believe with all my heart that my life is also worth *nothing* unless I use it all up for finishing the work *assigned* me. Over the rest of my years, however many they will be, I want to pour out my whole spirit, soul, and body like a trillion-dollar offering before God and humankind!

My biggest prayer since I became a follower of Jesus in 1991 has been, "Please, God, don't let me waste all of this potential on empty, selfish cravings. Use me—use *all* of me—for Your eternal purposes, until there is nothing left of me to give away. Then, after a full life, take me away from here most triumphantly, straight into my eternal reward!"

Today, I'm expanding this personal prayer to include others: "Please God, give each one of my friends and readers new courage, so they will pray and live just like this! Help them to spend every last fraction of their time, talents, and resources in the active service of Your worthwhile dreams for them. And when their lives are ending, give them a finishing wind so that they may kick it like champion Kenyan distance runners, and sprint wide open through the gates of Heaven! Give them that joy of knowing they left everything on the track of this earthly arena."

C.T. Studd is remembered for his shockingly passionate mission statement. As he carefully examined the fruitless lives of so many leaders from his era, he noticed how they grabbed for the painless tasks and played their whole lives pathetically safely. One day, while grieving over this malfunction, C.T. Studd penned the following legendary statement: *"Some people want to live within the sound of church or chapel bell; I want to run a rescue shop within a yard of hell!"*[20]

Just like Studd, I'm not looking for an easy life, but I must have a significant one. I don't need a boring set of lifeless routines, and I'm not emotionally attached to my couch. I want a crisis—and *not a little crisis!* I want to rush *to* the challenges everyone else runs *from*. Fruitless people squander their days slinging mud with all the other fruitless people who are going nowhere in life, but I don't have time for these shenanigans. I was born into the earth for this time, and I refuse to head for Heaven until I finish my heavenly assignment on earth. Again, this same passion existed in the apostle Paul when he said:

> *Not that I have already obtained all this, or have already arrived at my goal, but I press on* **to take hold of that** *for which Christ Jesus took hold of me* (Philippians 3:12 NIV).

MAKE ME A LEGEND

It seems to me that our society is way too *me*-focused. Do you feel the same way? Embarrassingly, it seems that we're generating fewer living legends today than at any time in all of human history. So we have a choice to make. Are we going to step up in a big way and give the next century something that inspires them into a fiery frenzy, or are we going to relax, knowing that some kind person will definitely exaggerate us at our graveside!

I'm not holding out for the pity of my loving descendants. I refuse to have my legend formed in compassionate exaggeration while everyone is weeping over my occupied casket. I want to live a life that's impossible for any level-headed person to believe; a life so bold that anyone who hears its truest, purest version will consider my story the biggest exaggeration they have ever heard!

As far back as I can remember, I've always pushed myself to dream beyond what is reasonable. I actually believe that God is my Father and anything is possible. I love scribbling my far-fetched dreams onto bright, blank canvases in my head, acting as if God thrills to birth every idea He conceives within me. When I consider my human limitations, I ignore them. When I inventory my limitless and legendary God-potential, I see a mix between Albert Einstein, Arnold Schwarzenegger, and Bill Gates! I have mind, muscle, and money! I have power like Moses and Influence like Samuel! By the grace of God, it's all true! *You should believe these very same things about yourself.*

Dear God, *make us Your legends!* May our biographies inspire a thousand or more just like them! May we so live that our decedents won't need a fancy funeral preacher to embellish our story—living every single day as we wish to be remembered. May we be the real things, the living legends of tomorrow's fairy tale world! When historians look back over our inspirational lives, may they say, "Now here was a person who traveled into the future, read through the pages of their own legend, came back, and actually pulled it off!" Lord God, please make us Your champions—selfless, compassionate, and sacrificial.

This is my prayer, my reason for writing this book, and my desire for every reader.

COMING UP

Never have we needed legends like we do today. In the chapters ahead, I'll tell you about the real crisis of our day, give you the tools you need to live like a legend, and charge you up with plenty of passion for getting there. So come on; let's push onward from average, to above average, to outstanding, to one in a million, to *one or two in a generation!*

Chapter 4

Tomorrow's Great Hope

Freedom is never more than one generation away from extinction. We didn't pass it to our children in the bloodstream. It must be fought for, protected, and handed on for them to do the same.

—RONALD REAGAN, 40th U.S. President[1]

ONE HUNDRED YEARS FROM TODAY...

...Long after our last breath, a generation yet to live will look back on this critical hour. Hurry up! Catch my hand, and together we will run to the place I've been spending so much of my time lately. I'm asking you to imagine that we've been translated into the future. As you look around at the people, you can't avoid noticing how their genetic features match yours, and you're overtaken with the reality that these are your beloved descendants. For ten seconds, the sheer awe of this mystical experience leaves you panting. Tingling all over, you wipe your eyes to make sure you don't miss anything; your curiosity has never been this heightened!

Not knowing how much longer this experience will last, your mind is engulfed with a few startling curiosities. Right now you must know: What kind of world are my babies living in? Is it a better world, marinated in love and peace? Or is it an unstable one, steeped in hatred and deep turmoil? Are they smiling or frowning? *Are they laughing or crying? As they look back over their tiny little shoulders at this generation, are they gazing with gratitude or glaring in bitterness? Who are they admiring for their advantages? Who are they cursing at for their privations?*

Have you ever given yourself a few hours to eyeball your future in this sort of way? One thing is for sure—your name may never find its way into their history books, but every move, even the slightest one, you make during your short span of time here on earth is creating the world of tomorrow. Clearly, the cowardly bystanders are never held in remembrance. History consistently honors the selfless pioneers who voluntarily forward vast segments of their personal pleasure into their future—the heroes who live and labor for dreams they never realize in their lifespan! These are the real champions of our civilization.

Don't relax yet; we still have one more stop on our way back to the present. From the future, let us now turn 180 degrees and travel back in time, all the way to the awe-inspiring world of 1837. Truly this was a salient dash of time, sadly disregarded by our 21st century populace. For more than 200 years, a legendary band of forerunners had been moving about the earth, contending for the 2.3 billion acres^2 of terrain that would become one of the most illustrious nations to ever exist—the United States of America. How easy it would have been for the founders to revel in their accumulated wealth and blessing, and deafen their ears to the piteous groans of their children and grandchildren to come. It would have been so natural for them to yield under the pressure of their fears and cower in the face of the unknown, to reach an awfully low sacrificial threshold, to offer up that which was convenient—and nothing more.

Fortunately for the hundreds of millions of sons and daughters living and thriving in the United States of America today, there are scores of legends radiating from our sacred chronicles—beautiful legends, men and women who were far too noble to shove us out of their charitable hearts. We are the present legacy of these great legends. Because of us, and *only* because of us, they never would have tolerated themselves if they had not gone all the way, if they had sold away these future generations for their own personal fantasies. Look around, my friend. Look into the endless amenities we enjoy in this fairy tale-like country. Our legendary founders purchased America the beautiful at a premium so much more costly than we will ever understand.

SACRED BRAVERY AND OLD-FASHIONED HONOR

Just after the American Revolution and the War of 1812, and during the time of the Indian Wars, John Quincy Adams, the sixth president of the United

States, sent a message echoing into his future. In 1837, while musing over the sacred bravery of his legendary contemporaries, he spoke to us with these impassioned words, "Posterity! You will never know how much it cost the present generation to preserve your freedom. I hope you will make good use of it!"[3]

From the pure richness of this classic statement, it's plain to see that President Adams wasn't living for himself. He and his friends were *dying* for us. Oh, the warmth of their love gently blowing over my thankful soul. Some days, when I think about this long enough, real tears collect at the bottom of my eyes. I can almost hear them whispering in my ears, "Chuck Balsamo— hey, little guy, we are the legends who built your Eden. Even though we haven't met, you need to know that we each carried a portrait of you in our right-front pocket. We held the dream of you deeply within our hearts. And even though it wasn't easy at times, somehow we found a way to love you so much more than we loved ourselves. Please don't ever take this for granted, because if you do, the blessing will be gone."

Every time I read quotes from people like President Adams and so many leaders and war heroes who forged my homeland, something beautiful breaks open inside of me. I'm uncommonly grateful to my predecessors for every blessing I enjoy. I am old enough to remember when schoolteachers still taught from the original version of our history. I still remember seeing God in the middle of our picture! I remember Him working brilliantly through so many highly committed Christian leaders. Our foundation stones were laid as biblical values were cemented together in Christian prayer. Despite recent efforts from the persuasive irreligious community to rewrite American history, our Christian heritage will never be forgotten. No matter how decisively today's humanistic society seeks to deny the God under whom we became one nation, it will never successfully eliminate the evidence of our Judeo-Christian origin.

Like it or not, our honorable ancestors were never ashamed of their sincere relationship with God. When they offended Him, they sought His forgiveness—publicly! When He blessed them, they thanked Him—also publicly! Consider the contrast between their words and actions, and those of the celebrity-leaders of today. Where did our ancestral legends' archetypal spirit go? Where is that shameless reliance on God we see modeled in our founders? How did we lose that sacred bravery and old-fashioned honor, that selfless and sacrificial passion they once had?

If you're keen for a sobering check of reality, mentally mute out the background noise and listen to the silence you've created. What do you hear? Most people only notice the unpleasant sound of their foremost personal problems. Yet, muffled behind the high volume of our 21st century way of life, there is a muzzled protest reaching out for a listener. Sometimes for me it is very faint, while at other times it overwhelms me, deafening my heart to everything else. If you should ever hear this protest, you may never get it out of your head!

Who is protesting? What is the complaint? Listen a little more closely, and you will hear the upsetting lamentations of the departed—their blood is crying out to us from the past. I believe our forbearers are increasingly agitated, tossing and turning in their unsettled graves. They willingly poured out every last drop of their consecrated blood that we may take up the gauntlet and carry their visions into future generations. Without a doubt, their fading reverberation seeps up through the soil of time: "Is anybody out there? Kids, can you hear us? What are you doing with our precious sacrifices? How much longer will you turn your noses up at our gifts of love while squandering your inheritance on empty pursuits? Soon enough, you will be joining us. Posterity! Even though it seems like you're going to live forever, your days are numbered. Very soon your time will be up, your brief episode in this cosmic saga will be over—and then what?"

THE RISE AND FALL OF AMERICA

My new friend, the more you listen to the media, and the more you interact with people, the more you will see that this generation has not yet accepted its responsibility in the conflict of the ages. We have not yet risen to the challenges of our day! We have not yet pledged our homes, our pleasures, our dreams, and our desires for the preservation of a God-blessed society.

Enslaving agendas have been slowly creeping in to endanger our freedom, demoralize our way of living, and terrorize our families and friends. Inch by inch, we've been moving the ancient boundaries set by our God-fearing founders. We've been dangerously drifting back into the oppression these legends fought so hard to overthrow—and if we're not careful, very soon it will all be gone!

Does this concern you? When strolling past a few carefree kids laughing and loving life on their school playground, do you ever consider the struggle ahead for them if we don't reinstate our godly heritage?

Let's reflect on the historical pattern found in the rise and fall of king-doms. Every world power to ever rise has fallen over time. Just look at Egypt, Assyria, Babylon, Persia, Greece, Rome, and the other super-kingdoms of human civilization. Sooner or later, they all drifted from the visions that rallied them. They became fat on their successes and lost their edge, while thinking they would lead the world forever.

So what does all this say for the United States of America? Is there some kind of warning we should be heeding? Are we missing the signs that signal the dangers ahead? Maybe we should keep on tricking ourselves into believing that everything will turn out differently for *our* super-kingdom. Maybe we can violate every last principle of blessing and longevity and hope that we can somehow outsmart the historical pattern. Will a nation so nurtured in God's loving embrace curse its righteous foundations and live? I have to wonder, *Is my generation just now witnessing the beginning of the end for this United States of America? In the not too distant future, will my friends and my children find themselves cloaked in dust and sackcloth, roaming through ravaged streets as they watch their self-assured nation plummet into captivity?*

A TROUBLING PROPHECY

Sometimes I feel figuratively possessed with Jeremiah's spirit, just another petrified prophet appealing to my calloused countrymen. Like Jeremiah, I also have an untamable fire burning in my restless bones. Sometimes I imagine myself growing the longest, grayest beard of all time and standing on every major city street corner in America with a megaphone shouting into the sea of faces, "Wake up, everyone! Turn away from your idols and stop living as if you have no God! With all your hearts, renew the covenants of your founding fathers. Hurry up, before it's too late—judgment is coming. America! We are standing on slippery ground at the slanted edge of a sweltering pit. In due season, our feet will slip, and down into the flames we will go! The only reason this has not happened already is because God is holding us up! Even though we have forsaken Him as few generations have ever done, He is extending His grace to us a little bit longer. But God's holy justice will not allow Him to do this forever. Very soon, He who holds us up will finally let go, and America as we have known her will be no more."[4]

Jeremiah was the prophet who preached in Judah while his people plummeted into captivity. Sadly, no matter how convincingly Jeremiah spoke, nobody listened; and Jeremiah lived to see his prophecies fulfilled. (For a full description of this atrocity, read the Book of Lamentations, written by Jeremiah.) Here is what's recorded about Zedekiah, the last king of Judah, as he ignored Jeremiah's warnings and misled his people the rest of the way into Babylonian captivity:

> He **did what was evil** in the sight of the Lord his God, and **he refused to humble himself** when the prophet Jeremiah spoke to him directly from the Lord. Zedekiah **was a hard and stubborn man, refusing to turn** to the Lord, the God of Israel.
>
> Likewise, all the leaders of the priests and the people became more and more unfaithful. They followed all the pagan practices of the surrounding nations, desecrating the Temple of the Lord that had been consecrated in Jerusalem. The Lord, the God of their ancestors, repeatedly sent His prophets to warn them, for He had compassion on His people and His Temple. But the people mocked these messengers of God and despised their words. They scoffed at the prophets until the Lord's anger could no longer be restrained and nothing could be done.
>
> So the Lord brought the king of Babylon against them. The Babylonians killed Judah's young men, even chasing after them into the Temple. They had no pity on the people, killing both young men and young women, the old and the infirm. God handed all of them over to Nebuchadnezzar. [Notice how this judgment came long after God had compassionately warned these people. The entire nation pushed away God's hand of protection and there was nothing else for them except the consequences of their godless actions.]
>
> The king took home to Babylon all the articles, large and small, used in the Temple of God, and the treasures from both the Lord's Temple and from the palace of the king and his officials. Then his

army burned the Temple of God, tore down the walls of Jerusalem, burned all the palaces, and completely destroyed everything of value. The few who survived were taken as exiles to Babylon, and they became servants to the king and his sons until the kingdom of Persia came to power. So the message of the Lord spoken through Jeremiah was fulfilled (2 Chronicles 36:12,13b-21a).

AN OPEN VISION

A few years ago, I was traveling southbound on U.S. Interstate 81, heading for the Roanoke, Virginia airport. My late father-in-law was driving, and I was in the back seat with Emily, reading my Bible and praying. As I looked to the east, I had an open vision. Missiles were falling out of the skies in the direction of Norfolk, Virginia. I remember thinking, *"How can this be happening on American soil?"* Even though I didn't receive an answer that day, I was positive that this was a vision of the future. God forbid that this day should actually come! If it does, we can be sure that all the earth will not believe what they see. Whenever I think about this vision, I ask myself, *Is there any way that any of us can do anything to prevent it?*

AROUND AND AROUND WE GO

No matter how good and loving God is, we often press the limits of His mercy, seeking to live as far from Him as we can while still meriting our big "mansion over the hilltop." Ever since the dawn of time, we've been spinning in circles in a clearly predictable cycle of freedom and oppression. From *salvation* to *stagnation* to *sin* to *suffering* to *supplication,* and back to *salvation* again—around and around we go. Even though the cycle is so obvious, we just can't seem to avoid it.

There's a good picture of this cycle recorded in Israel's history. Every biblical historian will tell you that the Jewish people have been spinning since the day they began. Right after Moses died, his successor, Joshua, stirred up the entire nation in faith, and finally they entered their land of promise under his leadership. After a fleeting moment of peaceful enjoyment in their Promised Land, the Bible says:

And the Israelites served the Lord throughout the lifetime of Joshua and the leaders who outlived him—those who had seen all the great things the Lord had done for Israel. After that generation died, another generation grew up who did not acknowledge the Lord or remember the mighty things He had done for Israel. The Israelites did what was evil in the Lord's sight and served the images of Baal. They abandoned the Lord, the God of their ancestors, who had brought them out of Egypt. They went after other gods, worshiping the gods of the people around them. And they angered the Lord (Judges 2:7,10-12).

Did you notice the obvious parallel between historical Israel and modern America? Take your time and read it again if you want. The cycle is there! Just in case you need a little more convincing, here is a short biography of the legend Nehemiah. As an Israelite growing up in captivity around 445 B.C., serving as a slave and a cupbearer to the king of Babylon, Nehemiah was a humbled man searching for big answers. In his urgent prayer, Nehemiah referenced the same period of Israel's history just mentioned. His prayer endures today as the clearest portrayal of this freedom-oppression cycle:

Our ancestors captured fortified cities and fertile land. They took over houses full of good things, with cisterns already dug and vineyards and olive groves and fruit trees in abundance. [Salvation] *So they ate until they were full and grew fat and enjoyed themselves in all Your blessings.* [Stagnation] *But despite all this, they were disobedient and rebelled against You. They turned their backs on Your law, they killed Your prophets who warned them to return to You, and they committed terrible blasphemies.* [Sin]

So You handed them over to their enemies, who made them suffer. [Suffering] *But in their time of trouble they cried to You, and You heard them from heaven.* [Supplication] *In Your great mercy, You sent them liberators who rescued them from their enemies.* [Salvation again] *But as soon as they were at peace, Your people again committed evil in Your sight, and once more You let their enemies conquer them. Yet whenever Your people turned and cried to You again for help, You listened once more from heaven.* **In Your wonderful mercy, You rescued them many times!"** (Nehemiah 9:25-28)

Oh, how far we can drift in so little time! It doesn't take long, does it? How often in my own life I've awoken from extended seasons of foolish pride only to ask myself, *How did I end up here?* God lavishes us with many undeserved blessings and somehow we always seem to take them for granted. We make bold pledges to be thankful, godly people for the rest of our lives, and yet even with a determined effort, sooner or later, the very things we cherished yesterday are ordinary tomorrow. You don't have to take my word for it; more than likely you have seen this a thousand times in your own life. When that which is precious becomes ordinary, it is replaceable.

More than likely, you're starting to wonder where America is right now in this cycle. Has the preciousness of our freedom become an ordinary thing? When considering our progress, can we honestly erase God out of our history and attribute our great, enduring success to the mere strength of humans? Sadly, just like Israel, "*...another generation grew up who did not acknowledge the Lord or remember the mighty things He had done for* [America]" (Judg. 2:10b).

Do you think our unbroken success could be lulling us into a downward spiral of spiritual *stagnation* and *sin*? Can it be that we've already progressed further into the *suffering* phase of the cycle than anyone has recognized? Can we legitimately overlook the increasingly widespread national adversity we've been sliding into?

In my experience, many Americans are fearful that if something doesn't change, we're going to spend many days ahead with our flags at half-mast. Globally, there is even talk of World War III. Terrorist groups have taken root in the Middle East creating nations within nations and making the task of policing our current "axis of evil" nearly impossible. Even though we have made great diplomatic and military progress, the spirit assassins fueling these fires remain unchallenged up to this point. Something big needs to happen soon to bring an end to their evil plans.

TOMORROW'S GREAT HOPE

Who's going to ride in and save the day? Should we sit glued in front of our televisions, pointing our fingers at presidents, legislators, and governors?

Or should we face the reality that our government is only a representation of our people, and that the blame for our struggling state of the nation is shared among our millions of citizens? When we look at the cross-section of our government, aren't we really looking into the mirror as a nation?

Take, for example, the economic slump that started before the 2008 elections. While we went after our nation's leaders (just like we usually do) with clubs and brass knuckles, so to speak, many people refused to admit fault. There are three simple ways to outlast a money crunch. We can increase earnings, decrease spending, or both. As radio and television host Glenn Beck said in one of his highly provocative presentations, "History has shown us you cannot spend your way to prosperity it just doesn't work. And that's what we are pinning our hopes on."[5] Instead of accepting responsibility for our decades of personal financial mismanagement, we command our government to *fix this problem right now*. We don't really care about where we end up morally or spiritually; just show us the *money* so we can keep buying everything that pleases our wanting eyes.

It seems that we've suffered enough pain to see our need for change. Yet most Americans are still addicted to borrowing. We cannot stop withdrawing fantasy dollars out of our future—mortgages, reverse mortgages, credit cards, personal loans, and loans against our retirement savings. Instead of devoting ourselves to the tedious progression of mastering money, we keep reaching into the future—raiding a generation not yet born! Without batting an eye, like spoiled apathetic children we demand that our political leaders magically increase the value of our real estate again, because we need another fix of luxuries and we're craving another loan! While I personally believe there are many things government can and should do to create opportunity here in our land, it is discouraging that many Americans refuse to accept personal responsibility for careless and unwise decisions and actions.

As long as we point our fingers in blame or cross our fingers in hope for some political hero to show up and make everything better, things will only get worse. I believe that the only real solutions to the various dilemmas of our day are wrapped inside of you, me, and all the other beautiful people who share our dream. We really are the last great hope of tomorrow!

Oh, I know it can be frightening to consider that a nation's survival can be resting on the shoulders of commoners like us. But it's important not to get nervous and throw away this book out of fear that you may end up enlisting in some revolutionary movement. For now, just consider that *you* may be one of the *legendary* prophetic deliverers of your day! Whether you're a stay-at-home parent laying it all on the line to maintain a flourishing home environment, a CEO leading your multibillion-dollar corporation into new horizons, or a retiree searching for significance, this is your trumpet call to action!

I believe that we are on the threshold of a "grassroots" phenomenon—a sudden rise of national problem-solvers from common places. The legends of today and tomorrow will appear out of nowhere (it will seem) with radical convictions and sudden influence! They will rally the dissenters, challenge the establishment, and obliterate the status quo. Do you believe this is possible? Can you see that it's already beginning to happen? How are you responding to it? Are you marching on the front lines or cowering in silence until the victory is secured?

I want to share with you one of my favorite quotes of all time. I'll bet you've read and heard it 25 times in your life, but it says so much to this generation. Theodore Roosevelt, America's 26th president, mulled over the cowardice of his day and penned these classic words:

> It is not the critic who counts; not the man who points out how the strong man stumbles or where the doer of deeds could have done them better. *The credit belongs to the man who is actually in the arena,* whose face is marred by dust and sweat and blood, who strives valiantly, who errs and comes up short again and again, because there is no effort without error and shortcoming, but who knows the great enthusiasms, the great devotions, *who spends himself for a worthy cause;* who, at best, knows, in the end, the triumph of high achievement, and who, at the worst, if he fails, at least he fails while daring greatly, so that his place shall never be with those cold and timid souls who knew neither victory nor defeat. (Emphasis added.)[6]

Unknown to most people, there is an invisible battle raging—the bloody collision between two very old kingdoms; a violent clashing between Light and darkness! Anyone who's been to this battlefront will scare the "hell" out of you. The casualties are mounting hourly. I believe that we're already living in a *post-moral era,* a day when good is evil and evil is good. Many churches no longer provide moral compasses and many are no longer appreciated as beacon of lights to the nations. Christianity is not effectively facing and solving the complex problems the modern generations are facing. It seems that Christians and Christianity have become outdated and unwanted, and more desperately in need of reform than we know.

But no matter how bad things may appear concerning the spiritual state of our society, buried deep beneath the dark, cold ashes of yesterday's awakenings, there remains a glowing ember of hope!

For several years now, I've participated firsthand in a very determined grassroots supplication movement. Thanks to people like Lou Engle and Mike Bickel, and a growing company of eccentric, Samuel-like[7] forerunners, beaten-down citizens all over America and around the world are starting to fast and pray—like there is no tomorrow! Can we gain enough momentum to turn things around fast enough? Can we stop the plague that is already underway? Without a doubt, our cumulative cries for help are rising up to God. In His mercy, God will answer us! Suddenly, seemingly out of nowhere, the legends will rise—the likes of whom the earth has not seen since the days of the prophets. Then perhaps, one legend at a time, we will lead our civilization back to safety.

> ...But in their **time of trouble** they cried to You, and **You heard them** from heaven. [Supplication] *In Your great mercy, **You sent them liberators who rescued them** from their enemies* [Salvation] (Nehemiah 9:27).

COMING UP

Without a doubt, the countless legends of today and tomorrow are waiting to be empowered. The real possibility of a much better future is well within our reach! All we have to do now is find these legends and give them a cause! In the next chapter I am going to upset mediocrity in an in-your-face kind of way. Just a few more pages, and you will be ruined for anything less than living a legendary life. Be brave.

Chapter 5

Exposed to the Bigger Cause

When a nation calls its prime men to battle, homes are broken, weeping sweethearts say their goodbyes, business are closed, college careers are wrecked, factories are refitted for wartime production, rationing and discomforts are accepted, all for war. Can we do less for the greatest fight that this world has ever known outside of the cross, this end time siege on sanity, morality, and spirituality?

—LEONARD RAVENHILL
Christian evangelist and author[1]

MEDIOCRITY INTERRUPTED

The long journey to legendhood always begins at the intersection of *crisis* and *curiosity*. An epic crisis collides with a curious citizen, and another legend is off and running! While the larger masses of people fritter away their best years muscling out hollow, personal initiatives and striving after passing pleasures, legends get hyped up with higher purposes along the way. Lesser dreams lose their luster when pitted against a bigger cause. For legends, the epic crisis is the bigger cause (and the higher purpose), and the day we first see it is the day we start breathing.

Today's world is overpopulated with grumblers. I'm not sure if you've noticed, but most people complain about even the slightest inconveniences. They're perfectly conditioned for the paths of *least* resistance. They want to be left alone! These idlers gripe and groan about every trending crisis. Some of them pretend to see nothing and know nothing, without the smallest inclination of putting themselves in harm's way.

Legends crave the front lines. We want to be posted wherever the personal risk of loss is highest because that is also where the possibility for making the greatest difference exists. One bona fide crisis is all it takes to launch us across a golden threshold, from a life driven by the aspiration of personal *destiny to a much fuller one* animated with the hope of *legacy!*

REDEFINING PURPOSE: DESTINY VERSUS LEGACY

While on the subject of *destiny* versus *legacy,* let me describe the contrast I see between the two. Ever since I can remember, people have said to me, "One of these days, son, if you can stay out of trouble and use your talents and gifts for good, you are going to change the world!" Influential leaders have often regarded me as a highly talented person with a winning personality. I'm telling you this to make a point. Please don't see me as vain or self-promoting. As the Scripture says, let someone else praise you and not yourself (see Prov. 27:2).

Believe me, it's thrilling to hear these kinds of things predicted about my life. The encouragement fuels my big dreams, but there is a danger. Sometimes, the dream of fulfilling so large a *destiny* overemphasizes personal accomplishment and reward. Without a doubt, most people want to make a difference for others, but if the truth were told, we are far more attracted to the perks of success than we're willing to admit. It's as if we want to save the world mainly because we want to rule the world we're saving.

I believe you can achieve a large, personal *destiny* and yet never establish a lasting *legacy.* There are plenty of self-centered heroes in today's world. At first, they're adequately satisfied with the thrill of being everyone's champion. They love the honors of riding into town on the back of their shiny, white horse like the *Lone Ranger* to the rescue. Initially, the honors they receive from saving the day energize them on to greater feats—but fame always loses its attractiveness with time.

I've found this to be true in my own life. In my mid-20s, I was blessed to be achieving on a high level. Everything seemed almost perfect. After all, I was doing what I felt I was *destined* to do. I wasn't any more self-centered than any other young, Christian man in my circle. At that time, I was a volunteer associate pastor and a large financial contributor in my home church. As an individual, I felt like I was thoroughly maximizing my effectiveness.

But there was something missing. I knew in my heart there was more to life than my *personal* achievements. Each next birthday reminded me about the briefness of life. My limited gaze gradually broadened from the ground in front of my feet to the distant horizon, far beyond my reach. That's when I learned about the *legacy* paradigm—and the bigger meaning of life!

Please don't get me wrong. I believe that everyone has a personal *destiny*. I am not suggesting that *legacy* is a replacement term for *destiny*. What I am suggesting is that *legacy* is a far more encompassing gauge of purpose.

Destiny says, "I am created to do something great; I need to discover what that is, so I can zoom around the world, be extraordinary, please my heavenly Father, sprint to my finish, and pick up the trophy at the end of my race."

Legacy begins the same way, and then adds, "The greatness of my destiny is measured by *what I pass on to the forthcoming generations*. I fulfill my individual purpose by building on the sacrifices of those who have gone before me, serving those who are with me today, and blessing those who will follow in my footsteps."

When talking about destiny, most people seem to focus on the *me* factor. Destiny makes me think about what *I'm* doing with *my* life and how well *I'm* doing it. We ask questions like, "What am *I* called to do with *my* life?" Legacy, by contrast, demands a shift in focus. Legacy makes me think more about *whom* I'm impacting with my life. Legacy asks the more beautiful questions like, "What are *my followers* called to do with *their* precious lives, and how can I leverage my destiny to better position *them* for *theirs?*" Destiny is mostly about *me*; legacy is all about *them*. Legacy awakens *me* to the much bigger cause of *them!* What a beautiful awakening this is!

MY FRIEND, JIMMY FLOYD

To illustrate this point, let me tell you about my friend, Jimmy Floyd. A few years back, he was the most enthusiastic softball player I had ever met. When I played on the team, Jimmy was the best player and I was the worst. Every time Jimmy Floyd walked to the plate with a bat in his hand, the pitcher gave a signal and the outfielders backed all the way up—but never far enough! I was right there cheering for Jimmy on the day when he dominated our local homerun competition. Still today, Jimmy's enthusiasm for sports is unprecedented. His athletic aptitude is legendary. One of my favorite things to do in life is bring up the wonderful world of sports in conversation with my dear friend Jimmy. Mention a single word about football, basketball, baseball, or golf, and he's happy! A few years ago, I asked Jimmy if he was getting excited about the coming softball season. Jimmy's humble response taught me much about legacy.

During that time, Jimmy's two children were just old enough to play catch with Daddy. Shockingly, Jimmy lost some of his desire for winning home run competitions and being the star player of our softball league. Was Jimmy excited about the coming softball season? His response, "I don't know if I'm gonna play as much this year." I was blown away, so I asked why, and he replied, "I'm more excited about seeing all these teenagers step up—and I'm really getting fired up about helping my kids enjoy the game!" Jimmy Floyd found his far more encompassing gauge of purpose—the *legacy* of his children, and of all children!

This is what legacy is all about—loving someone else's home run *more* than your own. It's about shedding your tears of joy when the next generation knocks one out of the park. At some point, the value of our lives will be measured by the advantages we pass on to the rising generations. Thank you, Jimmy, for illustrating this great principle. Your loyal friendship inspires me more than you know! I admire your love for Heather and the kids. Your whole life is a continuous lesson of godly character. John Maxwell says, "Teams make you better than you are!"[2] You, Jimmy Floyd, make me so much better than I am!

EXPOSED TO THE BIGGER CAUSE

To further develop my idea, I'm going to tell you a true story about a young and ordinary shepherd, years before he became one of the greatest kings of history. His name was David, and when our story begins, he was the youngest of eight brothers.

David lived during a time when Israel's very first king had spiritually and morally fallen away from God. Sadly, the once glorious King Saul was now on his way out of the palace. He was racing to an early grave, and nobody could stop him. Then there was a great prophet, Samuel. God sent Samuel to the village of Bethlehem, specifically to the house of Jesse. He went there with a highly classified message from God about what was going to happen in Israel.

At Jesse's house, Samuel was postdating one of Jesse's sons as Israel's next ruler. King Saul was being replaced.

After Samuel and Jesse had cut through the customary small talk, Jesse lined his boys up in front of the prophet. This was a huge deal for this humble family. One by one, Samuel carefully appraised Jesse's strongest and most qualified sons as he searched for God's chosen man. And God said to him, "The one I've chosen is not among these, Samuel. Learn to look at the heart, because I don't choose people by outward appearance. When you meet the young man I have chosen, you will know it because his heart will stand out more than all the rest" (my paraphrase; see 1 Sam. 16:7).

Finally, after seeing each of David's brothers, Samuel politely inquired, *"Are these all the sons you have?"* (1 Sam. 16:11a). Jesse responded in apparent confusion as he reluctantly acknowledged, *"There is still the youngest [David]...but he's out in the fields watching the sheep and goats"* (1 Sam. 16:11b). It doesn't take a professional family counselor to see what was happening. This man of God's choosing was not the most likely candidate. *Nobody* took David seriously, not even his own father.

As the story goes, David was finally called in from the fields. This was a holy moment! Can you feel it? Samuel studied the young man for a brief moment until he heard God say, "This is the one I have chosen! So get out your oil and anoint him now!" (my paraphrase; see 1 Sam. 16:12-13). Right away, Samuel reached for his horn of anointing oil, raised it high, and poured it lavishly down onto David's head, symbolizing David's invitation to the office of king and God's Spirit coming upon David's life. Whoa!

Can you imagine this kind of thing happening to you? The Bible says that every prophecy Samuel spoke actually happened, and none of his words ever fell to the ground unfulfilled. Can you picture yourself at work one day, just going through your ordinary routines, and out of nowhere you're taken by surprise, like David was, with a very credible prediction that you are going to become the next leader of your country?

Feel this with me right now—just as if you and I were witnessing this event, in real time, through David's eyes. Imagine a prophet of Samuel's magnitude traveling through your hometown, just to point you out! At first you're excited, but confused. You want to believe that anything can happen, but you're still you—just a small town guy or gal—but now with a king-sized fantasy. Being a world leader could be fun, and it sure would be rewarding, yet you reason, *Maybe I should let someone else deal with all that hassle! I'd better get back to familiar things like playing my harp and writing worship songs and herding my father's sheep. I'd better leave all this building tomorrow's better world stuff to someone else!*

Outside of playing his harp for King Saul and helping around the palace every once in a while, David did go back to life as usual. He kept on faithfully serving his elderly father in the fields, carefully executing his everyday jobs while developing his craft and character in secret—training himself to worship God like no one ever had, or ever would.

Life went on as usual—until *one remarkable day* that changed David's life forever. It's one thing to receive a prophecy. It's another thing to believe a prophecy and take your first steps into it.

In the backdrop, there was a war going on between Israel and the Philistines. The real problem with this conflict was a warrior named Goliath. The man was a giant, measuring over 9 feet tall! Just visualize that! Goliath wore a bronze helmet and a coat of armor that weighed over 125 pounds. He also wore bronze leggings, and he slung a bronze javelin over his back. The shaft to his spear was as heavy and thick as a weaver's beam, and was tipped with an iron spearhead that weighed fifteen pounds. He had an armor bearer who walked ahead of him carrying a huge shield. (See First Samuel 17:4-7.) Some people had to wonder if Goliath was even human!

Fear descended over the land like a bone-cold winter rain. It seemed like this was the end for Israel! Her most valiant warriors (including David's older brothers), her king, and her entire population were all *"terrified and deeply shaken"* (1 Sam. 17:11b). For 40 days, twice a day, morning and evening, the giant strutted in front of the Israelite army, mocking her God, humiliating her warriors, and threatening her people with a future of slavery.

If there has ever been a no-hope scenario, this was it! It was a problem far beyond the scope of human remedy, a burden too oppressive for even the king and his army. The battle was heating up fast; the burden was real. Yet for David, life was no more complicated than his regular shepherd's routine. Oblivious to the battle, sheltered from the reality of a national crisis, David had no idea how things were going to change for him.

Back in Bethlehem, Jesse commissioned David to rush some food to his brothers at the battlefront. He was supposed to deliver the food and hurry back to father with news of their condition. Little did Jesse know that in sending David to the front line, he would be exposing his son to the *bigger* cause.

As David entered the battle zone, he was traumatized by the images of Israel's finest warriors running from Goliath in dread! The morale of his nation had reached an all-time low. People must have been laid out facedown weeping and praying all over the fields. I can almost hear David's thoughts as he tried to process what he was witnessing: *Dear God, I wonder how long this battle has been going on! Here my nation is facing annihilation, and I didn't even have a clue! How could I have been so blind? How much longer is this giant going to taunt my people and humiliate my God before someone makes him pay?*

Weighing out the odds, David must have continued this internal discourse as any sane person would: *If our strongest warriors and even the king himself are "terrified and deeply shaken," then I would be out of my mind to approach this freak of nature! Maybe I should just hand over the food my father sent for my warrior brothers, and run home to Mama before someone else gets hurt! After all, I'm no good to anyone if I'm dead, right? Maybe instead, I should run away from here and never look back!*

Here's my guess about how this moment played out: As David moved dangerously far into the process of bowing to his fears, he must have looked back and sighed once or twice in the direction of his home sweet home; he must have reminisced about the day when Samuel had poured the oil on his head.

The reality of this predicament must have hit David hard. On the one hand, he must have wanted to run away like any ordinary young man might have. And then just in time, the voice of his inner legend boomed! *Hey, wait a minute! Maybe I'm standing here right now because I'm supposed to do something about this situation! Maybe, this is what Samuel meant when he said I was going to be Israel's next king.* Right there, it happened—an epic *crisis* collided with this *curious* young man; a burden was caught, and the *legend* of King David began!

Now that he was exposed, there was no stopping what would happen to David next. Curiosity and courage were pushing him away from the sidelines. By now, David's thumping, pounding, thrashing heart was crying out, *Oh, dear God, what's going on inside of me? No matter how hard I try, I cannot suppress this burden for another second! This is it. There's no turning back for me now. Enough is enough for this Goliath creature; he should have retreated while he had a chance. There is just no way I can sit here with my mouth shut and my hands idle while everyone I love descends into slavery! My country, my faith, my family, my future—everything is facing annihilation. If I don't rise to this occasion, my pretty, little sheltered life won't be worth living twenty years from today. I, the disregarded errand boy, was born for this very moment! If I die here, then at least I will die honorably in my arena, pouring out my own blood for the possibility of a better tomorrow!*

David did rise that day. He stepped onto the battlefield armed with nothing but a slingshot and five smooth stones. A young man with no military experience whatsoever brought down a giant and saved his country! *To be the man, you've gotta beat the man!* And the man on that day was Goliath—until a rising legend hit Goliath using the sling, then he cut off his head with Goliath's own sword! The power of that one courageous victory became the catalyst that triggered a pronounced series of events in David's life, and eventually led to the complete fulfillment of Samuel's long-shot prophecy.

Even though King David reigned in Israel more than 3,000 years ago, he is still remembered today by people worldwide. David was far from perfect, but he was perfectly in love with God! He is the primary author of the Book of Psalms—the largest book in the Holy Bible. During David's 40 years as king, he established the most glorious system of worship of all time, even to this very day. His military conquests were almost mythical!

David's son, Solomon, succeeded his father as king and built the most spectacular temple of all time. David's legacy is an eternal legacy. His life is celebrated in Israel's chronicles as the greatest human king to ever reign. David has his own city, *The City of David* (the oldest settled neighborhood of Jerusalem[3]), and his very own honorable title given from God Himself, *"a man after My own heart"* (Acts 13:22 NIV). For David, it all began the day he saw the bigger cause.

You have to be wondering if you could be that next David figure who rises to save your day. Maybe you're ready to dance with excitement right now, except you may also be wondering, *What is at stake here? What is this bigger cause Chuck is trying to show me?* So far, just five chapters into this manifesto, I have been merely hinting. But the more I express my dream, the more you will comprehend the bigger cause—and you will never lack exposure again. As you keep reading from here, the chances of walking away are more and more unlikely. Please be forewarned—these next few pages may trigger in you an extreme new spiritual devotion!

THE POST-CHRISTIAN DARK AGES

The moral and spiritual world as we have known it to this point is changing. To me it seems like the sun is setting on an era. The dusk of this past 50 years is turning to full night, and soon there may not be enough light to keep us warm and safe. For me, I can hardly bear the thought of my great-grandchildren fighting for survival in the coming *Post-Christian Dark Ages.* With this phrase I mean that our civilization is coursing its way into a long and punishing period of evil.

In the first chapter of Romans, there is a startling message about how far down people can slide, how evil they can become when they throw their fists up at God. I feel like its writer wasn't merely speaking about the spiritual and moral darkness of his own day; I believe he was pointing to an age when evil would devour like fire through the whole of its civilization.

If I'm right about this, then we are forewarned by the apostle Paul, of a coming spiritual dark age—a time when humankind will curse God and even the idea of God, claiming a humanist evolution that supersedes the need for a primitive God (see Rom. 1:18-32). In this coming spiritual dark age, people will become inwardly and outwardly *reprobate,* meaning that they will not be able to comprehend God or experience any kind of authentic relationship with Him.

During the Post-Christian Dark Ages, humankind will stoop down to such gross and humiliating evils that we will find ourselves plummeting into the darkness as we've never imagined. Read it straight from the apostle in his own convincing words, as the Holy Spirit inspired him:

> *Since they didn't bother to acknowledge God,* **God quit bothering them** *and let them run loose. And then all hell broke loose: rampant evil, grabbing and grasping, vicious backstabbing. They made life hell on earth with their envy, wanton killing, bickering, and cheating. Look at them: mean-spirited, venomous, fork-tongued God-bashers. Bullies, swaggerers, insufferable windbags! They keep* **inventing new ways** *of wrecking lives. They ditch their*

parents when they get in the way. Stupid, slimy, cruel, cold-blooded. And it's not as if they don't know better. They know perfectly well they're spitting in God's face. And they don't care—worse, they hand out prizes to those who do the worst things best! (Romans 1:28-32 MSG)

Is this happening to our world right now? God help us! Even with our multiplicity of religions and our craving for spiritual experiences, are even Christians becoming too sophisticated in our own eyes for a traditional concept of God? How have people become so incapable of distinguishing right from wrong? Look how so many people are forming a subculture that mocks and despises everything pure and good while celebrating every contaminated, evil thing.

Even though there's still a small, faint voice of conscience tugging at some of us, far too many people find themselves living today in ways they never wanted to live. This world is addicted to so many filthy, twisted pleasures. Government programs are failing. Millions are hopeless, they can't break free!

Do we really want to *do* this? Do we really want to find out where this road ends? We have no idea what were getting ourselves into.

SEARCHING FOR THE NEW WORLD

Sometimes I feel like Christopher Columbus, searching for another new world—but in a country that *once was!* When I discover this new world in all its glory, I'm going to give it to my children and yours as my loving inheritance to them. Just like Columbus pursued his ambitious dream, we must pursue ours, too! We have to raise our sails now and fly straight into the fiercest, uncharted seas, without flinching for even a second! And when that time comes, and we're face to face with the monsters, we have to banish them to the ocean floor!

With all my heart, I want our offspring to know all about the stand you and I took for them. I pray to God that they will always remember us as a selfless, sacrificing, and legacy-driven parent generation. I long to grant them a safer world, one that's free from terrorism and the threat of nuclear extinction; a world remarkably preserved in a spirit of innocence and free of godlessness, immorality, and ruin.

It may appear like Christianity is the antiquated religious movement of years gone by, but you and I can definitely make it the founding religion of tomorrow's America! Together we must reform the spiritual condition of our world and pass on a much *better* version of our great faith than the one we've been presenting these past 100 years. I'm talking about a Christianity that's not shunned, but rather greatly appreciated by the societies of tomorrow, *doing* so much more than just *telling* people how to live.

We have to become a modern *pilgrim* people—living powerfully and leading and serving our world through the timeless principles of our guiding Scriptures and God's Spirit living in us and working through us. We have to show our world a faith that courageously and relevantly approaches and solves the real problems of today—spiritual, emotional, family, social, economic, and *every category* of problems known to people.

We haven't much time left! Already the clock is set in motion. A blood-thirsty outbreak of sin and suffering ravages our planet. This is the world we've built with our decades of tolerance. Tonight, thousands of demonically stimulated father figures will molest thousands of innocent children, while you and I are safely tucked into our beds. Tonight, thousands of men, women, and children will be forced into the streets of our cities, to prostitute their bodies for another day's wages.

In this world tonight, too many teenage girls will lose their innocence to a charming young Romeo. Thousands more of our people, young and old, will overdose on drugs, die in drunk driving accidents, or commit crimes for which they end up behind bars. Multitudes of struggling marriages will tragically drift into that place of no return where numbness and hatred snuff out the love that once was.

Tonight, countless children will lie in bed awake, trembling through their fears of tomorrow—fears of their parents splitting up, fears of their homes being broken into, fears of drive-by shootings, and fears of emotional and physical abuse.

The ever-increasing evidences of the Post-Christian Dark Age are everywhere. This is our Goliath! Behold, the monster! Don't turn away. He's mocking our God, humiliating our warriors, and threatening all of us into a future of darkness.

EXPOSE THE MASSES—ASSEMBLE THE *LEGENDS*

We should build a camp right here at the rally flag of our shared dream. *Make Me a Legend* is the perfect rally flag! Here we can unify through our comprehensive list of common principles and purposes and synergize to save our world together.

It has been my experience that wherever there is one *legend*, there will often be a hundred more. Aspiring legends huddle until they hatch, and then they multiply. *Legends always beget legends!* In his inspiring leadership book, *The 21 Irrefutable Laws of Leadership*, John Maxwell teaches about The Law of Magnetism, which says, "Who you are is who you will attract."[4] Therefore, you and I have to *become* the kind of people we wish to *attract* so that we can *attract* the kinds of people we want to *become!*

If an eaglet hatches in a chicken coup instead of an eagle's nest, he will never fly. This is because the eagle learns to fly from imprinting, not instinct. He becomes identical to the creature that raises him. Humans are similar. If you really want to become a legend, then you have to get yourself to a legend's nest—quickly!

Together, everyone has boosted efficiency and range! This is the miracle of V flight formation in ducks and geese. I'm painting a picture of what can happen in us and through us when we assemble the *masses* to this life and world-changing concept. The potential power of what I'm suggesting is huge! To illustrate the point, let's talk about David again. As if his story isn't already hard to believe, just wait until you learn about David's mighty men!

It happened sometime after David slew Goliath and before he became king. Things were not going well for David at that time. King Saul's spiritual condition was rapidly deteriorating. Evil spirits inhabited King Saul's body and tormented him with depression and fear. Despite King Saul's failures, David loved and honored and served his king as faithfully as any person has ever served a king. David also joined the army and fortified his fellow Israelites with several impressive military wins. He was building up the kind of momentum one would expect from a rising world leader.

Sadly, the more successful David became and the more he blessed the king, the more the king hated him. What could have been a very discouraging time in David's life actually turned out to be a very necessary part of David's future dynasty. The time came when King Saul lost control of his anger for David, and he climbed down from his throne to hunt the man who served him best.

David refused to retaliate against his king. Trusting God with his future, David took the humble road out of town. Clearly, David hoped this move would calm the king's jealous rage against his rising fame. In a tremendous act of humility, David set up a temporary safe haven in the lowly but legend-like cave of Adullam.

As the Bible story goes, there was a common, growing discontentment among the people because of the way things were going in Israel. It was this unrest, coupled with the hope of a better tomorrow, that sent 400 men searching for a new dream. It was there in Adullam, during a most discouraging season in David's life, where the legends assembled! This group consisted of mostly family and a few friends and others who admired David's courageous spirit. None of these rough-edged dissenters looked anything like a legend in the making when they first placed their swords at David's feet. They were homeless and hopeless, all facing some kind of personal crisis. Many were struggling financially and had nothing of value to offer David except their loyal hearts.

Can you imagine being in David's sandals at this point? There is a prophecy that he will sit on Saul's throne as the second king of Israel, and yet in a homicidal outburst of jealousy, King Saul plunges into a violent hunt for David's life. Then David, while wanting to respect King Saul and submit to him as the legal head of Israel, runs and runs until at last he collapses onto the cold, dark, damp floor of a lonely, secluded cave of Adullam.

There in Adullam, David was safe from King Saul and away from other people; there he could carefully and prayerfully navigate his life through this very confusing, difficult time. Then, out of nowhere, hundreds of men with enormous problems start showing up at his cavestep—asking for a place to stay and a man to lead them. There, in his cave of misfit people and during a time when David's country yearned for a legend, he built his army of legend-people! Who could have possibly known that something that big was happening in that most unlikely place?

According to Second Samuel 23:8-39, David's mighty men were almost like the gods of Greek mythology, each one having a story too sizeable for even the wildest of imaginations. First there was Jashobeam, who once used his spear to take down 800 enemy warriors in a single battle! Then there was

Eleazar, who stood alone in battle with David, and without any other assistance wiped out enemy warriors until his sword stuck to his hand. The rest of the army didn't even show up that day until it was time to gather the plunder!

After Eleazar, there was Shamma. One time, when the Philistines were gathered against Israel, this legend held back the entire army all by himself as every one of his fellow soldiers fled to safety. What about Abishai? He once used his spear to slay 300 enemy warriors in a single battle. And Benaiah. He's the valiant warrior who did many heroic deeds, which included killing two Goliath-like warriors from Moab. Another time, on a snowy day, Benaiah chased a lion down into a pit and killed him with his bare hands! These guys were legends beyond belief!

And guess what? Every one of these *legends* came from the very same cave. Let me say this one more time: Wherever there is one legend, there will often be a hundred more! Aspiring legends huddle until they hatch, and then they multiply. *Legends beget legends!*

This brings me to the main purpose of this book: *I want to build a stronghold of legends! Then I want to expose them to the biggest cause they've ever imagined! Just like David rallied his mighty men, I want to rally the mighty ones in my generation! Just as Dr. Martin Luther King Jr. had a dream and shouted it loudly, I also have a dream to shout about: Legends unite! Amass yourselves in formation! It's time to save this world!*

Best-selling author Seth Godin details the surprisingly simple way this can happen in his book, *Tribes: We Need You to Lead Us.*[5] According to this intuitive man, a person can bring change to the entire world from the remotest places. Thanks to the Internet, geography is no longer a limiting factor. This means for example: it's possible to gather ten thousand legends out of one hundred nations and build a *one million-member legend tribe—from Stuarts Draft, Virginia or anywhere else in the world!*

I've been praying, with faith and determination, that my passionate invitation will echo to the remotest places of the earth—to people of every race, rich and poor, young and old, blue collar and white collar, men and women. Just like David, I want to form lasting and loyal *true love* relationships with my *legend* friends.

Sure, many of them will come into the tribe with an enormous degree of personal problems and not much more than an epic but unrefined divine potential. But I believe we will become mighty over time—and we will build tomorrow's better world together, one incomprehensible victory after another! Can you picture this? I certainly can! I've seen this *one* million-member legend *tribe* in a hundred visions, and I've been preparing myself to lead it for the past twenty years. Oh, the difference we will make together!

1,000 MILLION-MEMBER LEGEND TRIBES

Some might wonder if I'm dreaming too big and trying to get you to do the same. We have to consider how big our world is. Think about this: If one billion is also one thousand million, then 6.7 billion people is the same as 6,700 million people! So, even if my one million-member *legend* tribe should become a perfect reality, then I've still only impacted .0149 percent of the total world population.

Therefore, since this world's population is so massive and so in need of change, we should wish for the immediate formation of a thousand such legend tribes. That is: One thousand, million-member, legend tribes! Even then, we would only represent 15 percent of the total world population, reaching out to the other 85 percent. Maybe, instead of spending so much time calculating our risks and odds, you and I should stop everything and multiply our dreams by one million—right now! I'll talk about this more in Chapter 8, "Get a Dream."

Fellow *legends*, if we sleep now, we can be sure that this world we've been given will be handed to the next generation no better—and probably a whole lot worse than it was when we first received it. Humankind will have taken until there is nothing left for all who come after us, stripping the earth of so much more than ever needed, carelessly trampling down its beauty. We will die bloated with personal achievement and yet starving to death from a deprivation of legacy—the paradox of never really living for the bigger cause.

As loudly as I can say this, I'm appealing to anyone who will hear me now: Let's hurry out of our bedrooms with eyes wide open. See this current world as it really is, and see where it is really going. Our civilization is speeding down into hell with very little resistance to stop it. In America and in many other increasingly humanist nations, our tamed religion has little effect on the surging evils of our day. We have no idea what we're walking into. Look at the ground! A thickening darkness rises up over our ankles like the creepy death-fog in a chilling horror film. This is the beginning of the end unless we discover the new world soon! Can anyone hear me?

This is a very passionate message so far. But is it passionate *enough* to have any real shot at creating a better tomorrow? I think that it is! How about in your own life? Are you going to let these first five chapters permanently affect your way of doing things? Are you ready for a *now or never* transformation in your personality, character, and spiritual life? What about other things like your personal goals, values, and spending habits? Will you make the tough calls for the right cause? If you open up your heart, a new fire will ignite! As you're standing here in front of the bigger cause, let go of lesser dreams, and fully abandon yourself to the dream of a better tomorrow.

COMING UP

After researching the biographies of many past legends and paying attention to the people who are making the biggest changes in today's world, I've discovered the major differences between legends and everyone else. In the coming chapters I share what it actually takes to be a real-life legend. First, we will take a field trip to the birthplace of every legend. This is where the *legend* adventure really begins

Chapter 6

Hurry Up and Find Rock Bottom

We can make him better!
—ABC's *The Six Million Dollar Man* television series

MY CRAZY LITTLE THEORY

Being a *legend* can be the easiest and most natural thing you can do with your life! Yes, you read that correctly. Yet right away, a little voice may rise within you, deeming this theory far outside the scope of reality. Why is this? What if, sometime way before you and I could think for ourselves, the internal settings that run our lives today were programmed in a great, big labyrinth of deception? If you're like most people, ever since early childhood you've been brainwashed about the ease of failure and the difficulty of success. It's as if your whole life is a scheduled disaster or some mean prank, and nothing good happens without a tremendous struggle. Am I right? What if you've been struggling all this time when struggling isn't necessary?

I'm sure you've heard that old saying, "If you want anything good in life, you have to go *against the flow* to get it." Well, I'm suggesting to you that, contrary to popular opinion, maybe we're not required to go against some proverbial flow. Maybe somewhere there's another stream for us—an upward current, flowing aggressively into the land of our wildest dreams! Maybe there is a real-life utopia for each of us, a place where success comes naturally and failure is the challenge. Maybe in this potential stream, doing the right thing is effortless while doing the wrong thing actually requires a determined struggle. If we could ever find our way into this living river, our feet would be swept from under us, and real life would be ours for sure! Could it be? Intriguing possibility, isn't it?

THE STRUGGLE IS PART OF THE TRAP

Price Pritchett, author of more than 20 books, traveled through Canada in the mid-1990s; in his hotel room one day he got an amazing revelation. Here's the story in Pritchett's own words:

> I'm sitting in a quiet room at the Millcroft Inn, a peaceful little place hidden back among the pine trees about an hour out of Toronto. It's just past noon, late July, and I'm listening to the desperate sounds of a life-or-death struggle going on a few feet away. There's a small fly burning out the last of its short life's energies in a futile attempt to fly through the glass of the window-pane. The whining wings tell the poignant story of the fly's strategy—*try harder.*
>
> But it's not working. The frenzied effort offers no hope for survival. Ironically, the struggle is part of the trap. It is impossible for the fly to try hard enough to succeed at breaking through the glass. Nevertheless, this little insect has staked its life on reaching its goal through raw effort and determination. The fly is doomed. It will die there on the windowsill.
>
> Across the room, ten steps away, the door is open. Ten seconds of flying time and this small creature could reach the outside world it seeks. With only a fraction of the effort now being wasted, it could be free of this self-imposed trap. The breakthrough possibility is there. It would be so easy.
>
> Why doesn't the fly try another approach, something dramatically different? How did he get so locked in on the idea that this particular route, and determined effort, offers the most promise for success? What logic is there in continuing with "more of the same"? No doubt this approach makes sense to the fly. Regrettably, it's an idea that will kill him.[1]

Sadly, this story about the fly isn't really about some poor, little fly. It's the tragic allegory of a real-life tearjerker about you, me, or someone we love. If we take the time to replay our past few months, we'll be forced to acknowledge an awkward reality—that our seemingly private lives are up on some big screen surrounded by a great, big audience! Even though most people pass through life oblivious to the watchers, everyone has an audience.

More than most of us will admit we've been both the watcher *and* the watched. Unfortunately, I have known the misery of watching someone I love massacre themselves at the windowpane. Many times! I've lived through the disappointment of shouting a message of hope into the deafened ears of a hardened heart. You too?

Before going further, please stop and look around. Is somebody watching you right now? Are your family members and close friends listening to the desperate sounds of your life-or-death struggle in your frenzied effort to make something happen? Are your "whining wings" telling your poignant story—the burning out of the last of your short life's energies in a futile attempt to fly through the glass of some windowpane? Is there someone out there who loves you more than you'll ever know, praying for you like there's no tomorrow, crying late into the night over your tragic struggle?

When Jesus was here on the earth, He was a people watcher, and what He saw brought Him much pain. He had so much good to offer people, and no matter how amazingly He presented it, some of them just never got it. They broke His heart, as Luke records:

> When the city came into view, He [Jesus] wept over it. **"If you had only recognized this day, and everything that was good for you!** But now it's too late. In the days ahead your enemies are going to bring up their heavy artillery and surround you, pressing in from every side....All this because you didn't **recognize and welcome** God's personal visit"** (Luke 19:41-44 MSG).

This portrait of Jesus crying is so real to me. I can almost feel the tears of Christ cascading down over my impassioned spirit as I synchronize myself with His burden. There is pain in the heart of God when people turn their noses up at the new life He offers them. This is why Jesus was weeping. He had just spent three and a half years preaching His heart out, loving everyone more than anyone had ever loved them, and pleading with that generation to stop throwing away their precious lives.

Jesus wrapped His compassionate, loving arms around the rejects of His day. Rich or poor, it didn't make any difference to Him; Jesus never turned people away. He accentuated the high value of their children, He took away their emotional pain, and healed their sickened bodies; He even bowed to wash their feet in unparalleled humility. Jesus invited everyone into the river of life. Yet many still rejected His love. Instead, they held tightly to their desolate lives until their season of grace had ended and there was nothing left but the mirage of achievement and a looming, fearful exit into eternity.

HOVERING OVER ROCK BOTTOM IN THE PIG PEN

Isn't it sad and ironic to think about how much God loves us, and how we spend so much of our lives running and hiding from Him? Why do we muscle through our days in human strength, only turning to God when we have nowhere else to turn? Why do we make Him our last resort? Why?

We live in a time when anyone claiming a close relationship with God is shunned as a "religious fanatic." This modern world makes it seem as if the only people who actually use the Bible as their guiding light are the *Jesus freaks*. It's like we're telling God to leave us alone so we can live as we see best, without having a responsibility to some heavenly Father. Take a look at the beautiful story Jesus used for describing this insanity:

> To illustrate the point further, Jesus told them this story: "A man had two sons. The younger son told his father, 'I want my share of your estate now, instead of waiting until you die.' So his father agreed to divide his wealth between his sons. A few days later **this younger son packed all his belongings and took a trip to a distant land, and there he wasted all his money on wild living.**
>
> About the time his **money ran out**, a great famine swept over the land, and he **began to starve.** He persuaded a local farmer to hire him to feed his pigs. The boy became so hungry that even the pods

*he was feeding the pigs looked good to him. But **no one gave him anything.** [Tough love] ...When he **finally came to his senses,** he said to himself, 'At home even the hired men have food enough to spare, and here I am, dying of hunger! **I will go home to my father** and say, "Father, I have sinned against both heaven and you, and I am no longer worthy of being called your son. Please take me on as a hired servant"*" (Luke 15:11-19).

Can you see why this message was, and still is, such an important message from Jesus? Millions of people who have never heard about Jesus have heard His story of the Prodigal Son. I think it's so popular because everyone has served time in the pig pen, haven't we?

Of course, not everyone in the mud is perceptibly trudging around in some extreme state of human deprivation. There is a vast sea of prodigals who *seem* to have their lives together—living in nice homes, driving nice cars, and having nice careers—while the *real* truth is that they're torn to pieces on the inside. No matter how successful we become in this world, nothing ever truly satisfies when our connection with the Father is broken.

Almost every day, I see people who are worn down with hard life in the pig pen. Some of them have spent so much time in the mire they've started to oink, grunt, and squeal at their own reflection. Their weather-beaten hides are bone dry and callus-covered—coarse, like sandpaper. They look thirty years older than they are. In a haze of misery, herds of these history-maker hopefuls drift into the wastelands with very little chance of return. They stopped liking themselves a long time ago; their dignity is shredded, and they feel like they have nothing and nobody to live for.

God forbid that you're up to your neck in the slop right now, reduced to a fraction of the amazing person you once were or could be, gasping for your life under the unbearable consequences of a big series of wrong moves. I've seen this happen so many times to so many people. Nobody ever plans a trip to rock bottom. Everyone gets there while trying to go somewhere else.

THE WORST THING ABOUT DECEPTION

I remember not too long ago, I was praying and even crying about several off-course people scattered through my wide circle of acquaintances. Just as I lived prior to my salvation in 1991, these people had thrown up a scant, five-second thought about God, and then went on living dangerously with their fingers crossed. They didn't know it yet, but they were racing straight into hell without any doubt over their chosen course of direction. They needed to be rescued—and I really wanted to rescue them!

During this time, I was meditating almost daily on this verse:

> Satan, who is the god of this world, has **blinded the minds** of those who don't believe. They are **unable to see** the glorious light of the Good News. They **don't understand** this message about the glory of Christ, who is the exact likeness of God (2 Corinthians 4:4).

Look at the key phrases from that verse: *blinded the minds, unable to see,* and *don't understand.* Isn't it scary to admit how often we've confidently devised idiotic plans, only to find out later how far off we were? Over and over again, we drive ourselves to dead ends because we're too prideful to stop and ask for directions. Even worse is the frustration of trusting an inaccurate source of information—the wrongness of being hoodwinked! At first glance, the wrong path usually feels perfectly natural. After all, *everyone's doing it,* right? But how can we know for sure that *everyone's going in the right direction?*

The prodigal son Jesus talked about was also confident in his plan! There was no doubt about it; he just knew his life could be so much better if he didn't have to suffocate under his father's rules. He felt that his father was somehow holding him back from the better things in life, that if he could just break his father's restricting grip, he would be a free man with limitless opportunities.

That is when the journey to destruction begins. An unchecked false impression grows into a faulty belief that inevitably steers us in fatal directions. We become stubbornly emboldened in our feeble stances, and we make bad decisions; yet we refuse to talk about alternatives because we're 100 percent convinced that we are right. The worst thing about deception is not knowing when you are deceived! As the proverb says, *"There is a path before each person that seems right, but it ends in death"* (Prov. 14:12). The

Contemporary English Versions puts it even more clearly, *"You may think you are on the right road and still end up dead."*

THRESHOLDS OF PAIN

It's so disturbing to consider how much pain most people are willing to endure. Numbed to the reality of their predicament, they keep on wishing for a miracle without changing direction. When anyone attempts to offer a sensible way out, they hold tightly to the deception and run as fast as they can in the wrong direction.

It's as if these suffering people are trapped in another realm, incapable of communicating with the outside world; they are unable to feel, paralyzed with agony, deaf to the voice of common sense, and unresponsive to the guiding voice of God. There they are, sinking deeper and deeper; down and down they go! All along, everyone watching them wonders how much worse things will get before they see how much better life is for everyone at Daddy's house. Plainly, some people have a towering threshold for pain, and so they never comprehend the severity of their scenario until they slam headfirst down to rock bottom!

A few years ago, while preaching for three nights in Kenya, Africa, I spoke from one Bible verse every night—John 10:10, which is one of my all-time favorite verses. It says so much in two short sentences! Jesus said:

> *The thief [the devil] comes only in order to **steal** and **kill** and **destroy**. I came that they [every disciple of Jesus] may have and enjoy life, and have it in abundance (to the full, till it overflows)* (John 10:10 AMP).

Here is Jesus again making everything so clear. In those sentences, He describes a world besmirched with evil. He lets us know of a violent spirit-enemy who thrills to tyrannize us in a living hell.

Apostle Peter says this also when he writes, *"Stay alert! Watch out for your great enemy, the devil. He prowls around like a roaring lion, looking for someone to devour"* (1 Pet. 5:8). What a pathetic job description. The devil's mission is to keep people far away from God so he can steal, kill, and utterly destroy them for all eternity.

WHERE IS GOD WHEN WE NEED HIM?

You may be wondering, if God is so great, then why doesn't He do something about the devil and all the evil in this earth? That's the age-old question, isn't it? I'm afraid the real answer might be too simple for most people to grasp its rightness. You see, I believe in God; I also believe that He is a good and loving God. I believe in His explanations of the past. I follow His instructions for a blessed present life. I believe in His promise of an eternal future. What God does in our world and in our personal lives is always done for our best—in the light of eternity.

Because there is a devil who influences the desires and actions of so many humans, we're all making bad moves that lead to awful consequences. Sometimes, we suffer the awful consequences of our own bad actions. Sometimes, our bad actions create awful consequences for other people. Other times, we suffer the awful consequences of other people's bad moves. And yes, because of this, bad things do happen to good people. But, even though bad things happen, we don't have to stay down when we're knocked down. We don't have to accept a defeated existence.

This will come as new news to some people. God has flattened the evil powers that once ruled the humankind. All by Himself, God through His Son Jesus Christ made it possible for *everyone* to have a restored relationship with Him. We were wasting away in our sins, absolutely incapable of satisfying God's righteous laws, and Jesus Christ lovingly and willingly lowered Himself down to this fallen world. As one of us, He did what we couldn't do for ourselves. He lived sinlessly and died sacrificially for all who trust Him as Lord. Jesus is the ultimate Man of the universe! Because of Jesus, we *can* become the children of God; and as such, the devil no longer has a legal right to destroy us. Because of His love and power, we *can* overcome *all* of life's challenges!

God doesn't want any of us to suffer and die without hope. We don't have to live like unwanted orphans when we have a Father who cares so much about us. Even though we cannot see His physical body, we definitely have a wonderful Father in Heaven who is always standing at the door, waiting for His sons and daughters to come back home! God's arms are always open to us. We see this in both the Old and New Testaments of the Bible:

> *The Lord has appeared of old to me, saying: "Yes, I have loved you with an everlasting love; therefore with lovingkindness **I have drawn you**"* (Jeremiah 31:3 NKJV).

And:

> *Then Jesus said, "**Come** to Me, all of you who are weary and carry heavy burdens, and I will give you rest"* (Matthew 11:28).

One of the amazing things about Father God is that He will give us our inheritance so we can go do whatever we want with our lives. Yet, great freedom always comes with great responsibility. And with our freedom, we can choose to go our own way and do our own thing, and we can shut God out of our lives—as long as we can endure the pain.

What a Father we have! He makes us homesick in many imperceptible ways. He's the gentle whisper in our cluttered hearts during those fleeting moments of silence. Faintly, we can feel Him nudging us to open our unused Bibles. He's the nagging co-worker who invites us to church every Sunday. In the middle of every disaster, He is that warm and peaceful voice, telling us there has to be a better way.

So, *where is God when we need Him?* He's right where He's always been! The natural next question: *"Then why isn't He helping me?"* Because you asked Him to keep His nose out of your life when you raced out of town with your inheritance, remember? I know, people don't usually say it like this, and I'm sure you never intended to say it like this either, but somewhere along the way, you wanted to live your own life—to go your own way. I hope this doesn't sound too harsh, but I'm just trying to set the record straight on God's behalf. It's like the church sign that says, *Feeling far away from God? Guess who moved?* Sadly, it takes most people a very long time at rock bottom before they realize this. The problem is never on God's end. Our Father is always reaching out.

THE TURNING POINT

Once you've really been there, you will always remember rock bottom as the Eden of your re-creation! Even though right now you may be gasping for air, only a few seconds from flat lining your way into eternity, rock bottom is a *wormhole* in the core of hell that transports the dead back into the land of the living.

While rock bottom will always be the low mark of your life, it is so much more—rock bottom is the starting location for your next exciting journey. So no matter how bad things might be going in your life right now, go ahead and free your heart to hope again! This moment is the end of your life as it has been to this point, but *it need not be the end of you.* Change your perspective! Be optimistic about all the suffering you're going through, for this can be the start of something wonderful—it can be all *upward* from here, if you just do the right thing at rock bottom.

In my own life, I've been shocked with how fast God can shift the momentum back in my favor. It's nothing for God to work a 24-hour miracle! It doesn't matter how far down you've fallen; if you're serious about returning home, this is the moment when God steps in like a superhero to the rescue. He's been waiting for this moment all your life, and here it is! Father is livid with your enemies! He's been anticipating the rock-bottom prayers you're now praying. He's never forced Himself on you before today, but if you'll open your heart, He'll rush in like a gale-force wind! Open the doors and windows as wide as possible—let the fresh, spring air in! This is a new season in your life!

Swooping down out of nowhere, it would seem, with His bare hands He will tear apart everything that has been making you cry. Stop trembling in fear! You're safe now. You've come under the omnipotent protection of *God.* Just reach out and take your Father's hand. Be still for a moment and let Him have a look at you. God specializes in fixing broken people and shattered circumstances. God is the restorer of broken dreams and the giver of new ones! No broken person is broken beyond repair. Every person is fixable! Yes, God can fix *you!*

To best illustrate the points I've made, let's remember that familiar nursery rhyme Humpty Dumpty.

HUMPTY DUMPTY

Humpty Dumpty sat on a wall.
Humpty Dumpty had a great fall.
All the king's horses and all the king's men
Couldn't put Humpty together again.

Have you ever taken time to mourn the demise of this helpless, shattered egg? I have. I remember hearing about Humpty Dumpty when I was a kid, and I always felt sad for him. It felt like there should have been a Humpty Dumpty sequel, but it never came! Whenever Mom would tell me this rhyme, I would think, *If all the king's horses and all the king's men couldn't help, why stop there? Why did these people give up on Mr. Dumpty?*

Then, one creative morning, I found new hope for poor old Humpty Dumpty. It made me feel so good! I thought, *What if we went to the king and asked for help? After all, we've tried all the other options; so what do we have to lose? It makes perfect sense that if the horses and the men couldn't do something, then still maybe the king could get Humpty back on his feet!*

But nobody thought about calling on his majesty, did they? Of course not, because this is the way we are. We try every other option before we ever consider going to the God who made us. If Humpty Dumpty had reached out for the king at his rock bottom, maybe this death rhyme would have a happy ending.

Have you ever thought about how morbid this story is for a tenderhearted six-year-old? "There was this happy egg who fell off a wall and died a brutal death on the concrete sidewalk. *The end!*" And then we say, "Good night kids; *sweet nightmares!*" Forget about blaming today's violent video games for the rise of violent crime, we have *Humpty Dumpty* to blame!

You know I'm exaggerating, but I'm trying to make you laugh a little while I make a serious point. I do hate to amend this classic rhyme, but we can't just walk away from Humpty Dumpty while he's suffering like this! We have to *do something*.

Just like the egg, we are all just one great fall away from breaking apart! I suppose it's good for us that Humpty Dumpty sat on his wall and had his great fall. We can relate to this, can't we? Maybe we should be so fortunate as to fall down off a high wall and break apart at some point. Otherwise, we could spend the rest of our lives sitting just a few feet above rock bottom. *Everyone falls.* It's what happens *beyond the fall* that makes the difference. For some, the fall is the end. For others, it is just the beginning. Humpty Dumpty could represent any one of us. I guess that's why I feel so compelled to give the rhyme a happy ending:

> *Humpty Dumpty sat on a wall.*
> *Humpty Dumpty had a great fall.*
> *All the king's horses and all the king's men*
> *Couldn't put Humpty together again.*
> *Then, when it seemed the story was over*
> *Along came the King Himself.*
> *He did what the horses and the men could not do,*
> *He worked His kingly work on Humpty and made him brand-new.*
> *Humpty Dumpty never sat on the wall after that day.*
> *He leaped and he danced*
> *And he thanked the King, as he went on his merry way!*
> *And Humpty Dumpty lived happily ever after!*
> *The End*

WRITING YOUR HAPPILY EVER AFTER

What about the rhyme of your life? How is it going to end? Don't tell me you're going to stay with those same worthless remedies you've already tried a hundred times before. You don't have to lie there, fragmented, strewn across that cold, hard concrete sidewalk. Don't you want to try something different? Instead of wasting the rest of your life calling for the King's horses and men, are you ready to see what the King can do? Just a few added verses, and you can turn your *death rhyme* into a *fairy tale!*

In Psalm 20:6-7, the psalmist David encourages people to put their trust in God alone for deliverance when he says:

> *Now I know that the Lord saves His anointed; He will answer him from His holy heaven with the saving strength of His right hand. Some trust in chariots and some in horses; but we will remember the name of the Lord our God* (NKJV).

Really, where are you putting your trust? Where are you going for answers to life's problems? Is your heart crushed and your mind frustrated, because you've spent a long time looking for love in all the wrong places? This reminds me of when I was a kid riding in the backseat of my mom's Buick Skylark. Every time the radio station played that 1980 Johnny Lee country music classic, "Lookin' For Love," my mom would turn the volume up. I don't think I'll ever forget the lyrics to that song!

I spent a lifetime lookin' for you.
Single bars and good time lovers were never true.
Playin' a fool's game hoping to win.
Telling those sweet lies and losing again!
I was lookin' for love in all the wrong places.
Lookin' for love in too many faces.
Searching her eyes, looking for traces
of what I'm dreamin' of.[2]

We have to stop living in singles' bars and sifting through the good time lovers, playing the fool's game and hoping to win! There is only one place to find the love and help we need. Request the King! Go ahead and make your appeal to the high court of Heaven! Ask God for His mercy. Ask for His help. He will come and do for you what nobody and nothing else has ever been able to do for you before.

Today you may feel like the worn out fly, beating your head against the window. Or maybe you're the young man, far away from home, feeding with the pigs! Maybe you're just like Mr. Dumpty—you've fallen, you're broken, and you can't get up. Even though this might be a very painful place, this is the very *best* place you've been in a very long time! This is when you encounter the glory of your King. This is your turning point. It's that fascinating moment when the winds shift in a new direction!

Fortunately, I'm not merely articulating some pleasant-sounding theory. I've had more than one highly successful rock bottom comeback over my past 40 years. Every time it seemed like there was no way I would live to see a better day, and I reached for God's great mercy—He never let me down. Not one time! It is at rock bottom that all our accumulated pride is stripped away.

It's there that we become most useful to our God and to our world. Rock bottom has to be one of the seven wonders of the universe!

Whether you're a worn-out businessperson, a burned-out drug dealer, a teenager struggling to find yourself, or a soon to be ex-spouse trudging through a nasty divorce, this can be your comeback! With only a fraction of the effort you're now expending, you could be just a few months away from the better world you're longing for. Don't be uncertain! Move away from the closed window and toward the open door! Hurry up and go back home to Father! Call out to the King! And live again—this time the way you always knew you could!

COMING UP

If you've had the guts to face the realities I've presented in the book so far, you're going to love what's next. In Chapter 7, we're going to chat about developing a *legendary* work and life ethic.

Chapter 7

Earn Your Keep

You dream and you wish with all your little heart, but remember, Tiana, that little star can only take you part of the way. You got to work hard too, and you set your mind too. Just promise your dad that you will never lose sight of what is really important.

—TIANA'S FATHER, *The Princess and the Frog*

THE DEADBEAT EPIDEMIC

It's a front-page story—fast becoming a large-scale, countrywide crisis. Will this be the end for us? Yes, of course, unless we get up and do something. It seems to me that *freeloaders* largely outnumber *breadwinners*; and one person can't carry ten deadbeats in today's expensive world. This isn't about one or two lazy people. We have an epidemic on our hands! Deadbeat dads, moms, and kids, deadbeat workers and bosses, deadbeat politicians, deadbeat Americans and Europeans—deadbeat *people!* Everyone has a few friends or family members with onset deadbeat tendencies. Some of us may even have it ourselves and not know it yet. Hurry up, cover your mouth and disinfect your hands! Put on a yellow mask and a pair of rubber gloves. It's spreading!

Certain mutant strains of this disease have already built a vaccination resistance; nothing seems to effectively knock it out. Initial symptoms include: an exaggerated longing for rest, a lost desire for work, an inability to get off the couch, and a decreasing concern for the well-being of one's family, community, church, and country. Even worse, DB massacres ambition, rendering its victims useless. People infected with a full-blown case of DB face the ultimate danger of mutating into zombified carcasses of deadweight burden to the rest of society!

As for my family and me, we would rather die a bloody death at the front lines of today's hottest battles than to live in the false comforts of self-preservation. God forbid that we should even slightly deviate from our dreams. God forbid that we should drag out our days knowing that our lives matter for no cause beyond our own survival. I cannot bear the thought of scrounging off of anyone else's hard work for even a single day, without putting back something far more valuable in the days that follow. No, instead I pray in earnest that God will expend every last ounce of us Balsamos—that He will feed a hundred nations and many generations with the great quantity of plunder acquired with our calloused hands.

Naturally, there are times when we all need to live on the efforts of others—while recovering from a serious injury, after the sudden loss of a job, or during some other category-five catastrophe. During these hard times, we should never feel guilty for accepting a few handouts. Instead, we should thank God for the blessing of friends, families, and charities, and pay special attention to the way it feels to be loved by others. Then, right after recovery, we should emerge with newfound compassion to make a bigger and more lasting difference in our world!

LEGENDS ARE NEVER LAZY—NOT EVER!

I can see how all this fanatical talk may come across as if I'm trying to take you a little too far. Yet, if we really want to leave this world a better place, we need to be the kind of people who react obsessively against laziness. First, we have to *seek and destroy* every lazy impulse within ourselves. Then in great humility we have to do whatever it takes to help shake it from our friends!

Because legends exhibit an insistent ambition to get things done, they create humongous waves of conviction for everyone in their proximity. Legends are live wires described by such spirited terms as provocative, invigorating, energetic, and captivating. With the slightest contact, they awaken the dead! The whole world loves to watch legends, because they are inspirational, motivational, and highly contagious! These are some of the reasons I want to become a legend in my generation. In the paraphrased words of the *legendary* 18th century evangelist John Wesley, "I want to *catch on fire with enthusiasm* and let the world come watch me burn!"

Don't get me wrong. I'm not opposing down time whenever a productive person enjoys it. If we work hard, we should play hard! In fact, the more diligently we labor, the more frequently we should rest and play. After all, *"The sleep of a laboring man is sweet"* (Eccl. 5:12a NKJV).

In the social code of Hebrew civilizations, there was zero tolerance for idle citizens. The saying of their day was, *"The one unwilling to work shall not eat"* (2 Thess. 3:10b NIV). They also taught, *"...if anyone does not provide for his own, and especially for those of his household, he has denied the faith and is worse than an unbeliever"* (1 Tim. 5:8 NASB).

Simply put, in those days, if you had mobility, you got up every day and worked or you were shamed right out of the community.

My First Job

Even as a child, I loved to work. I couldn't wait to get up in the morning and do something that would make life easier for the people I cared about. I even found great satisfaction in paying for my own toys. Believe me, I had my problems, but cleaning my room, helping around the house, and holding down a job were never issues for this precious little angel.

My first job was picking up trash for my mom's boss. I was only about ten at the time. One of the highlights of working that first job was being able to shop for presents *with my own money* to give away at Christmas. I wish you could have seen me that Christmas day. I walked tall into Grandma's living room with my sack of gifts. I felt like Santa Claus!

As each relative opened my special gifts that year, I smiled so big a banana could fit in my mouth sideways. My mom seemed even happier than me. I'll never forget her telling everyone, in her proud, motherly tone, *"Now, this one Chucky bought with his own money!"* During this time I learned a powerful, eternal principle that still drives me today—how much more *fun* it is to *give* than it is to *receive*.

I'm guessing that some people have never experienced this defining pleasure—not as young children, and not even as maturing adults. This is how the deadbeat disease latches onto its victims. It comes early in life, at the time when we first develop the aspiration to earn our keep. When this desire isn't acted out and then celebrated, it is suppressed; and if enough time passes without correcting this, we gradually drift down a path to full-blown *bumhood!*

While some people work very hard to improve our world, hordes of slugs and slugettes plunk themselves down and prop up their feet, demanding every kind of free ride available. If we don't awaken the inherent desire for carrying our own load, we will become unnatural creatures—men and women without a single ounce of dignity. Little by little, we will cultivate a selfish disposition, one that has no problem living fat on the handouts of productive citizens.

MY BIZARRE PASSION FOR LEARNING

Recently I received my current academic transcripts from Life Christian University and found that after I finish this manuscript, I will have achieved a total of 204 college credit hours, and I will have finally earned my Doctor of Ministry degree. Here's the breakdown:

- Undergraduate Studies—120 credit hours, GPA 3.73

- Graduate Studies—36 credit hours, GPA 4.0

- Post-graduate Studies—48 credit hours, GPA 4.0

Not too bad for the class clown who barely made it out of high school, and who never read a single book cover to cover until age 19! I lied on every book report and squeezed my way through English with a string of low Cs and Ds. When I was younger, I hated the classroom. I refused to read because I felt that I already knew so much; to me, school was a big waste of my work and social time. Then I hit the real world, and I struggled unbearably! Thank God it didn't take me long to see how much I had to learn.

Here I am two decades later, and wow, how things have changed! My passion for learning is a work of God's grace. Sometimes, when I think about where I came from, it's as if I'm hearing about a man I've never met! Believe me, this radical degree of transformation can happen to anyone. Once the mind is awakened, it rarely goes back to sleep. All a person needs is one good book to get the learning started—the rest is history!

I know this is going to sound super-spiritual, but it's true—the Bible is the very first book I ever completely read. By the time I was 21, I had devoured it—cover to cover—several times. I was reading ten to twenty chapters a day at times. On one quiet Saturday, I read the Book of Daniel three times and the entire Book of Jeremiah—all in one sitting! I began a routine that was popular back in those days—reading and meditating on one chapter of Proverbs each day. I swallowed down every morsel of insight I could pull from every chapter. By the grace of God, I've maintained this same commitment to reading the Bible for more than 19 years now; *it has been life-changing!*

I'm sorry if this sounds like a mountain of bragging, but I hope to rouse within you this same acquired love for learning. Think about it—you're reading a full-sized book, written by a guy who never read a book in his life before the Bible at age 19 except maybe *Clifford the Big Red Dog* and a few dinosaur pop-up books that don't really count. Maybe you didn't do your best in high school either. There is still time to learn—it's amazing what a mature adult can learn and add to classroom discussions. There are many colleges and universities that offer online learning opportunities in every area of interest.

In my early 20s, I began taking Bible college classes, and I haven't stopped studying theology and ministry since then. At age 24, I caught something important from my world-renowned real estate coach, Mike Ferry—his rare appetite for new information. I'll never forget how much it inspired me every time Mike spoke of the number of books he read each month and how committed he was to multiplying his effectiveness. During that time, I started reading at least four books a month—a habit that has stuck with me. Thank God for people like Mike Ferry! Attending his seminars was so much more to me than the profound information he presented; it was really about catching his passion. To this day, I've never met a man more inclined to learn.

After this book is published and I have received my Doctor of Ministry, I will continue to read a few books a month for the rest of my life. And I will complete another 45 post-graduate credit hours to earn my Doctor of Philosophy. Beyond this, I might study law or medicine, or something else that will help me better understand government, society, or certain intriguing aspects of our physical universe. Hopefully, I'll form a writing team and we'll publish a hundred books or more. I'd like to learn classical piano and study new languages and learn how to communicate in sign language for the deaf.

I certainly plan to study and experience God for the rest of my life! I want to know everything a human can know about Him before I head for Heaven.

I will never, ever stop learning. Neither should you. No matter your age, I pray that you will make a radical move toward learning, just like I did. Today, I hope my thirst for education inspires you just as much as my real estate coach, Mike Ferry, inspired me. Maybe you'll enroll in night classes at a community college. Maybe you'll register for classes at a trade school or enroll in Bible college or law school. Maybe you'll commit to some other fascinating field of study online. I do hope you start to up your game, and keep upping your game from today forward.

Really, who are we to brag in this 21st century compared to the legendary students of centuries past? Please consider John Wesley—the great evangelist from the First Great Awakening and founder of the Methodist church. In the course of his ministry, John Wesley "rose daily at 4 A.M., was preaching at 5 A.M. so working men could attend his services…traveled 225,000 miles, mostly on horseback, and preached over 50,000 sermons." That's 1,000 sermons per year for 50 years (or three per day)! Simultaneous with this preaching schedule, Wesley "wrote 233 books on all sorts of subjects, including some health remedies (*Primitive Medicine*, in use for almost 200 years) and one of the earliest texts on electricity!" He published "fifty volumes of theology called the *Christian Library*…a complete commentary on the whole Bible…composed hymns which live to this day." John Wesley left behind him 750 preachers in England and 350 in America; 76,968 Methodists in England and 57,621 in America."[2] We should be shocked to new life with biographies like this one.

A FEW GREAT QUOTES ABOUT LEARNING

I am learning all the time. The tombstone will be my diploma.
—EARTHA KITT

Man's mind, once stretched by a new idea, never regains its original dimensions.
—OLIVER WENDELL HOLMES

I don't think much of a man who is not wiser today than he was yesterday.
—ABRAHAM LINCOLN

Anyone who stops learning is old, whether at twenty or eighty.

—HENRY FORD

Wisdom has built her house; she has carved its seven columns. She has prepared a great banquet, mixed the wines, and set the table. She has sent her servants to invite everyone to come. She calls out from the heights overlooking the city. "Come in with me," she urges the simple. To those who lack good judgment, she says, "Come, eat my food, and drink the wine I have mixed. Leave your simple [foolish] ways behind, and begin to live; learn how to use good judgment" [be wise]. (Proverbs 9:1-6)

—KING SOLOMON

EVERYONE CAN BE PRODUCTIVE

Do you ever think, *What's the use? Nobody really cares anymore, so why should I care so much? Nobody really works hard anymore, so why should I work so hard? If nobody really values truth anymore, why should I sacrifice so much to preserve it for them?* So many times throughout this project, I have feared that I might be wasting my breath. Would anyone take me seriously in a world that mocks and martyrs its zealots? I've often wondered: *Will any lasting change come from me throwing this tiny, sterile message out into a vast sea of polluted ideas? Do I have even the slightest chance of building a better world?*

Then I realized that every time a sincerely devoted person starts somewhere, anywhere, change has a chance. Everyone can make a difference if we believe in a better tomorrow according to God's plan for our lives.

It has been said that the best way to swallow an elephant is to eat it one small bite at a time. Several years ago we sent our daughter, Heaven, to clean up her bedroom after a month's worth of neglect. After she was gone for more than an hour, I went to check her progress. To my astonishment, there was no progress at all. In fact, she was sitting in the middle of the room on a mountain of dirty clothes, crying in sheer hopelessness. Being the great father that I am—at times—I wiped away her tears and convinced her that the room would be on its way to perfection just as soon as she started somewhere. Within an hour, Heaven and I were ready for a visit from the president!

Even though I don't always bounce into action when opportunity knocks, here is the moral to this story about my daughter: Productive people love to get the show on the road. While everyone else sits around pouring out the tears, productive people motivate change. People love it when we step into their situations, because they know we won't accept failure. Whether it's in a child's bedroom, a small community boardroom, or the U.S. House of Representatives, all it takes is one productive person to get the cleaning underway.

What if every reader of this book spends two or three fewer hours on the couch every day? What if a half-million of us spent these newly created hours cleaning and significantly upgrading our personal domains? What if we volunteered in our churches or mowed grass for a widow in the neighborhood? What if we invested our time visiting the neglected elderly folks at a local nursing home or taking food to a struggling family?

Believe me, the lives of the diligent are fun and full! Just beyond that La-Z-Boy recliner, there is a great, big world of beautiful people praying for assistance from someone just like you. So rise up and burn your couches, all ye couch potatoes! You're being summoned to a lifetime of great adventures!

BE OUTSTANDING EVERY DAY—NO EXCEPTIONS

Throughout my three decades in the work force, I have discovered a very exciting secret to success. I used this secret to become a top-selling insurance agent (within months of starting in sales). This secret won me the top available salary for a tree climber within months of putting on the spikes! I used this secret to become one of the top-producing real estate agents in the nation. So far it's given me a huge advantage when speaking and leading, and I believe it's going to make me a legendary writer! My secret is not that complicated. Anyone can learn it.

Here's the secret: *Be outstanding every day—no exceptions!*

Sounds simple enough, doesn't it? In a world where many people range from incompetent to average, you have to become *outstanding every day—no exceptions.* Please notice the two simple commands given in this statement.

1. *Be Outstanding.* Determine that your performance will not be deemed typical or even slightly above average. Your

performance will always be far better than great—you are *outstanding!*

2. *Every Day—No Exceptions.* You can be counted on every day of your life—*no exceptions!*

I believe that in today's society, it is almost unfair how easily an outstanding and productive person can dominate any field of employment. Anyone who sets out to be *outstanding every day without exceptions* will most assuredly ascend each and every career ladder he or she sets out to climb. Life is so much fun for these kinds of folks. They spend their lives climbing; every step is progress. Even disaster works in their favor, though this may not always initially seem to be the case. *Outstanding every day—no exceptions* kinds of people live from one promotion to the next one all the way up to the day they are promoted to eternity.

If you're working at Chick-fil-A, make the finest and fastest chicken sandwich your lunch crowd has ever tasted! On days when you are not feeling well, keep your pain to yourself; quietly deal with it, and with great devotion put out no less than 110 percent. On those days when you are a basket case because of some big emotional crisis, give 110 percent! Throw away all the excuses for not performing; and for the rest of your life, refuse to be like the rest of the crowd. Sure, even the most outstanding people in the world have a moment so crushing that it wipes them out for a period of time. But don't let anything keep you down for any longer than necessary. Remember, you are a *legend*, so live up to your commendable title!

LEGENDHOOD IS HANDICAP ACCESSIBLE

What about all the people who feel like their Creator has ripped them off? Now I'm shining the spotlight of this discussion onto anyone who does not seem capable of doing as much as everyone else. Should we deem a person incapable of high achievement just because he or she is confined to a wheelchair, is learning disabled, or is blind or deaf? No way! Has our society grossly underestimated the tremendous potential of our handicapped community? Yes, we have! Is there any room in the chronicles of tomorrow's legends for a handicapped hero? I say without hesitation, *yes.*

I have a vision for my handicapped friends: I see thousands of Helen Kellers bursting from obscurity to bless the world! Maybe you have never been taken seriously before now—I believe you will rise during the next decade and astonish the mightiest people. I see handicapped business moguls and handicapped world leaders, handicapped presidents of universities, handicapped physicians, attorneys, and famous actors. I even see new breakthrough medicines for incurable diseases coming from you guys!

History is on your side. Take, for instance, the legendary Helen Keller.[3] When she was nineteen months old, Helen Keller contracted an illness that left her deaf and blind. But, by age seven, Helen created a sign language to communicate with her family. Anne Sullivan, who was also visually impaired herself, taught Helen to communicate. She learned Braille and used it to read English as well as French, German, Greek, and Latin. Eventually, she learned to speak. Not impressed yet? At the age of 24, Keller graduated from Radcliffe College magna cum laude, becoming the deaf-blind person to earn a Bachelor of Arts degree!

Even though I cannot praise Helen Keller for her progressive, liberal worldviews, I cannot praise her enough for modeling such a productive spirit. In her very full life, Helen traveled worldwide, was a friend of presidents, and became one of the most well-known women of all time. *The Miracle Worker* movie based on her life won rave reviews and awards, and in 2003 her likeness was stamped onto Alabama's state quarter.

Helen Keller is remembered for saying, "I am only one, but *still* I am one. I cannot do everything, but *still* I can do something; and because I cannot do everything, I will not refuse to do something that I *can* do."[4] She also said, "It is for us to pray not for *tasks equal to our powers*, but for *powers equal to our tasks*, to go forward with a great desire forever beating at the door of our hearts as we travel toward our distant goal."[5]

As you read or listen to *Make Me a Legend*, may your limitations shrink in the face of your enormous potential! This section is not only written for the benefit of those who are most obviously disabled. It is for anyone who even slightly lacks the physical mobility, mental aptitude, special abilities, or the dazzling looks of all the other near-perfect people in our world. I'm not pretending to know what it's really like for everyone. I can't imagine how often some people have been reduced by the low expectations of other people. I can't imagine how many times you've cried yourself to sleep, wishing your beautiful spirit could inhabit another body. All I can say is that I can feel God reaching out to you through me right now. He loves you so much, just the way you are!

Legendhood really is handicap accessible. Cheer up my good friend, you *can* most definitely help build tomorrow's better world. *Stop dreaming handicapped dreams!* There is a unique, divine purpose for every person. You can *earn your keep* in today's world. All you have to do now is free yourself from all the imagined restrictions of your handicap(s) and start to believe and live as if anything is possible for you from now on. *"Then Jesus said, 'Did I not tell you that if you believe, you will see the glory of God?'"* (John 11:40 NIV).

THE DOMESTIC ENGINEER

While covering the topic of earning your keep, I have to mention what I believe is the most indispensable category of human productivity—though their profession has never been listed in the annual *US News and World Report* list of best careers. I'm talking about the power of the domestic engineer, more commonly referred to as *the dedicated Mom.*

Solid research by Salary.com showed that in 2006 a stay-at-home mom needed $134,121 per year to be adequately compensated for her multiple roles and her 91.6 hours of weekly toil. The mom who works outside the home is given an estimated value of $85,876 for her 49.8 hours of mom-work per week.[6]

Amazingly, every one of these sometimes underappreciated women does what she does for a whopping annual salary of zero dollars and zero cents. Not a big deal, because Mom doesn't work for dollars; she does what she does for the personal satisfaction of seeing things go well for the people she loves. Without applause or other appropriate acknowledgment of achievement, Mom chooses to work her wonders in the shadows of the visible triumphs of her husband and her little ones!

Over the years, I have heard many moms say how increasingly insignificant they feel in this career-driven era. Many live confused and discouraged about their purpose and their future. I bring this up because I feel a great deal of compassion for the remarkable workers of this under celebrated profession. We should validate their significance in this modern world.

This is how God feels about moms: *"She carefully watches everything in her household and suffers nothing from laziness. ...Reward her for all she has done. Let her deeds publicly declare her praise"* (Prov. 31:27,31).

To all the industrious moms out there, I say, *Thank you!* Even though you may not have the achievement trophies to prove it, you are the *legend* behind the *legends!* Don't allow society to make you feel insignificant or underproductive. You are earning your keep—and so much more!

Dearest reader, please do me a big favor—for the rest of your life, never let another mom pass through your circle without publicly declaring her praise. Make it known to them that their sacrifices matter, that their everyday responsibilities are critical to the health and welfare of the family. On Mother's Day and every day, let us better appreciate mothers and do everything we can to respect and defend their importance.

A HUNT FOR SIGNIFICANCE

The next few paragraphs are devoted to the wiser, older generation. Why do many Western cultures put pressure on their prime-timers to fade from the workplace when they have finally accumulated a real aptitude for success? If the average U.S. life expectancy is now 77.9 years[7] and many of us are going to live well into our 90s, why are we retiring our finest employees in their late 50s to early 60s?

I feel like we've been brainwashed about the apparent blessings of retirement. Many Americans not only dream of retiring, they often fantasize about the possibility of an *early* retirement. From early on, we have been conditioned to believe that the earlier we retire, the more fortunate we will be. Retirement dangles in front of us like a bright orange carrot. Many work so hard in their 20s, 30s, and 40s only so they can rest when they reach the *retirement finish line.*

Several years ago as one of my very good friends was creeping up on his own retirement, I could tell there was something he wanted to tell me. As he eased into the conversation, he described several of his lifelong achievements. He explained that in spite of them, there was still something missing. That's the first time in my life I heard about the concept of *significance.* Even though my friend had no idea what his significance was going to look like, he was positive that he had not found it at the time of that conversation.

I felt a large degree of unrest in my senior pal as he longed to channel his passion and all his years of education and experience into something significant. Thanks to his transparency, I was blessed to comprehend something well beyond my maturity level at that time. It was right there in the front passenger seat of his new black Suburban that I heard the unspoken burden of so many retirees: "Please don't let me die before I contribute something significant!"

Shortly after this special time with my friend, I was in California at a Mike Ferry real estate conference. Since this particular conference took place during Mike's fiftieth birthday, he shocked his eager audience with a rare degree of optimism, dedicating an entire session to outlining his life plan for the next fifty years. I will never forget what Mike said to us that day. He gazed at his eager audience. You could hear a pin drop. We were on the edge of our seats. Then Mike said, "I've spent my whole life gaining the wisdom necessary to achieve real wealth, and here is how I am going to do it...." When many people start prearranging their funeral at 50, people like Mike Ferry write a detailed plan for achieving *significance*.

I wonder if the concept of retirement, as it stands today, actually sets us up for a premature departure. An extreme example of this is when a wife dies soon after the passing of her husband, maybe because she no longer sees a substantial purpose for living. I have to wonder, too, how much longer and more successfully we would start living if we planned on making our best years beyond 50.

What if we could reenlist some of these retired employees back into today's marketplace? What if we could culture a new way of viewing the aged people in our land, one that celebrates the possibility of phenomenal achievement between the ages of 60 and 90? There are countless examples of men and women beginning a lifetime of achievements well within their retirement years. These examples exist in both secular and biblical history; each one adds credibility to my proposal.

TO SIGNIFICANCE AND BEYOND

Two great biblical examples of aged *significance* are Abraham and Sarah. Abraham lived a normal life; but then, *at age 75* while all his friends were probably spending their pensions and prearranging their funerals, Abraham *finally* received the prophecy of a lifetime! I'm sure he must have felt like the message came about fifty years too late. Little could he have known at that moment how much God was able to do in his life after age 75! Abraham and Sarah had prepared their whole lives for the *legendary* decades still ahead!

Without hesitation, the couple packed their belongings and left everything to follow God's command to them. Nothing else seemed to matter. Abraham and Sarah were pioneering for a prophesied country and the promise of significance. And then, *another twenty-five years later,* this legendary couple finally whipped the odds and did the impossible, giving birth to a son as promised by God. (See Genesis 21:1-5.)

The territory God promised to Abraham became the land of his descendants and home to the great nation of Israel. Abraham and Sarah's retirement children multiplied like the sands of the seashores and survived unparalleled plots of annihilation to endure as God's beloved Jewish people.

During the following 75 years, Abraham outlived all other seniors in his circle, and he saw his miraculous lineage multiply. At 175 years of age, Abraham left the earth in peace, knowing the legacy of his *significant* existence.

All this happened because a man in his mid-70s refused to retire when he still hadn't found what he was looking for. You and I should also do the same. We should memorize the following verses from Psalms and refuse to die until we have achieved *significance!*

> But the godly will **flourish like palm trees** and **grow strong** like
> the cedars of Lebanon. For they are transplanted to the Lord's
> own house. They flourish in the courts of our God. **Even in old
> age** they will still produce fruit; **they will remain vital and green**
> (Psalms 92:12-14).

If you're over 50 and you still haven't found what you're looking for, don't ever stop searching for it! Don't waste away in boredom and loneliness, waiting around for some incurable disease to take you down—search for a new dream! Rather than eating up the money you've accumulated during your working years, leverage your great wisdom and multiply your nest egg by a hundred times or more. Then leave it to the incoming generations. Proverbs 13:22 says, *"Good people leave an inheritance to their grandchildren...."*

Don't get me wrong. I'm not trying to take away your right to kick back and feast on the fruits of your labors. Go ahead and do what you like—take vacations, enjoy eating out and going to the movies, spend time lavishing your grandkids! Just know that you don't have to cease being productive to enjoy your second 50 years. Do cease from hard labor. Leverage your influence wisely; for instance, start a small business, invest in real estate, author a book, become a coach, or enter into ministry. Do something significant that you may have spent the first half of your life dreaming about. This way you will stay young and vibrant, earn a hundred times your keep, and really know what it's like at *significance* and beyond!

LOVE YOUR WORK

If you are really going to be a legend, then you must love work. Even though it's true that most people are more successful when they find work they enjoy, legends love all work in general. As I have said before—honestly, I *love* hard work!

The kind of work I do doesn't matter so much. Give me a podium, a microphone, and an audience, and I will deliver my messages with peak energy day and night until I can't stand up another minute. Give me a shovel and a rake, and I will work blisters onto my hands and feet, loving *almost* every minute of it. Believe it or not, I enjoy working just as much as relaxing, and sometimes even more than that. In fact, I can't imagine living without a demanding assignment.

Some will argue that happy workers are workaholics. I believe that's a whole lot better than being a couchaholic. So, don't feel bad for people who love their work, and please don't try to counsel this out of us. Trust me; the benefits of loving your work and earning your keep in this lazy, modern world are way beyond listing.

Because I've always loved my work, I've always enjoyed a great abundance of unapologetic leisure. Whenever I'm working, my head is in the game for every second of it. When I rest, I have the time of my life with the people I love most. So, loving our work is actually the means to living a balanced life. When we are at work, let's love our work and do it well. When we are not working, let's love our families and friends, and live it up with them.

Wow, this was not the kind of chapter you want to read with a big fat bowl of ice cream. It was aggressive because it needed to be. Hopefully, the message is the wonder vaccination needed to successfully neutralize the deadbeat disease lurking everywhere. Hopefully, from today forward, fewer and fewer people will mooch from the efforts of our hard workers, and more and more of us will love our own work and earn our own keep!

Hopefully, more and more of our nation's potential *legends* will jump up off the couch and multiply their personal output a hundred-times right away. Don't be afraid to run hard after significance. You can do it and you *will* do it! Go out and add tremendous value to your family, your church, and your country. Even though your contributions won't look big to some people, you will know you gave your all.

Coming Up

One of the best ways to jump-start our productivity is to find something to live for—a worthy cause, a noble mission, or a God-inspired dream. Most people find it difficult to get up and work hard with a happy smile and overcome the many obstacles to success, if they never fully understand the real reason they are working so hard. In the next chapter, I'm going to share the wild story behind my big dream. And, hopefully, I'll provide all the inspiration you need for seeing or clarifying yours!

Chapter 8

Get a Dream

If I don't get the goose-bump factor when I'm reading it (the script) than I can't do it.

—RUSSELL CROWE, Actor

FACE DOWN ON THAT COLD, INDUSTRIAL TILE FLOOR

That night, under the chairs in a pond of tears, I had vowed to God that I was not leaving that spot without a dream. I was 20 at the time, a confused young man with a strand of mistakes varnishing the backdrop of my life up to that point. How did my world become so complicated already?

With a passing glance into my childhood, it would have been impossible to figure out why I wasn't the happiest person alive. When I was 12 years old, my parents purchased a campground, and we migrated south from the Big Apple (New York) to the Old Dominion (Virginia). This strategic move sheltered us kids from the dangers of city living and gave us an opportunity for togetherness as we operated our family business. At least that was the plan.

Here I was, just entering my teenage years—a respectable young lad moderately hyped over the coolness of owning a personal resort. We had a five-acre fishing lake and a very big pool with a really nice diving board. Every Friday and Saturday night, we hosted live concerts for hundreds of campers and locals. We had our very own video arcade stacked wall to wall with all the latest games—and pool tables, air hockey, pop-a-shot basketball, and the claw animal machine. Oh, and we had a grocery store supplied with every kind of junk food on the market—and cool tractors, horseshoe tournaments, exciting weekly activities, and everything else a kid my age could ever want!

For me, life at the campground was very good at first, and from the age of 13 to 15, things only got better. Our 44-acre oasis was sold out every weekend—and for my girl-crazed friends and me, there were girls everywhere! Spring, summer, and fall, that place was our very own paradise city. I remember talking my parents into letting me sleep in the tent for most of the camping season—this way I could sneak off the property and party the nights away. Yet the more I partied, the emptier I became.

Just like most American families, we had our dysfunctions, and as a young person in the wonderful world of dating I had my fair share of painful relationships—each one took its toll on my tender little heart. Even though I had a loving family, great friends, and every tangible object of my desire, I grew increasingly unsettled and so hopeless about my future that twice I tried to end my own life. Once was with my dad's .357 pistol. I remember walking into his bedroom, pulling the gun out of his bedside table, and putting it to my head. Still to this day I am positive I put enough pressure on that trigger to fire—but nothing happened.

A second time, I went into my bedroom on a midsummer day with a partially-used bottle of Extra Strength Tylenol. It was the biggest bottle they sold back then—and I swallowed down every pill. As I started to fall asleep, I remember praying the very first heartfelt prayer of my life when I told God, "I changed my mind and I want to live!" Thank God, He answered that prayer and I woke up a few hours later throwing up. I was terribly ill for a few days—an understatement. On both occasions, I wrote long good-bye letters blaming everyone for my pain. On both occasions, I was spared.

With a casual outside glance, people couldn't tell how far down I was sinking. At home, I was one of the most responsible kids a parent could hope for. My mom and I were best friends. Barbara Lynn Dobzeniecki Balsamo— what a lady she was! She and I talked about everything, and I do mean everything—we kept no secrets from each other. She even knew about that one time when… (Naah.) She loudly applauded my strong work ethic, because I toiled like a real man every day, mowing the grass, cleaning the pool, fixing broken picnic tables, and cleaning bath houses—three times a day. I also ran the camp store, helped my dad fix broken water lines, cleaned the ashes from a few hundred campfire rings, and did just about everything else that came with running a large campground.

At school, even though I spent so much time in Mr. Case's office, the assistant principle—and my stack of suspension notices measured something like four inches thick—my teachers secretly adored me. I was a phenomenal runner, winning Virginia state medals in both cross-country and track. I ran a mile in the low four-minute range and had a most impressive letterman's jacket decorated from top to bottom on both sides with patches and medals.

I started drinking alcohol just before my thirteenth birthday at a school graduation party—twelve Milwaukee's Best beers and a permanent scar on my forehead and my left knee to prove it. By the time I was old enough to drive, I could drink most of our campground drinkers under the picnic table any night of the week.

At 16, I passed an undercover police officer across the double yellow lines at close to 100 mph—and tried to outrun him in my four-cylinder Chevy S-10 pickup. When the chase began, I honestly thought it was a prank of one of my heartless buddies. His mom worked for the rescue squad and she had a flashing light on the car he drove that night. But those flashing *blue* lights were no prank! When I finally pulled over, my friend and I were commanded to the ground with guns, and I was charged with five accounts of reckless driving, including driving in possession of two pints of grain alcohol. They took away my driver's license and made me go to alcohol recovery classes, which only made things worse because none of the people in my group wanted to be in those classes. During the "smoke" breaks we bragged about our crimes, mocked our counselors—and broadened our party networks.

THE GREATEST AMERICAN HERO

Despite my harmful ways, I always had a strong desire to do something good with my life. Do you remember the television show, *The Greatest American Hero*? It aired for a few years in the 1980s, and I loved it! In the story line, a regular guy ends up stumbling upon a UFO one night where he's given a superhero suit and a mandate to rescue the downtrodden. The actor who played the lead role was a skinny, white guy with a big blond afro—just like mine! Everyone in my family could see the resemblance, or so they told me. I'm thinking I was barely eight at the time, and oh how I would dream about becoming the real-life Greatest American Hero someday! For an hour or so each night, I lay awake imagining myself flying around the world—defending justice, beating up the bad guys, and saving the lives of hopeless people.

At the time, my only concept of God came from my Catholic grandmother and my mom. Every night, Mom would bring me a glass of water and tuck me in, and she would remind me to dream of what it was like in Heaven. I wasn't even positive there really was a God, and even when I did believe, I never once thought that He had some great plan for my life.

I believe, though, that with each new episode of that crazy television show, God was connecting with me. He was announcing my future—and I was clueless! All I really cared about those days was dressing up in those orange and red Hot Wheels pants and racing up and down my driveway in my super cool Big Wheel—and in the strangest way, God was always there. The great Creator of everything was telling me that I would be a great American hero one day—flying around the world defending justice, beating up the bad guys, and saving the lives of hundreds of thousands of helpless, hopeless people! I have no doubt that millions of kids are getting messages from God just like I did—about a heavenly calling they won't understand until later in life.

ENGAGED IN THIRTY SECONDS

Just after my high school graduation, I reunited with Emily Elizabeth Wall—the love of my life! Emily was one of those "wild Richmond gals." Her parents conveniently stayed at our campground while building a hunting camp when Emily was just 13. I will never forget the day she walked up to the counter and gave me the pleasure of "checking her out"—with her purchase, that is.

After Emily bought her Snickers and headed back to the pool, my friend Tommy and I started fighting over who would be the first one to go talk to this drop-dead-gorgeous newcomer. I pulled rank out of sheer desperation—and Tommy graciously manned the cash register while I walked over to Emily.

We both felt love struck that afternoon as we talked together in front of that big, red barn. I laid down my bravest pickup line ever, "Hey! Will you please marry me?"

Without a moment's hesitation, Emily tossed back her stunning purple and red streaked hair, and she smiled just like it happens in all the fairy-tale proposals. Then she postured up and replied matter-of-factly, "Sure, if I can pick out the china pattern!" She is the only girl I ever used that line on, and amazingly it worked! I got the girl and she got her china pattern—four china cabinets and counting!

Emily and I tried our very best to stay close even though we lived 100 miles apart. We wrote each other one or two romantic love letters a day for something like six long and lonesome months. Long distance telephone rates were outrageous back then. We did not have email, Facebook, or cell phones with text messaging—and eventually we grew apart. For three whole years, it seemed as if the love we found to be so true that first day was only a memory sealed in time.

But this was not the end for us. Eventually the high winds of passion and romance blew over us again. Just after my high school graduation, we fell crazy in love—this time it was very serious! Our relationship was explosive. Our highs were very high and our lows were very low! In one minute we were playing and laughing until we couldn't breathe, and then a second later we were "breaking up forever!" We were way too physically attracted and definitely not committed to any kind of moral standard—so Emily became pregnant. It was terrifying for both of us. She was only 17, and I was just turning 19—and we were having a baby.

We were married in my grandparents' back yard, standing on top of an old creek bridge on August 11, 1990—and we lived happily ever after. Well, not really—because neither of us had been to rock bottom yet. Little did we know just how close to disaster we really were. It wasn't long before we were falling out of love and into hate—sliding into the divorce of no return!

The pressure of life was unbelievable during those days. Emily had to finish her senior year of high school in a new town, at a new school, and with a baby. She attended cosmetology school at nights, worked as an apprentice hairstylist, went to her prenatal doctor's appointments, cooked dinner, and took care of our home. I worked multiple jobs, trying my hardest to support our new family. We no longer had time to play and laugh. We had regrets. As you can imagine, the honeymoon didn't last long! Just before our first Christmas, tears were falling, love was lost, and we were both looking for the fastest way out! Emily found an attorney, and we were going our separate ways. Neither of us really wanted to be apart; we just could not find a way to end the fighting.

One night during that painful time, I fumbled across an episode of *Little House on the Prairie* and thought, *If Emily and I could just get a little religion in our home, maybe we could work things out and someday we could have a family like the Ingalls'*. Looking back now, I know that God planted these thoughts. He was reaching out to both of us in many unassuming ways and we were on the brink of reaching back!

There were three primary forces impacting us positively at that time. First was a group of kind and loving volunteers at the local pregnancy help center.[1] After the free pregnancy test, Emily received a free Bible and one of the volunteers, Amy, started sending handwritten letters of encouragement to us. Then there was our bold, redneck neighbor Dale—the guy who high-beamed us with his great bright Jesus smile every time our paths intersected.

In addition to Amy and Dale, there was one old high school buddy of mine—he really made the difference! Just as soon as my heart started opening up to God, Kevin was the first person I thought to call. Even though a few years had passed, I had not forgotten that unexpected September day when Kevin first came into school claiming he "found Jesus" at a summer youth camp. None of Kevin's friends were happy about his experience. I'll bet that I was the unhappiest of all! In fact, I did everything I could to lure Kevin off that straight line he walked so well.

Here I was, just two years later, pitifully humbled and on the phone asking Kevin to show me the way. Thank God he stood his ground in high school and did not weaken in the face of all that peer pressure. Thank God for people like Kevin, who gladly forfeit friends and reputation and everything else to live their faith right out in the open for all to see. It was about one month into our near-divorce encounter, while on the telephone with Kevin, that Emily and I invited Jesus into our hearts! It was the night of February 17, 1991, at 10:15 P.M. EST, to be exact!

We were so happy that night! Emily was on one phone and I was on the other, both with puffy, wet cheeks. I remember when we got off the phone, she ran from the bedroom and I met her from the living room—and we hugged for what seemed like hours, crying in each other's arms. At last, when it seemed like there was no help for us, God dove headfirst into our blazing inferno, scooped us up in His loving arms, and blasted us out the other side of rock bottom. What new confidence we had that night, knowing that our lives had finally taken a turn in the right direction!

BACK TO THE TILE FLOOR

Within a year of that 1991 spiritual encounter, I was on a grand scale quest for the meaning of my life. Why had God spared me so many times? I had friends who were killed in drunk driving accidents after leaving the same parties. Another friend died from a drug overdose sitting right beside me in the same motel room, doing the same drugs. A few of my friends even succeeded at suicide. And there I was, an unlikely survivor, miraculously still standing.

My Greatest American Hero dreams were back—stronger than before. What had started years ago as a curious feeling deep inside my preadolescent heart was beginning to shake me up! I started to experience an uncommon awareness of God. The One I so eagerly pursued during those first months was now pursuing me. He was watching every move I made, following me everywhere I went, waiting for that perfect moment when He and I could have a heart-to-heart conversation about the future. Somehow, I recognized the importance of what was trying to happen and I gave myself to God like a spiritual junkie. Every fix left me longing for so much more!

The time was nearing midnight. The band was still playing as a courtesy to me. My curiosity was far beyond its bursting point. I was starving for answers to the questions God Himself had loaded into my heart. I mumbled in built-up desperation, "God, here I am at this Saturday night Bible study asking You for answers. For some unknown reason, You spared me—and I know that when You made me, You had something very specific on Your mind. Emily and I have just come from rock bottom, and we are both ready to serve You faithfully for the rest of our lives. Please don't ask me to wander around aimlessly for even one more day. Just a glimpse, please give me just a picture—a snapshot of my future!"

You see, once we are stripped all the way down to nothing, we are in the perfect position for a bona fide message from God. We don't care what it is, we are ready to do anything—just give us purpose! The portal for divine interaction opens; our ears become high-powered antennas divinely attuned to the channel where God transmits His grand-scale messages! We find ourselves hearing things, until we wonder if we might be going crazy!

During these times of spiritual amplification, we start to appreciate all the simple things we never noticed before—like sunsets and star-filled skies, chirping birds, and the splendors of a flower garden. Our eyes fly open to a million new spectrums of beauty! All the years of blindness are finally over and for the very first time, we can see! "Hey everyone, I can see! Look at all the meticulous details of this infinite universe! All the new colors and shapes and creatures and images—and God!"

This is where real living begins. Just days, weeks, or maybe a few months beyond rock bottom, the legendary progression starts to pick up speed. The dream comes, often as everyday images fighting to be noticed in our hurried, cluttered hearts. Every time we lend all of ourselves to these creative moments, we come out of them with the dreams that shape history!

For some, before the dream, their scanty lives drift along without purpose or direction, tossed around by the winds of uncertainty. Tens of years pass by while they expend their meaningless days, sometimes with high achievement and self-gratification, doing nothing of great and lasting significance. On the outside they appear adequately contented, even overly satisfied, but on the inside they long for a dream!

THE HELICOPTER VISION

Well, God did speak to me that night. He shattered that irritating cloudy glass ceiling between the two of us. On the floor and under those chairs, my eyes had never been so tightly shut—yet, it seemed as if I was yanked into my future undetected, onto the scene of a world-scale event—eyes wide open!

The first thing I noticed was a helicopter flying low over a large city. It had a remote news camera mounted underneath, scanning the world below. As I looked down from the helicopter, I could see skyscrapers lining both sides of the street. And from one building wall across the sidewalk, across the road, and across the other sidewalk all the way to the other building wall—I saw crowds of people throughout the city.

As the helicopter proceeded northwest, I could see that there were massive speakers and television screens every 30 yards or so. Everyone seemed to be frozen in time over what they saw and heard. We flew until the street we followed reached an intersection. It was like some kind of square, or roundabout, with streets running out from it in several directions. When I saw the other streets, I noticed that there were just as many people on each street as far as my eyes could see. Their attention was riveted to the screens with fascination.

After I caught my breath from the shear awe of this occasion, I remember looking toward the middle of the square where I noticed a grassy area with a humble platform. It looked like a live concert had just taken place. There had to be millions of people gathered into this city for whatever was happening. The helicopter switched into silence mode—and I looked down to the platform.

Truly, I had no preconceptions about what I was about to witness. In this vision, I could see through the lens of the news camera as it began zooming down on center stage. I could see instruments and speakers, and a tall man standing in the middle of the platform with a microphone in his hand. Just a little more zoom and chills ran over my whole body as I came face to face with myself, orating like a world leader! It was me, standing tall and speaking confidently, while the audience was listening to my every word. Could it be?

At this point the vision seemed to be so much more than a vision—it was a live event actually happening, somewhere in the future! My tears were now forming a little puddle on the floor as if a lifelong dam of emotions had ripped open. Oblivious to anything else happening around me, a sudden stillness settled over my heart and from the stillness came a voice, "Chuck, follow my plan, you will impact all these people for Me—and you will shape *world history* before you leave the earth!"

END THE SCHIZOPHRENIA

I have to wonder if I'm out of my mind for spending so many pages boring everyone with all the personal details of my life dream. You picked up *Make Me a Legend* to better define yourself, right? I guess maybe I'm gambling on the chance that as you experience my story, strong desire will surface for your own unique story.

The dream you just read is my dream. It's what makes me an original. Thankfully, none of you can ever be me. Because you are an original as well! Even if you're not absolutely convinced yet, God is right now at the edge of

His imperial throne ready to infuse you with a dream so original it will end your schizophrenia forever!

Of all the key biblical characters, none better describes the need for a life dream like Jacob, grandson to the great patriarch, Abraham. Scripted halfway through the Book of Genesis, Jacob rushes onto the scene in a frantic outrage, striving so badly to be somebody that he ends up hoisting the identity of his older brother, Esau. As far back as Jacob could remember, he never wanted to be himself.

Jacob salivated at the dream of being Esau because as the oldest brother, Esau was promised what seemed to be the greater inheritance of his father's estate. Jacob was all messed up! Countless preachers have pointed to Genesis 25:19-34 as the perfect text for describing an identity crisis. Can you imagine being the remembered as the most insecure person of all time?

For me, the saddest thing about this unhappy young fellow is that he didn't need to steal his older brother's identity. Jacob already had his own unique prophecies—epic prophecies predating his birth. Jacob was predicted to have far greater eternal influence than his older brother. Yet, instead of believing the prophecies and trusting the God who gave them, Jacob created years of torment for himself through the terrible insecurities that fueled his actions. Even though God orchestrated many opportunities for Jacob to discover his own uniqueness and appreciate it, Jacob just could not see it until much later in life. Here was a man who wished to be anyone but himself.

In a very short summary of Jacob's life, he tricks his blind father into blessing him with his older brother's inheritance—an irrevocable blessing this was! Jacob then relocates to a distant land in fear of being killed by his rightfully enraged brother. Here, living under the constant guilt of his wrongful actions, Jacob gulps down a few barrels of his own medicine when his new father-in-law swindles him repeatedly and for many years. Finally, after too many years of complicated living, an exhausted Jacob heads for home.

It was on one very dark night of this petrifying journey that a most devastated Jacob had all he could take! Without a doubt, this was a rock-bottom moment. After sending his family to the other side of a creek—all alone, Jacob fires off his distress prayer—my interpretation:

> "Um, hello? Is anybody out there? Hello, God? It's me, Jacob, and I need You right now. Please don't let me do this to myself

anymore. Tonight, when I get finished praying to You, I must walk away from here knowing who I am! I have been living a lie for most of my life and tonight You are the only One who can tell me the truth. Please God, tell me who I am. Please, tell me why I am still alive. I am here for as long as this takes, with my face in the dirt—my trembling arms are wrapped around Your strong ankles and I can't let go until You bless me with my very own unique identity! Please God, I am so tired of playing Esau. For the rest of my life, I just want to be Jacob, no matter what that means."

The significance of what transpired under the stars that night could never be overstated. God certainly responded to Jacob's cry of distress. Just as He always does, God far exceeded Jacob's expectations by changing his name to Israel. The name Jacob means one that supplants or undermines. God was now saying to him, "Jacob, I am going to grant your humble request and you are no longer going to live as one who supplants or undermines. Tonight, I am changing your name to 'Israel,' which means one who wrestles with God and overcomes. I am upgrading you in this one very significant prayer session, My son. And you will never struggle with your identity again!"

We have to wonder how much better things would have gone for Jacob if he had scheduled this meeting earlier in life. Just like Jacob, too many people fail to appreciate their uniqueness until they have become exhausted trying to be like everyone else. It amazes me to see just how much more successful people become once they know who they are. In just *one night,* a crushed man became a conquering nation! Usually that is all it takes—just one long, dark, desperate night. In Jacob's case, a mighty legend struggled through many days as a second-rate imitation, not knowing that one night and a new life dream could change everything!

I would say the greater part of our society lives and dies in a Jacob-like pre-metamorphosis form. They are the Jacob who never blossomed and the Israel that could have been. It happens so often because few people ever push for God's dream like Jacob did. Let's be very honest. Besides a surface glance at Rick Warren's best-selling book *The Purpose-Driven Life,* most people never really wrestle with God about their identity. Our world is covered with millions, even billions, of striving Jacobs sleepwalking through the wastelands of meaninglessness, perishing without a clear life dream, doing what they do only because there is nothing better to do—whatever, wherever, whenever, until finally they retire to their pine box caskets.

KEEP YOUR DREAM PURE—DON'T EXAGGERATE

Maybe you already have a life dream, and maybe your dream seems minuscule when compared to other grander ones. Maybe you're tempted to underestimate your personal value because everyone else seems to have so much more going for them than you do. What if your whole reason for being here is all about helping someone else's dream fly? What if you have been training all these years to assist another big dream? Are you ready to jump up and down over that picture? Would that kind of dream still motivate you to live and sacrifice like a legend so that you can become the very best "second person" your world has ever known? Do you see what I am getting at?

I have met and known countless strivers in my lifetime. In fact, I have been one! I know what it is like to look down on a huge life dream—like it's never good enough. I know the restlessness of striving after some other person's more electrifying dream. We all want to be electrifying—and we should be! I am talking about that striving-induced agitation that keeps people deadened from the completeness of a pure heavenly calling. With peace and confidence, we should be able to say, "Yes! I now know who I am—and it might not look like much to others, but this is really me!" Then we won't end up driving everyone around us crazy with our strenuous exaggerations.

People don't usually realize (until it is too late) that exaggerating a dream usually makes it smaller, not bigger. So my advice to you is this: Be very careful not to reduce your dream through exaggeration. Always dream big, live bold, and make a difference! Love and serve the God who promises, *"with God all things are possible"* (Mark 10:27 NKJV). Just be very determined about keeping your life dream as pure as you can. Because really, the size of a dream does not matter—clarity does! Oh, and keep it biblical, too. Don't fall into the trap of thinking you are some reincarnated ancient prophet bringing a new religion to the earth. Pray about everything—keep yourself in check by keeping God in your heart, mind, and spirit.

This element of exaggeration really is a dangerous thing to play with—sometimes it can be deadly. Here is why. I believe that God graces each person to carry out their own life dream, whatever it may be. So when people exaggerate themselves into things they are not created for, they risk exhaustion. Someone may say, "OK Chuck, what if my dream leads me out into the remotest regions of some volatile third world county, and as a missionary I will have to offer myself to a life of danger and sacrifice? Would this be fair when I could just as easily invest my same talents to the creation of a multibillion-dollar company—one that funds a thousand missionaries? Why does one person get to carry out his life dream living in a 10,000 square foot presidential suite while I have to live in a grass hut and eat repulsive foods for most of my life?"

Now you are asking the right questions! I believe God graces you to enjoy *His* dream for your life. In other words, if God has called you to be a missionary, then He will satisfy you in grass huts and grief-stricken lands. You will taste all the majesty of God's amazing grace as He dwells in those humble shelters with you. Every time you walk through that curtain door, you will be happier than you could ever be in a Ritz Carlton Hotel. If God calls you to start up that multibillion-dollar company, then His amazing grace will satisfy you too, despite the insufferable pressures of business leadership! Every dream has a cross and every cross comes with—grace. Neither money nor possessions nor any other thing will ever yield a satisfied heart apart from the grace of living in God's specific dream for you.

CONFIDENCE IS ATTRACTIVE

Our present world is overcrowded with insecure people who drive everyone around them crazy and waste the best years of their lives salivating at the identity of someone else. If you really want to make a difference in your world, you need to get a dream and confidently pursue it—because history belongs to confident people! Nobody likes to spend time with people who crave attention and affirmation. Am I right? Whether it's moral or not, the more uncertain you are about yourself, the more attention you need, the less attention you will receive. Get a dream, because confidence is attractive!

Are you blazing ahead with the clearest version of your life dream? Have you taken the time yet to wrestle with God until the break of dawn? If it takes a few weeks, a few months, or even a few years—the time you spend looking and listening for God's dream is time well spent. Don't put this off any longer—the striving has to end right here.

Ding, ding, ding! It's time to wrestle, Jacob—this one defining moment changes everything for you! As a million mondo-sized goose bumps race up and down your back and arms, stretch this out! Make it last! Take massive, immediate action before this opportunity passes. This morning, today, or sometime tonight—politely dismiss everyone and everything out of your personal space, lower the shades, lock your doors, and wrestle. Go after a new name—and don't let go until you get it!

COMING UP

Look how far we have come in just eight chapters! "Whooah, we're half way there! Whooah, living on a prayer! Take my hand and we'll make it—I swear!" –Jon Bon Jovi

You may have to change your clothes before you turn the page! Put the book down, go to your bottom dresser drawer, find your dirtiest work outfit, get out your work boots, and pick up your shovel. I'm not joking! In Chapters 9 and 10, we are going to dig the deepest hole ever. Then, we will dive to the bottom of the pit and start laying a foundation extravagant enough for your exciting future!

Chapter 9

Build an Extravagant Foundation: *Why?*

If I had eight hours to chop down a tree, I'd spend six hours sharpening my ax.

—ABRAHAM LINCOLN, sixteenth U.S. President

PATIENCE

There she is, towering above the first sentence of the first paragraph of this ninth chapter. One tiny little word staring you down—so intimidating she is! Patience! Brr, so chilling. Every time a person tells me, "Chuck, just be patient," or, "Chuck, you're too anxious about everything—you should pray for patience!" Every time I get stuck in heavy traffic and I start to breathe heavy and say mean things to the other drivers, and one of my tranquil passengers snickers and says, "Chuck, God must be trying to teach you a little patience! Try to relax and it'll be OK."

Hearing this turns me into an animal. Aggghhh! "You know what? Just buckle your seat belt, and sit there quietly in your passenger seat, Mr. Cool! And please do not use the P word in my car ever again. Do not say it in my house either. Consider yourself warned. The next time you say *patience* in my presence, I will have no choice but to wash your mouth out with soap!"

Have you ever felt like you were going to snap like this? Even just a little bit? OK, maybe I am exaggerating to make a point. I'm wondering though, *Am I the only one in a hurry?* Do you have a "patience phobia" too?

Several years ago, I envisioned myself standing tall on a gigantic international platform, giving a fresh start to millions worldwide. Instead of being there, I was actually awakening to the reality of another average day—all alone on my back yard patio, still typing my no-name heart out, wondering if anyone would even want to read this book by the time it was finally finished. I knew I was carrying a right-now message, and I feared my topics might not even be relevant if it took much longer to complete. No matter how many focused hours I dedicated to this task and others, time had become my enemy! I felt like a slow-motion person in a fast-forward world!

Now the book is in print, and, as you can tell, my life dreams are very clear. This may sound a little strange, but it is as if I have already lived in my future! I have already voyaged into the horizon—and if even one tiny fragment of my life vision doesn't happen just the way I have already experienced it, I am afraid that I may somehow feel defrauded. Sometimes I am taunted with the vast dissonance between my dreams and the baby steps of progress I have enjoyed to this point.

On one very discouraging day, a dear friend sent an email inquiring about the progress of our church and ministry. Here was my reply to that email, and the nucleus of this chapter:

> Dear Bennett and Jane,
>
> Things are going really well here with us. Even though I have been poised since the first six months to start building a radiant skyscraper, God still has us shoveling dirt and laying blocks—every long, grueling day, shoveling dirt and laying blocks. We are building an unprecedented foundation like nothing I've ever seen! It's so enormous, so *extravagant* as far as foundations go! Reluctantly, I admit how humiliating it is to keep informing my supporters that we are still working on the foundation here!
>
> It seems illogical to be building *down* for so long. It is taking forever, and I am more anxious than ever to start reaching *up* toward the vast blue skies. Despite my impatience, I am beginning to see God's brilliance here. This extravagant foundation we are resting on today is masterfully constructed—built to support something of legendary proportions. God has been surrounding us with people of impeccable character—and He's been very careful to tear out any blocks we have recklessly

laid—the ones that will not be able to support the magnitude of vision we are about to erect!

THE DIRTY PART OF THE JOB

Nervous people demanding split-second results; this is our world. When today's achiever cannot measure results in terms of above-ground progress, they usually jump ship in search of something far more immediately gratifying. It is comical to watch how enthusiastic people are when they first encounter a sizable dream like ours. Springing up so quickly—out of nowhere, unreservedly committing their blood, sweat, and tears to nothing more than a well-pitched proposal—only to fizzle as they calculate how much longer it could take before they will be able to personally benefit from the dream.

Building foundations takes a very special kind of people. Building extravagant foundations takes the rarest people of all! Successful foundation workers possess a remarkable degree of foresight. With bizarre enthusiasm, they bed down in dirty places for however long it takes to lift a towering dream into the air. They have counted the cost, knowing they may never experience the pleasure of standing on their own platform. Foundation workers accept responsibility; they request responsibility—for the dirty part of the job!

Throughout history, former generations have given up everything to lay the foundation for a better tomorrow. Sadly, their better tomorrow is our better yesterday. Even though we may feel especially enticed to kick back and freeload off whatever remains from their selfless labors, we must welcome our commission to labor insistently for the greater blessings of our future generation. We should consider it a great honor to sacrifice just as they did—underground for most of our lives, sweating in dirty places for the hope of a better tomorrow. Possessed with dreams, people like us stand up firm on little more than the intangible possibility of what could be, and that is more than enough for us—the legends we hope to become.

Recently I was having a conversation with my son about his purpose in this world. At 19, he is thinking and praying about so many things these days. At 39, I am thinking more and more about the kind of world I am creating for him and my daughter and for their future children. On some days, it seems as if my life is moving way too slowly—as if my lofty dreams are still a few lifetimes away.

Have you ever considered what might happen to your dreams if you die sooner than expected? Maybe you are uncomfortable thinking of such things, but for me, it is very enlightening. Sometimes, your progress is more easily identified when you look beyond your funeral—even 20 years beyond your funeral—or further than that! I am not a perfect person and neither are you, but I hope that when our lives are over, people will say, "Those people had the dream of a better tomorrow. They sweated their lives away in dirty places, seldom tasting the fruits of their own labors. They stood so firm on nothing more than the intangible possibility of what could be—and now, look at this extravagant foundation they have left for us!"

If the only thing you and I leave behind is a new foundation, then we should be able to rest in peace. If we have to spend our entire lives in the dirty places, we must know that it is worth it. We must demonstrate a deep confidence in the generations behind us, that they will make our efforts count for something—and that when the time is right, they will stand up tall on the platform we have built for them!

THE MIRAGE OF AN ALLURING SHORTCUT

Just like many others, I am always attracted to the mirage of an alluring shortcut. Don't get me wrong; I do believe in the real possibility of a quantum leap.[1] These happen when we are faithful to dominate every square centimeter of a growth phase—all the way to a graduation ceremony. In this process of faithfully completing lesser assignments, God promises that He will promote us into far more enlivening ones.

> *The master was full of praise. "Well done, my good and faithful servant. You have been faithful in handling this small amount, so now I will give you many more responsibilities. Let's celebrate together!"* (Matthew 25:21)

In this passage in Matthew, Jesus makes a huge promise to each of God's *faithful* servants. From Jesus' statement, we can know that God is always testing for progress. It does not matter that nobody else in the entire universe gives you the attention you feel you deserve. God is the giver of promotions. One touch of His favor and everything can change for you! Don't worry about being overlooked, because God never misses faithfulness. When you pass a level, God will call you up from the crowd and onto the platform to be lavished with honor in the presence of all your peers. He will promote you to infinitely higher degrees of ability and responsibility. When that time comes, you have to stand up tall, without hesitation or false humility—and take God's hand, turn on your biggest smile, say good-bye to yesterday, and leap with everything you have!

My warning in this chapter is against the danger of seeking a promotion before you have mastered a level. I'm talking about the danger of overestimating your progress, the hazard of forcing your way onto higher levels before you are strong enough to thrive there—the hazard and humiliation of self-promotion. You and I both know the embarrassment of seating ourselves at the head of a table only to realize we were sitting in somebody else's place of honor. This is a perfect portrait of a forced promotion. It fluffs our minds with false hopes and dashes our hearts to pieces, as we are asked to move back down the table. This is always a very painful, big waste of time.

> When Jesus noticed that all who had come to the dinner were trying to sit in the seats of honor near the head of the table, He gave them this advice: "When you are invited to a wedding feast, don't sit in the seat of honor. What if someone who is more distinguished than you has also been invited? The host will come and say, 'Give this person your seat.' Then you will be embarrassed, and you will have to take whatever seat is left at the foot of the table!" (Luke 14:7-9)

The more impatient you are, the more shortcuts you will encounter. As you yearn for them, they reach for you! On some days, there seem to be a hundred shortcuts whispering to me from every direction. This is especially true when my passions are heightened as the urgency of my mission puts pressure on my devoted heart. When I see and hear the oppressed people in this world, the people I was born to rescue, pushing their way into my dreams, pleading to be helped—I long for shortcuts!

I don't want to be shoved to the butt of the table any longer than I have to sit there, because perhaps like you, I feel my country needs me now. As I listen to presidential speeches, I find myself wishing that I could have just 30 minutes to address my countrymen and women. Every time I feel like I'm getting close to achieving my dream, there is another freaky delay, some bizarre obstacle that sets me back a year. Sometimes, I am afraid that I may surely pass away before I lay hold of the influence I was born to wield. Yet I cannot fall prey to these urgent impulses and lose my head in a manic hunt for shortcuts. Neither can you! I think this is what the prophet Habakkuk must have been getting at when he said:

> This vision is for a future time. It describes the end, and it will be fulfilled. **If it** [the vision] **seems slow in coming, wait patiently, for it will surely take place.** It will not be delayed (Habakkuk 2:3).

SHOOTING STARS

Captivating the masses, blazing brightly against their motionless backdrops, smoldering out in a short second or two—thus is the fleeting spectacle of a shooting star! Certainly you have noticed how fast today's superstar burns up and then fades away. Everyone built on a poor foundation of twisted intensions and rotten character always ends with a humiliating collapse.

Tragically, too few people stay on top once they get there. The whole world stands at attention as each new history-maker hopeful graces the scene. Yet, more quickly than each one rises, they plummet from their heights, mutilating thousands in their wake. There is no way to fully measure the damage caused by each shooting star. King Solomon explained it like this, "*A righteous man falling down before the wicked is as a troubled fountain, and a corrupt spring*" (Prov. 25:26 KJV).

Innocent people suffer when stars collapse! Every time another high profile leader falls down in the sight of millions, God is mocked for it. In the last book of the Bible, satan is described as the "accuser." He is just like a drama-hungry news reporter who is constantly searching for the next shameful story. Just like satan, wicked people love it when godly leaders fall into sin. Their unjustified case against God is fueled with our human weakness and hypocrisy.

True, a big part of this problem comes from the exaggerated value we place on famed humans. Still, the protest is valid. With greater influence comes greater responsibility. The higher a person climbs, the more fanatically everyone else wants to learn from them and imitate them. In light of this, we should be very careful not to place a shameful smudge on God's good name—especially as we become "highly esteemed" in the eyes of others. Wouldn't it be tragic to fall hard and knock out more people on our way down than we lifted on our way up?

Consider the great evangelist Billy Graham. Clearly, Graham's extravagant foundation has always been a high priority in his life and ministry. Reverend Graham is a great orator, but more than that, Billy Graham the man is great person of integrity. I want to be more like him than any other Christian leader. Just like Billy Graham, I think the apostle Paul must have been safeguarding his integrity when he said, *"I discipline my body like an athlete, training it to do what it should. Otherwise, I fear that after preaching to others I myself might be disqualified"* (1 Cor. 9:27). Paul did not want to end with a humiliating collapse!

As I mature, I am beginning to appreciate my long road to *legendhood*. I am beginning to understand the high value in making my mistakes now, right here in the privacy of my own back yard! I want to learn from today's sins and reinforce everything in me that is still too feeble for the pressures of national scrutiny. At all cost, I must avoid becoming another statistical shooting star. Let's do this together!

OVERNIGHT SENSATIONS

"Would you look at that lucky guy—out of nowhere, he's an overnight sensation!" We have all heard this sort of bitter chatter before. It really does appear like some people are born with unfair advantages. They sweep the playing board in record time, leaving the rest of us scratching our heads. If we do not put these thoughts into perspective, we will find ourselves envying their instant successes rather than focusing on our own dreams.

Since foundations are constructed below the surface and out of the public eye, we often do not hear much about them. We do not usually recognize the value of a rising *legend* until the rest of the world is singing their praises. We usually wait for the crowds to point out our stars, and then we look right next door to us, wondering where that mystery person came from! It is so true—legends are invisible right up to the day they are noticed!

A few years ago, I was trying to work this all out in my own mind when I turned on the television and happened upon Bishop T.D. Jakes preaching one of his slam-dunk sermons! In that message, Bishop Jakes spoke very openly about his foundational years. I cannot tell you what an inspiration this was for me—to watch and listen as this living *legend* spoke of his humble beginning.

During this candid presentation, Bishop Jakes carried his audience to the place where it all began for him—all the way back to the remote hills of West Virginia. The man of God held nothing back, describing the dirtiest moments of his average, everyday life—just years before becoming an influential pastor of a megachurch in Texas.

Spilling over with that Jakes kind of humor, he told about one of his clunker cars from those good ole' days. He claimed that car was such a pile of junk, he would park it down the road from the churches where he was speaking and walk the rest of the way to the services so nobody saw what he was driving! Some would call him vain for placing too much value on outward appearance. I say thanks for the honesty! I believe the sermon was titled, *Fake It Till You Make It!*

Here was a celebrated preacher describing the agony of his intense former poverty. He told about the many threats against his family, such as the people who hated him and busted out his windows with rocks in the night. He meticulously reenacted (with words) the sore highlights of his long and tedious journey to greatness. I was hanging on every word. And toward the end of that message he said something I will never forget. Jakes explained how he continues to preach the same sermons today that he preached long before he was famous! This confirms my belief that *legends* are powerful long before they are noticed!

Do not be fooled by some blown up fairy tale and undervalue the decades of hard work and dedication overnight success requires. Even though I am one of the most impatient people ever, I am constantly asking God to pull me back when I get too far out in front of His plan.

If a million people rave over this first book of mine so that I become the next overnight sensation, I will never forget the 468 months of schooling it took to get me here. I will never despise my day of small beginnings—my hunk of junk cars and busted out windows. It might have been nice to grow faster, but God's timing really has been perfect! So, here it is again: "If it [the fulfillment of your vision] *seems slow in coming, wait patiently, for it will surely take place. It will not be delayed"* (Hab. 2:3b).

THE CHINESE BAMBOO—BASED ON A TRUE STORY

Somewhere today in a far away land lives the tiny little seed of an impressive kind of tree. Planted in the soils of far-east Asia, this unique species of the Chinese Bamboo starts out as just another average seed. Similar to other seeds his age, he carries the genetic potential of growing up to be a big tree one day. He sinks downward into the earth and vanishes out of sight. It will be a long time before he is freed from the confines of his dark and dirty beginning!

Longing for the sky, there is no time for distractions; our little guy has lots of work to do. The wait would be far more bearable if every other seed would grow just as slowly. Perhaps his impatience is set off as hundreds of fellow seeds start shooting up into the air at once! An entire forest graduates from the ground while our Chinese Bamboo seed quietly encourages himself, "That's OK. My time will come."

A year passes and all the Chinese boys and girls gather to appreciate the beauty of all the other flourishing and flowering trees, while young CB (Chinese Bamboo) is commanded to wait his turn. Even though it doesn't seem like it, God has something very special in mind for him. Due to the profound uniqueness of his *growing cycle,* CB is cautioned not to aim for the stars right away like his other seed friends.

Another year goes by. "Can I grow up now?" CB asks God. "Keep working on your roots little guy! Trust me, and when the time is perfect, I will release you from the ground." Year three passes and then year four—and you guessed it! Absolutely no sign of progress from the surface, only a gentle command, "Stay in the dirt and keep working on your roots!" By now, birds start to nest on the maturing braches of CB's tree friends! It would almost seem that poor little CB is going to spend the rest of his life as nothing more than an intricate root system.

Then it happens! During a time when all hope has nearly perished, suddenly and seemingly out of nowhere, an overnight sensation is born! Blasting upward, breaking free from the hardened ceiling hanging over CB's head, up into the sky like a speeding rocket, another Chinese Bamboo screams toward the heavens! Nothing in year one, nothing in year two, nothing in years three and four, and then in year five, all the waiting pays off big as CB becomes the talk of the forest when he rises 90 feet in 6 weeks![2]

Don't you just love stories like this, true stories, hardly believable? Every time I think about the Chinese Bamboo, I recover my resilience to continue underground as long as I am stationed here! Somehow I just know that my own 90 feet in 6 weeks is right around the corner. Maybe it is happening right now! As long as I work hard and keep my heart right in the dirty places, sooner or later, nothing will be able to keep me grounded, not even my own hesitations. Suddenly and seemingly out of nowhere—boom—90 feet in 6 weeks and another *legend* will grace the earth!

On that day when I am so high up that I can barely see the ground, I will know that my roots are massive! I will glance down, smile big, and thank God for my dirty years and an extravagant foundation I can always count on. So keep on dreaming with me, all you who are growing intricate, strong root systems, because your very own 90/6 is closer now than ever before!

30 YEARS OF ROOTS FOR 3 YEARS OF FRUITS

Though He was God, even Jesus refused to spring up into ministry before he had a root system. Jesus modeled this extravagant foundation principle to absolute perfection. If you think about it, Jesus expended His first 30 of 33 earthly years on *waiting* and *watching*. During this time, He affectionately engaged Himself with humanity, absorbed the deepest teachings of the Jewish Rabbis, and faced every temptation. Even though He had the solution to every problem, Jesus did not perform a single miracle for 30 years!

Who can really imagine what it must have been like for the almighty Son of God to *wait* and *watch* while the world around Him suffered? During this time, the Bible says, *"And Jesus grew in wisdom and in stature and in favor with*

God and all the people" (Luke 2:52). Jesus built the most extravagant foundation of all time!

When the time finally came for Jesus to rise, He was positioned for incomprehensible impact. During His brief earthly ministry, Jesus was the spotless sin offering and Savior of humanity—past, present, and future. From the day Jesus started the ministry phase of His life, it only took him three years to get the job done. Three years—it blows my mind!

When you think about everything Jesus accomplished in three years, it is too far-fetched for most people to believe. Yet, this is exactly the kind of thing God wants to do through you and me. He wants to build us underground for much longer than we prefer, so He can raise us up suddenly and permanently!

Really, what *can* God do through you and me in a short time, once we have built our extravagant foundation? The Bible promises every child of God, *"Now all glory to God, who is able, through His mighty power at work within us, to accomplish infinitely more than we might ask or think"* (Eph. 3:20). Infinitely more than we might ask or think! A boy's father once asked Jesus if He could do a miracle for his son. To that Jesus replied, *"What do you mean, 'If I can'?"* Jesus asked. *"Anything is possible if a person believes"* (Mark 9:23). There seems to be no lack of desire or ability on God's part.

Maybe our lives are far less impressive than the life of Jesus because we have them upside down. Instead of imitating the model, maybe we are trying to produce thirty years of fruits on three years of roots? I think we are. It is no wonder that most great people end up burning out!

COMING UP

Hopefully you have been well enthused about the intriguing world of foundations. If you sincerely want to renovate your existing foundation and turn it into an extravagant one, the next chapter shows you how!

Chapter 10

Build an Extravagant Foundation: *How?*

If you have built castles in the air, your work need not be lost; that is where they should be. Now put the foundations under them.

—HENRY DAVID THOREAU

PASSING INSPECTIONS (GRRR...)

While I write this book, we are building an addition on our house. The foundation was recently finished, or so we thought! According to our county code, we needed the building inspector's approval before starting the next part of the project. I still remember how we waited for the inspector with our fingers crossed that day—hoping he would flash onto our property, nod his head yes quite a few times, and leave us to start on the fun stuff!

I wish I could tell you we passed that inspection, but that would be very far from the truth. No, the by-the-book inspector flunked our foundation almost immediately.

At first, I felt slightly peeved because it seemed like he was slamming us on every little part of the project. *I mean, come on! Didn't we do anything right?* So I decided the next time that he came to inspect I would turn on my charm and try to distract him with a pile of sweet-talk, and hurry him through this irritating process. After all, I really did not care if everything was *perfect*. Emily and I had been dreaming about this addition for many years. We just wanted the man to sign off on our progress so we could hurry up and build our long-anticipated sunroom. The room was finally becoming a reality, and this perfectionist was throwing a big wrench in our momentum!

While I was venting to one of my friends, he did what most good friends ought to do in situations like this. He delicately pointed at my dilemma from another angle! It is so humbling when this happens, isn't it? You call on your friends so that you can have someone to agree with your conspiracy theories—and they end up siding with the conspirators! *Grrr!*

Thankfully, this individual created a tremendous paradigm shift for me that day. He gracefully educated me about the value of inspectors and explained how it is the inspector's job to *"make sure your sunroom floor doesn't collapse while you're hosting all of your* beloved *friends and ministry leaders during your annual Christmas party."* What an eye opener!

In the world of personal development, people are often disqualified because of certain hazardous weaknesses in their foundations. Building an extravagant life foundation is so much like the situation with our sunroom addition. At first, everything may seem very adequate in our own estimation. We often feel confused or frustrated every time our best effort is not good enough. Sometimes it seems like we will never finish our foundation. But, if we ever resort to sweet-talking our inspectors instead of making things right, we may spend our whole lives wondering why all our middling works keep toppling into rubbish!

Through many years of trial and error, the building inspector's office has created a detailed checklist intended to guarantee our long-term safety. How thoughtful! Still frustrating, of course! Needless to say, I no longer sweet-talk building inspectors and no longer try to rush them around the blemishes. I now appreciate the worthwhile service of our friendly neighborhood inspector. Long live the inspector's office!

THE EIGHT-POINT INSPECTOR'S CHECKLIST

You think your foundation might be ready for another inspection. Are you sure? Before we prematurely schedule your appointment, let's put your progress to the test. I sincerely hope you are right and that your foundation really does pass the test. If not, at least you will have an accurate punch list of all the necessary modifications.

The following is a very basic eight-*point inspector's checklist*. I have created this list from my numerous years of failing inspections! Even though there are 100 items or more on the full-length version, these are a few of the crucial ones. So, slow down and read these next several pages with careful eyes. Don't be tempted to skip ahead! Double-check your work; make sure it is just right. This eight-point self-examination will save you and the Big Guy a whole lot of time, and I am sure you will both appreciate that!

ONE—THE CHARACTER TEST

Over the years, I have been widely criticized for consistently promoting unskilled people instead of the more "obvious" candidates. I believe that a man or woman of impressive character and unrefined talent will always trump the ones with obvious skill and inadequate character. This is because it takes a few years to many decades for talented jerks to make even minor adjustments to their struggling characters, and only a few days to a few weeks for people of great character to master new skills. Don't get offended; we all get a little jerkish sometimes!

Have you ever witnessed the unfortunate scenario of a team superstar pouting on the sidelines just a few yards away from all the real action? Every time we kneel to figure out what is going wrong for one of these outraged big shots, it is plain to see how poor character is benching them. Instead of taking responsibility for their personal defects, they place the blame on everyone else for "not recognizing true talent." Ask any coach about this challenge and you are sure to get an earful!

Because of the breakdown of the family unit, substandard parenting has left many with a lifetime of character glitches to deal with. Gossiping parents, bitter friends, untold exposure to abuse and neglect—all have ways of programming character viruses into people's souls. Since many have been raised like this, they are blind to the destructive nature of such traits. They go on through life oblivious to the fact that they are personally sabotaging every real shot they get at succeeding. Until they come clean and make the daring commitment to go for a character overhaul, they will never enjoy lasting success.

Even though I have made it sound like real character transformation is difficult, it can happen. You can become the acclaimed legend from your suffering lineage—the person who turns the Titanic around! In this next season of your life, you can annihilate whatever determinisms you have inherited. You can wipe out patterns of laziness, drunkenness, and perversion. You can overcome anger, lying, cheating, and gossiping—and all other destructive strongholds now hovering over you and your beloved family. You can become the head in a long list of hard workers and successful entrepreneurs! You are the chosen one, the fountain of a new and beautiful legacy, a plentiful spring flowing into a new river of generational blessings and pouring a few hundred years into your future.

In the words of Daniel Defoe, "The soul is placed in the body like a rough diamond; and must be polished, or the luster of it will never appear"[1] There are a few simple things you can do to get the polishing underway. First, you will need to carefully select a person who absolutely adores you—a friend you can hire for the dirty job of locating your character discrepancies. Do not get mad when they give you the truth. This person needs to be the confrontational type, willing to hurt your feelings when necessary. If they are humble and aiming for character transformation along with you, this is a great big plus! After your character transformation alliance is created, start with one or two deficiencies at a time, and with all your heart pursue the transformation.

TWO—THE PERSONALITY TEST

A few years ago, my children and I were watching an Olympic qualifier race, and for each event we picked athletes to cheer for. In one particular event, we unanimously decided to cheer for the same person. As we listened to each one talk during their pre-race interview, we made our selection with ease. During the interview, one contender was grossly immodest with the reporter, contrasted with another who "felt blessed and humbled to be there." We instantly wanted the "nice" guy to win because we thought he would best represent our nation to the rest of the world—and we could not bear the thought of this other nasty person strutting up on the platform to be lavished with such an honor.

Just like my kids and me, people usually cheer for the person who seems to be most deserving of victory's honor. We can become fans during one 60-second interview. Why? Because attitude is everything!

Which one of these two athletes best replicates your personality? Are you a likeable person—one who creates instant fans with every 60-second interview? Are you able to hit it off with a diverse assortment of people? Do others naturally gravitate in the direction of your magnetic personality? When you walk into a crowded room, does everyone thank God in their hearts that you have arrived, or do they curse the moment?

Do yourself a favor. Please go to the nearest mirror right now and stare at yourself for a few minutes. Pay special attention to your eyes, mouth, and cheeks. Do you have a happy face or is it mad, scared, discouraged, or perhaps indifferent? Does your face say, "You're a loser" to every person you meet? Or does it say, "Hello beautiful person, I'm so excited to be here with you!"

Our faces are formed by our resting attitude—they showcase our innermost feelings about others and ourselves. Arrogant people carry their heads tilted upward with a condescending smirk on their lips and cheeks. Depressed people communicate a dark, infectious frown! Happy people project an illusion, like there is a brightness beaming from each of their 20,000 facial pores! Generally speaking, faces showcase personality!

On May 12, 2008, *People Magazine* did a feature on the one hundred most beautiful people and asked each one to reveal the secrets of their uncommon attractiveness. While many were giving tips about how they get their hair and makeup just right, there was one comment that really stood out as profound. Jennifer Lopez, referencing her fairly recent plunge into motherhood, stated, "My babies make the world new again; there is nothing like happiness in your soul to make you look and feel beautiful. I've heard you have the face God gave you until you are 25, and after that you get the face you deserve. True beauty comes from goodness, kindness, and strength of character."[2]

Wow, go back and read this quote once more, paying closer attention to the comment about our faces! *"I've heard that you have the face God gave you until you are 25, and after that you get the face you deserve."* Amazing, Jennifer Lopez! Thank you for believing that blemishes of the soul should not be painted over and that real, natural beauty comes from the healthy condition of our personality and character. This is such a great beauty tip! It reminds me of a great proverb, *"Like a gold ring in a pig's snout is a beautiful face on an empty head"* (Prov. 11:22 MSG).

If this book were wholly dedicated to the subject of personality, I would spend far more time covering things like creating a positive posture, developing a firm and confident handshake, learning to nod your head yes more often, developing a good sense of humor, learning to ask more questions, figuring out when to talk and when to listen, and training yourself to smile all the time! Maybe another day?

Personality is so important because we will never change the world unless we master the skill of relating with a wide spectrum of people. I still remember the highlights of my high school graduation. During the ceremony, one of the speakers said, "If you're going to succeed in life, remember this one thing: Always look out for A-number one, because nobody else will!" I'm sure you have heard that sentiment before.

Phrases like that have a way of arousing an aggressive degree of independence. The speech was somewhat helpful to me, especially while I built the courage I needed to leap into my future; however, it did not take me long to realize that looking out for A-number one was not going to get me very far.

On the contrary, if I am really going make a big difference with my life, then I need to forgo that aggressive obsession for A-number one and start to build meaningful relationships with other people. You should do the same. From this moment forward, start to value others on a much higher level. Be fanatical about it! Get started building your dream team or join a team that is already underway. Become a master of relating with people and watch your life take on a whole new and far greater level of significance.

If you are to become tomorrow's next great legend, you need people to like you. Even Jesus, though His life and message contrasted and collided with the polluted norm of His day, still He *"grew in wisdom and in stature and in favor with both God and all the people"* (Luke 2:52). If you think about it, quite a few people persecuted Jesus and some hated Him with a vengeance; but this was never due to a malfunction of personality. Jesus was hard to hate, because Jesus perfectly related with people. His personality was and is unfaultable.

The best way to improve our personality is to aim at becoming more attentive. Attentiveness is defined as "mindful, observant, and heedful of the comfort of others."[3] To become more attentive, you need to train yourself to become far more aware of the wants and needs of others. Decide now to make this one of your highest aims in life—to bless others!

> *Don't be selfish; don't try to impress others. Be humble, thinking of others as better than yourselves. Don't look out only for your own interests, but take an interest in others, too* (Philippians 2:3-4).

Here is another small tip for beautifying your personality—marry a happy person, invite a few happy friends into your circle, and pray they rub off on you! This is one of the special keys to my happy personality. In my opinion, I was raised by the happiest, most creative and adventurous mom, I married the happiest, most creative and adventurous woman, and I continually surround myself with the happiest, most creative and adventurous friends I can draw into my personal space. Like this, all I have to do is flow with it. Beautiful things grow in beautiful environments. No wonder I'm turning into such a great man!

THREE—THE SUBMISSION TEST

Submission is especially a problem for Americans. To our own detriment, many believers know very little about praying for the country's leaders. We know very little about honoring and encouraging our leaders. We seldom give ourselves entirely for the realization of a leader's dream. Too many people obsess over the president's high throne—never realizing that life as a leader is a sacrifice, not a reward.

Very simply, I believe there are two kinds of people—those who will do almost anything to *be* important and those who have already *been* important long enough to despise the hassle of it. Half are striving for some kind of throne while the rest are living in the nightmare of a crumbling kingdom. Most leaders are far more burnt out than they are willing to admit. They are more than willing to step down, *if* they can just find a worthy replacement. The truth is that it's no fun leading a society of rebels.

Sadly, each person has to be in charge of something before he or she realizes how overrated *importance* really is. The goal here is not to discourage people away from an honorable calling to leadership. I just want to generate a sudden, towering respect for existing authorities—before anyone else rams their way into leadership with a wrong attitude. I can't tell you the number of times a person has said, "I'm going to start my own church and be the pastor you never were." It happens a million times each year in churches and in businesses.

If every discontented laborer were unexpectedly exalted (uncalled and unprepared) into some sizeable leadership role for just one year of his life, a necessary paradigm shift would occur. We would suddenly live in a far more submissive world. People would return from this experiment with a permanent admiration for leaders everywhere. There would be far less striving and far more synergy—a society blessed with harmony, recovery, and breakthrough.

True leadership is a role of serving, one that demands quite a bit of blood. Enduring leadership requires *legendary* obedience to a genuine calling. So trust me when I say, "Enjoy *following* as long as you can. Prove yourself with a broom and a dustpan. Never do something you will regret for an early promotion. Instead, let every promotion naturally find its way to you!" Trust me, if you're doing the right things long enough, promotion will happen.

Are you an expert follower? Are you generally the compliant, supportive type, or are you always demanding an explanation from your leaders? Do you often find yourself caught up in negative conversations about your leaders behind their backs—secretly campaigning to your fans about how differently you would do things *if you were in charge?* This kind of insubordinate activity will surely cause you to fail the inspection.

Most of us have faked out past leaders—being submitted in action, while remaining rebellious in attitude. Submission is so much more than a series of outward actions. True submission is an attitude of the heart. If you are going to pass this part of your inspection, you will need to stop striving and trust God with your future. Don't ever forget, *"The king's heart is in the hand of the Lord, like the rivers of water; He turns it wherever He wishes"* (Prov. 21:1 NKJV) and, *"For exaltation comes neither from the east, nor from the west, nor from the south. But God is the Judge: He puts down one, and exalts another"* (Ps. 75:6-7 NKJV).

No matter who is leading, God can and will promote you when the time is right, when you are humble, submissive, and obedient. Trust me; I know how difficult it can be submitting to certain leaders. I bet we've all had a few *doozies* in our lifetime. But we must not let the bad experiences of our past lessen our obedience to biblical principles. We are responsible for our own actions—despite how well or poorly we are led. God promotes obedient, compliant followers—never rebels. Jesus is our great example:

> *When they hurled their insults at Him, He* [Jesus Christ] *did not retaliate; when He suffered, He made no threats. Instead, He entrusted Himself to Him who judges justly* (1 Peter 2:23 NIV).

Therefore, God elevated Him to the place of highest honor and gave Him the name above all other names (Philippians 2:9).

FOUR—THE SERVANT TEST

Who wants to be subjugated under the dictatorship of a power-crazed tyrant? No way, not me! A dictator is a leader who failed servant school, but graduated anyway. We must become servants first, leaders second. Jesus taught His disciples about servanthood as if there was nothing in the entire universe more important than serving. He didn't just teach servanthood, He modeled it in a most distinguished manner. Jesus, in my opinion, is the greatest Servant Teacher of all time. Philippians chapter 2 has to be one of the most inconceivable chapters of the entire Bible. To this day, even after years of reading and studying the Bible, I am still left scratching my head over these next few verses:

> *You must have the same attitude that Christ Jesus had. Though He was God, He did not think of equality with God **as something to cling to**. Instead, **He gave up His divine privileges; He took the humble position of a slave** and was born as a human being. When He appeared in human form, **He humbled Himself** in obedience to God and died a criminal's death on a cross. Therefore, God elevated Him to the place of highest honor and gave Him the name above all other names* (Philippians 2:5-9).

Why would God strip off His rights and privileges when He came to earth? What a risk! At a fast glance, this doesn't seem intelligent or necessary. Why would God kneel before this lowly human race and serve us to such humiliating degrees? How could God be omnipotent from His knees? We cannot comprehend this because we humans feel like big power is the product of radical domination. The farther we all drift from God's way of doing things, the more we fail to see the profound mystery behind Christ's humiliation.

In God's universe, omnipotent power is not expressed by dominating over people but in bending down to lift them up. Thus is the brilliance of Christ bending down to wash His disciple's feet (see John 13:5), and giving His back to a lead-tipped whip (see Mark 15:15), and yielding Himself to a brutal crucifixion (see Mark 15:21-38). Many people back in that day and still many more today view the cross as a huge glitch in God's supreme power, a sign of God's weakness. Yet, the exact opposite is true. Serving is the highest demonstration of power! Jesus was trying to teach this, but many saw Him as weak.

The cross is a symbol of God's boundless love, a demonstration of His omnipotent power—the supreme ruler, sacrificing everything for the express benefit of His beloved ones! His lowly service, although difficult to comprehend, attracts us to Him! Today, 2.1 billion[4] of us serve Him as Lord, and not because He beats us down into submission like so many of our earthy rulers. Instead, we joyfully sacrifice our lives for Him, and we seek to serve His will with all our hearts, because our God loves us like no other! He is the ultimate Leader, showing His power in bleeding out for His worshipers. Leadership like this is easy to follow and serve!

Back in the early 1990s, in the days after I first committed my life to Christ, servanthood was the biggest Christian theme being taught and preached. Servanthood was modeled by all the great preachers worldwide. This is when church people had an edge on everyone else. Having and demonstrating a servant's heart was the remarkable quality that set us apart as the true followers of Jesus. Back then, a good Christian person would not even think about aiming for a high office without first scrubbing toilets for a few years. This was the climate of my spiritual upbringing.

We were taught to sacrifice our lives without the hope of reward or honor. We didn't fight for the front spot in a church picnic food line. Like well-trained waiters and waitresses, it was our sheerest pleasure to refill cups and clear off tables. We fought for the brooms and vacuums, and we smiled like pigs in mud over the privilege of taking trash to the dumpster. Call us brainwashed, but we wanted to be the last servant standing—so everyone else could enjoy the blessing of our loving service.

In this 21st century, there seems to be a far different kind of attitude. Servanthood is the forgotten virtue. Even among today's most aspiring Christians, some seem to be looking for the straightest, fastest path into the highest leading roles—and for all the wrong reasons. What is really scary is that some have learned to sound like real servants when they say things like, "I'm not doin' this for position or recognition, I just want to be a humble servant. In fact, I really don't care if I have to clean toilets for the rest of my life—I just want to be more like Jesus." Sure, there are still a few authentic servants who actually mean what they say. Sadly, though, some say these things because they have heard this is the right way for a good Christian person to talk. They sound and look like servants, but deep in their hearts, some servant leaders in this modern world want to lead as fast as they can so they never have to serve again. It is like this in companies, churches, governments, and families. If there is no huge fun factor, and if there is no big potential of payment, and if there is no promise of immediate promotion, the menial jobs will not get done.

One of the things I have always appreciated about belonging to the Christian church is the opportunity we create for service. Since our Great Commission encompasses so much, we create tremendous opportunities for everyone who wants to do something positive with their lives. Through the love and power of many good people working together in the church, we can alleviate much of the hopelessness and suffering in our world. We have been the greatest source of blessing in past times, and I never want to see us lose this great distinguishing quality.

I've often wondered how so many children of great world leaders grow up with an awful disposition of entitlement. It is sad to see some of the most sacrificing leaders ending up with the laziest and most egocentric kids. In recent years, this has become a topic of growing concern while raising my own biological and spiritual children. We Balsamos are not that big of a deal right now—we still clean our own house, and we don't have a driver, a butler, or a personal chef—but we are lavished with honor and service from many special people within our ministry.

Oh sure, we like to believe we are a family of servants—but we have been living in various degrees of success for most of our kid's lives. Despite our very humble beginning, our two children mostly know about the more recent years when we were rich with real estate income, or when we've led teams of leaders and servants inside the church. They have watched their dad stand before hundreds of audiences. They've watched thousands of people from all around the world take radical actions based on my lectures. They aren't old enough to remember when Emily and I sacrificed our blood, sweat, and tears for another man's vision. They don't remember our days of mopping floors and cleaning toilets. Though we still bow to serve in every way possible, cleaning toilets is no longer our primary serving role.

Emily and I serve more today than ever in our lives. But our current category of service isn't easily comprehended. Now that we operate in a high church position, we are not able to spend nearly enough hours serving in the ministry of helps—definitely not enough time for our kids to catch a serving attitude. Therefore, in order to prevent this disposition of entitlement with our own children, we have had more deep conversations with them about selflessness and service. If we could go back and change anything over the past ten years, we would clean more toilets with our kids.

For me, the highest honor in this life is to be known by God, my family, and this whole world as a good and faithful servant. I can think of nothing greater. So here is my advice about passing the servant test: develop the truest kind of servant's heart possible, and once you get it, never let it go! Keep yourself willing to reach down and get filthy dirty for other people. Whenever your service is rejected, because it most certainly will be, remember, "The true test of a servant is how you respond when you're treated like one."[5]

It's easier to think like a servant when we are at the bottom. The real challenge comes when we climb and prosper and our ego escalates. So watch out for the ego monster! Spend your whole life blessing others, no matter how important you might become. Do this especially when there is no talk of recognition or compensation. Then with each new promotion, you will really be a bigger blessing. Because I expand this topic in Chapters 15 and 16, I'll let it rest for now. Thank God, right?

FIVE—THE FAITH TEST

It seems to me that some people have an invisible force shield surrounding their lives. They cruise through their obstacles with incomprehensible ease. Nothing fazes them for more than a second or two. These exceptional people are always calm, cool, and collected—experts at turning bad situations into bizarre breakthroughs. Their health is always good. Money and favor chases after them. Everything they place their hands on turns to gold.

After spending a little time with a few of these lucky dogs, I have discovered that this stroke of luck is not luck at all. And thank God for the rest of us—their kind of Midas touch (without an obsession for gold) is available to everyone. It doesn't matter how bankrupt a person is. Anyone can be trained to see (and seize) the golden opportunities that exist. Anyone can rise to the top, from the bottom. It's the same concept behind turning lemons into lemonade. If you and I are going to change the world like legends, we must learn how to do this!

Usually, "lucky" people are "lucky" because they actually believe this is the way things are supposed to be for them. They expect the whole universe to conspire in their favor as they fearlessly advance. When these believers awake in the morning, they whisper "Boo" and their demons faint! They passionately believe they cannot fail because they are protected and provided for through an unseen host of spiritual forces. God Almighty is always present with them, perfectly guiding their steps—straight into the lushest, greenest pastures around. You won't convince them otherwise.

These people have a concept of God that is different from that of most others. They actually see Him as a heavenly Father who is good and loving, a Father who wants the very best for His cherished children. They *expect* to be healthy and wealthy. They *expect* to live long and happy lives. They *expect* people to love them and support their noble dreams. They *expect* their marriages to be blissful; they *expect* their children will turn out exceptional. Whenever bad situations arise, these people *expect* to slap down anything and everything that dares threaten their sacred future. Boo!

Then there are the people who live in the "unlucky" camp. The people there seem to crave disaster. They don't accidentally fall into bad times—they attract destruction because they don't know how to live without it. These hardship junkies trudge through life like zombies, hobbling around in a pig pen of negative energy, always talking sickness and disadvantage; they are professionals at locating the rotten part of every circumstance. What a contrast! These people spend most of their miserable days crying about how often they are overlooked and defrauded by all the cold-hearted people in this cruel and unfair world.

I am not suggesting a life without adversity. Jesus said, "...*Here on earth you will have many trials and sorrows. But take heart, because I have overcome the world*" (John 16:33). Legends are overcomers! When faced with adversity, they stand in faith and stay to their course. Despite our intermittent adversities, we must establish our belief system on the authority of God's World. If the Bible says that we can raise a *shield of faith* over our lives, then we should figure out how to do that! Consider the following verses:

Therefore, put on every piece of God's armor so you will be able to resist the enemy in the time of evil. Then after the battle you will still be standing firm. Stand your ground, putting on the belt of truth and the body armor of God's righteousness. For shoes, put on the peace that comes from the Good News so that you will be fully prepared. In addition to all of these, hold up the shield of faith to stop the fiery arrows of the devil. Put on salvation as your helmet, and take the sword of the Spirit, which is the word of God (Ephesians 6:13-17).

*Those who live in the shelter of the Most High will find rest in the shadow of the Almighty. This I declare about the Lord: He alone is my refuge, my place of safety; He is my God, and I trust Him. For **He will rescue you** from every trap and protect you from deadly disease. He will cover you with His feathers. He will shelter you with His wings. **His faithful promises are your armor** and protection. Do not be afraid of the terrors of the night, nor the arrow that flies in the day. Do not dread the disease that stalks in darkness, nor the disaster that strikes at midday. Though a thousand fall at your side, though ten thousand are dying around you, **these evils will not touch you*** (Psalms 91:1-7).

The *shield of faith* is perfectly described in the Book of Job as a *hedge of protection* surrounding the main character's utopia (see Job 1:9-10). There is no question about it—Job was the richest man of his day. Everything this man touched turned to gold! Job had one of the greatest shields of all time. If you've ever read the story, you are definitely shaking your head yes right now!

Job's hedge was impenetrable as long as his faith remained intact. Nothing could get to him! The man goes all those years almost like Adam and Eve in the Garden of Eden—and then, out of nowhere, Job's houses burned to the ground, all of his children died, and his entire wealth was wiped out in a single day. Everything was perfect in Job's life—until the day when fear opened the gate for disaster. Job said, *"The thing that I feared has come upon me!"* (See Job 3:25.) And how right he was. Just like a destroying insect, fear gnawed its way through Job's hedge until there was no shield left to keep disaster away.

Faith and fear are two very real, opposing forces. Every person operates to some degree in one of the two, primarily—never in both for very long. These are the two possible default programs for your existence—unconsciously determining the general outcome of your life. Before having a real shot at being legendary, we have to build a thriving hedge of faith around our God-ordained futures.

To do this, we need to greatly expand our concept of God. We need to develop a strong confidence in His love for us and in His desire to make us legends. We need to see Him as the God who heals, the God who performs miracles, the God who provides and protects, the God who is all-knowing, all-powerful, and occupies all places at all times. If we take the time to do this, we will reap a lifetime of God's protection, power, and presence. People will call us lucky and we will tell them, "blessed."

SIX—THE LEADERSHIP TEST

Are you ready (and willing) to process an exaggerated, unfair share of complaints, curses, and false accusations? Can your heart keep beating as your most beloved friends formulate your harshest hater circles? Are you tough enough to be scrutinized from every angle, betrayed a thousand times, mostly underappreciated, and always overworked—and still wake up every day with a great, big smile, thrilled to be everyone's lowliest servant?

I have just a few more questions. Can you consistently formulate brilliant solutions for sophisticated problems and keep on dreaming big as the last man or woman standing while everyone else on your team screams, "Mutiny and Retreat!" In addition to your own careless actions, are you willing to accept full personal responsibility for the careless actions of others—even when it is humiliating and expensive? Can you do these things and still maintain an admirable personal life and a model family—without lowering your morals and compromising your testimony?

If you are up for these challenges, you might be ready for leadership!

Whenever I think of leadership, I think about a teenager from the Bible who scored unbelievably high on the leadership test. His name: Joseph. Joseph was a leadership prodigy. At the age of 17, his jealous brothers sold him into Egyptian slavery—just like that!

Amazingly, Joseph navigated through the painfulness of rejection like a seasoned champion, and bitterness did not wreck his future. Joseph held very tightly to his God-sized dreams, even when he was left for dead, sold into slavery, and sent into prison without a single fan in all the world. He succeeded through every crisis he endured. While serving as the purchased slave of his Egyptian slave master, this young man Joseph ascended to the highest position of honor—and he did in a very short period of time.

> The Lord was with Joseph, so **he succeeded in everything he did as he served** in the home of his Egyptian master. **Potiphar noticed this** and realized that the Lord was with Joseph, giving him success in everything he did. This pleased Potiphar, so **he soon made Joseph his personal attendant.** He put him in charge of his entire household and everything he owned. From the day Joseph was put in charge of his master's household and property, **the Lord began to bless Potiphar's household for Joseph's sake.** All his household affairs ran smoothly, and his crops and livestock flourished. So **Potiphar gave Joseph complete administrative responsibility over everything he owned.** With Joseph there, he didn't worry about a thing—except what kind of food to eat! (Genesis 39:2-6)

I love this story! It is very inspirational—how a teenage slave could unchain himself from a seemingly irreversible, no-hope scenario like this one. Here was a young man beaten into the lowest of human classes who then rises to the highest, most honorable position in his slave master's house. Joseph's uncommon ascent was clearly the product of Joseph's uncommon leadership ability!

In this success story of biblical proportion, we see the limitless potential of effective leadership. We see how fast and how high a person can rise. This is how a person races up the ladders of success—from the very bottom to the very top, again and again! Joseph brought absolute perfection to every task entrusted to his care. *"When Joseph was there, he* [his master] *didn't worry about a thing—except what kind of food to eat!"*

Joseph's success didn't end in Potiphar's house. What made him great in one place made him great in every place. Joseph went on to lead as Prime Minister of Egypt, because Joseph was a great leader and a true legend.

Fortunately, there are many great books written on the subject of leadership. So, instead of trying to write a book within a book about my one hundred secrets to effective leadership, I highly recommend you purchase the top ten or fifteen best-selling leadership books and educate yourself. Don't put it off; do this today. I also want to encourage you—and even pressure you, if I must—to start leading something—anything. One very simple key to passing this leadership test is to start somewhere and thrive with each leadership assignment you take on. Once you master one assignment, look for something far more challenging and master that as well. The bigger the challenge, the better the opportunity for proving yourself. So, get educated, find a good mentor, get some experience, and lead the way!

SEVEN—THE MONEY TEST

I'll begin this test with a very strong Bible verse.

> *If you are faithful in little things, you will be faithful in large ones. But if you are dishonest in little things, you won't be honest with greater responsibilities. **And if you are untrustworthy about worldly wealth, who will trust you with the true riches of heaven?** And if you are not faithful with other people's things, why should you be trusted with things of your own?* (Luke 16:10-12)

Gulp—that Scripture passage contains a crucial principal. To think that God really gives us *"the true riches of heaven"* based upon how well we do on the money test. Of all things to test us on—please God, anything but money! Am I right?

In Matthew 6:21, Jesus said, *"Wherever your treasure is, there the desires of your heart will also be."* From this we see that God is always watching what we do with our money—because our money trail spotlights the true condition of our heart. So God says to us, "Once you learn how to do the right things with the currency of this earth, I will be able to trust you with 'the true riches of Heaven!'" I think this is a brilliant move on God's part.

Learning how to manage money might be the biggest test of all. If it's a big deal to God, no wonder it is so much of a challenge to us. We need to become far more committed to the process of mastering money. According to Jesus, there is no way of getting around this. It is the secret door of access to the mysterious *riches of Heaven!* Who really knows what that means, but I am totally interested in being trusted with them.

To pass this test, you need to become a dedicated student of finance. Don't worry; I'm not talking about a college degree. I'm saying you'll need to read a few good books about things like budgeting and investing, career building, self-discipline, and biblical giving.

Rich Dad, Poor Dad by Richard T. Kiyosaki is one of my favorite financial books of all time. In my opinion, it is a must–read! You will learn to use your *employment income* to purchase assets before luxuries. You will be taught the value of deferring luxuries—until you are able to purchase them from your *asset income.* Kiyosaki teaches his readers to see every dollar placed into the asset column as your very own full-time employee—one that earns you money around the clock for the rest of your life. I encourage you to purchase this delicious morsel of literature, and wolf down every succulent bite of it as soon as possible.

Do you know someone who has already passed the money test? Maybe you can ask them to mentor you for an hour a week. Or, maybe you can schedule an introductory appointment with a local financial advisor. Be creative, over-enthusiastic, and highly optimistic! No matter how bad things look for you, start somewhere and start now!

Most of all, meditate on what the Bible says about financial stewardship. Thoroughly comprehend how every blessing comes from God, to us, for the express purpose of His eternal plans. Make absolutely certain that you are cheerfully offering to God the first and best of everything coming into your personal storehouse. This point can never be overstated! I have never met a real-life legend who wasn't also the biggest giver in their circle of influence! Legends give back hundreds, thousands, millions, and even billions more than they keep for themselves. Proverbs 11:24 says, *"Give freely and become more wealthy; be stingy and lose everything."*

EIGHT—THE TEST OF TEACHABILITY

This is it—the eighth and final test! By now, I bet you are trying to calculate how much longer it will take before you will be able to pass all of these tests—and finally graduate from this sophisticated school you've been talked into! Maybe you had been the biggest school hater ever and this exhausting marathon of study has you broken out in hives! I was a big school hater myself—back in the day! Believe me, I can feel your pain! In blunt contrast with this school-hating disposition, there are some people in this world (the legends) who obsess for the newest information and the deepest educational experiences. They have developed the rare skill of learning something powerful every day.

Until people fully recognize their many inadequacies, they will never grow very far beyond average. You did say you wanted to be a legend, right? Legends are highly teachable individuals. They are the first to listen, usually the last to speak. While everyone else impresses the crowds with everything they know, legends usually say the more perfect things at the more perfect times, because they "seek first to *understand*—then to be understood!"[6]

Please tell me you are not a "big fish in a little tank" type of person. Please also tell me you're not one of those "big, fat know-it-alls" with all of the first answers and none of the great questions. Proverbs 18:13 warns us about the danger of living like this: "*Spouting off before listening to the facts is both shameful and foolish.*" If you have read this deep into the book, I have to assume you want to become the smallest fish of a much larger tank? Yes? Me too! Let's go there together!

> *Wisdom shouts in the streets. She cries out in the public square. She calls to the crowds along the main street, to those gathered in front of the city gate: "How long, you simpletons, will you insist on being simpleminded? How long will you mockers relish your mocking? How long will you fools hate knowledge? Come and listen to my counsel. I'll share my heart with you and make you wise. I called you so often, but you wouldn't come. I reached out to you, but you paid no attention. You ignored my advice and rejected the correction I offered*" (Proverbs 1:20-25).

> *Wisdom has built her house; she has carved its seven columns. She has prepared a great banquet, mixed the wines, and set the table. She has sent her servants to invite everyone to come. She calls out from the heights overlooking the city. "Come in with me," she urges the simple. To those who lack good judgment, she says, "Come, eat my food, and*

drink the wine I have mixed. Leave your simple ways behind, and begin to live; learn to use good judgment" (Proverbs 9:1-6).

These verses from Proverbs chapters 1 and 9 are two of my favorite passages in the Bible. I could end this segment right there and not say another word; and if you would promise to meditate on those verses until they became part of you, this test of teachability would never be a problem for you again!

Do you sincerely appreciate wise advice and honest critique? How about when it comes through an arrogant messenger? Legends don't just tolerate wise advice and honest critique—they thirst for it! They don't just learn from their mentors, peers, and apprentices; they learn from any person who offers a valuable tip. They even learn a lot from those who dislike them.

Some say, legends ask way too many questions, almost like they are going back through the "terrible twos" stage. They constantly ask "Why?" Whenever they stumble, legends are quick to take responsibility for their failures so they can figure out how to do it better next time. This is why legends grow so much faster than others. *"Instruct the wise, and they will be even wiser. Teach the righteous, and they will learn even more"* (Prov. 9:9).

To pass this test, you have to accept full responsibility for your own destiny! Hurry up and create a comprehensive list of all the necessary skills you lack today—especially the obvious ones. Stop faking yourself out! If conditions are less than desirable, educate yourself for something better! Stop making excuses about why you are at the bottom. Come all the way out of ignorance—as fast as it can be done! Then you will no longer be grounded to this current level. You will learn, and grow, and thrive—for the rest of your *legendary* life!

FOUNDATIONAL EXCELLENCE

As large sections of this modern world crumble to pieces because of gross mediocrity—anyone can stand out. Build an extravagant foundation, and you will lead this incompetent world with ease, and make it better in every way!

It seems that in some ways we have become a foundationless generation; the evidence is in the flimsiness of our shabby accomplishments. *"The wicked build houses as fragile as a spider's web, as flimsy as a shelter made of branches"* (Job 27:18). As I have already mentioned, I am terrified about the future of my home nation when "Made in the USA" is no longer a seal of international value.

Yes, we have seen tremendous recent improvement in the American auto industry, and the world seems to be glancing in our direction with a brief glimmer of enthusiasm. But we cannot let it stop there. The United States and the American people have to strip all the way down to our foundations—and re-covenant, reform, recover, repair, refresh, rebuild, and renew. This is my prayer! Psalmist David said, *"If the foundations are destroyed, what can the righteous do? The Lord is in His holy temple, the Lord's throne is in heaven; His eyes behold, His eyelids test the sons of men"* (Ps. 11:3-4 NKJV).

We have to build our lives on something that will stand upright in tomorrow's precarious world! If we do not immediately and urgently repair our compromised foundation, and if we do not revitalize our founding faith and somehow recover our founding values, then we will hurl our legacy onto a rotten platform—and the time will surely come when everything we have built and everything they will build will come crashing to the ground!

Here is what I see. In recent years, America's foundation has been pulverized and greatly weakened from enemies lurking within our own borders. Right out in the open, our history is being rewritten by a reckless but influential band of godless, amoral leaders—men and women who no longer respect the enduring foundational ideals of our founders. Even though most Americans still place a very high value on our founding faith and the morality it once created, the voice of a few is sledge-hammering away at our foundation in order to suit their own anti-American, anti-Christian beliefs. Sadly, they are stealing the minds of ignorant citizens, reducing us to a fraction of what we once were.

God spoke a great promise through His prophet Isaiah when He said, *"Afflicted city, lashed by storms and not comforted, I will build you with stones of turquoise, your foundations with lapis lazuli* [sapphires]" (Isa. 54:11 NIV). I claim this promise for my country and my people. Dear God, rebuild us with stones of turquoise on a foundation of sapphires! Let us shine brightly for You again as we once did—one nation under God, a City on a hill giving light to a dark and troubled world!

MICHELANGELO AND THE SISTINE CHAPEL

Legendary artist Michelangelo was contracted by Pope Julius II to paint the ceiling of the Sistine Chapel in the Vatican in Rome, Italy.[7] The Pope proposed twelve large figures of the apostles. But Michelangelo chose a more complex design that was eventually comprised of hundreds of figures and took four years to complete, finishing in 1512. For almost five hundred years the painted ceiling has been heralded as one of the finest art works of all time. About 20,000 visitors a day[8] tour the chapel to marvel at Michelangelo's genius.

According to an article on the Wikipedia website:

> Contrary to popular belief, Michelangelo painted the chapel ceiling in a standing position, not lying on his back. According to Vasari, the work was carried out in *extremely uncomfortable conditions* from his having to work with his head tilted upwards. Michelangelo said, "If people knew how hard I worked to achieve my mastery, it wouldn't seem so wonderful after all."[9]

While a few baffling structures like the Roman Coliseum, the pyramids of Egypt, and Michelangelo's ceiling of the Sistine Chapel endure for hundreds, even thousands of years, most structures created by man are gone within a few generations. *Legendary* structures awe humankind for centuries because they were built to do just that!

No matter what you aim for in life, take your time getting there. Like Michelangelo, carry out your work in extremely uncomfortable conditions when necessary. Build an extravagant foundation for an enduring legacy—so that 500 years from now, 20,000 people a day will be admiring your life's great works! Slow down and live in the moment. Have fun, make memories, and keep a journal—so that all who come after you may know the price, process, and pleasure behind your lasting success.

COMING UP

The *funnest* chapter of the book!

Chapter 11

Celebrate Your Progress

Celebrate what you want to see more of.
—THOMAS J. PETERS, American writer

FRENZIED FANS AND HOME FIELD ADVANTAGES

Everyone loves to watch a huge crowd of maniac fans as they elevate their team into a never before seen phenomenon of strength and skill! Most of us have been right there when sports history was made, knowing that our hyper raving pushed our beloved teams over the edge during their defining moments!

More than likely, everyone has experienced the sheer pleasure of cheering like there was no tomorrow, and we just knew that if we fans held anything back in the stands, our dear players would be mutilated on the field right in front of our eyes. What a rush of adrenaline! We could not hold back; they needed us like they needed their lungs and legs, and when it counted the most—we always came through for them!

So many professional athletes commit to their profession primarily because of the very enticing *multimillion-dollar contracts*. But really, how many of these athletes would want to compete in professional sports without stadiums and fans? Imagine you are Tom Brady, quarterback for the New England Patriots, and you're playing that crucial game of the season against your arch rival, the Indianapolis Colts, in an empty stadium without television coverage—not one moment of applause, no mascot or cheerleaders, not even a small delegation of family and friends.

There you are with nothing but the sound of colliding pads and the heavy breathing of your teammates and opponents. Even with all the money in the world, who could get energized about this game? Sure, there would still be a few fanatics who would keep on playing for the "love of the game" and a few more who would stay dedicated for the luxury it affords. However, we must wonder how much time would pass before many of these non-applauded superstars would start looking for something else to do.

> *Two people are better off than one, for they can **help each other succeed**. If one person falls, **the other can reach out and help**. But **someone who falls alone is in real trouble**. Likewise, two people lying close together can keep each other warm. But how can one be warm alone? **A person standing alone can be attacked and defeated, but two can stand back-to-back and conquer.** Three are even better, for a triple-braided cord is not easily broken* (Ecclesiastes 4:9-12).

Truly two *are* better off than one; they do help each other succeed! Anyone who falls alone is definitely in real trouble! I hate to see people all alone, struggling to encourage themselves day after day without a single fan. Fans create the ambiance of a universe worth living in. Just like the soundtrack of an Academy Award-winning film, fans are the unassuming essence many fail to appreciate, yet everyone feels the sheer immensity of their contributions.

Life is so much more animated when people are screaming their heads off on our sidelines. Whenever circumstances turn bleak, our trusty fans help us bust a miracle! Fans are the mysterious blast of energy behind all underdog wins. Every scrape, bruise, and break is no big deal—as long as we can feel *just five minutes* of thunder in the stadium! Thanks to our fans, we are always conscious of how amazing we already are and how much more amazing we are on our way to becoming.

SPECIAL THANKS TO MY FRENZIED FANS

It is a well-acknowledged fact—Green Bay Packer fans are *legendary* in professional football, going so far as baring naked bellies painted in their team colors and raving like lunatics through entire games at sub-zero temperatures! I know it is hard to believe, but some of *my* frenzied fans are even more fanatical than that! If you didn't know any better, you would think I pay my friends to cheer for me. They never hold anything back. Whenever I stumble and fall, they never let me stay down longer than it takes to catch my breath. I can't share about frenzied fans without publicly appreciating mine:

> Dear friends, what a blessing you have been to my family and me. You have carried us on your shoulders with pure love and high expectations. Again and again, in the face of certain tragedy, you have gifted us with victories beyond belief. Thank you for always making an exaggerated big deal over every small sign of progress. Whenever our confidence ran out, you gave us yours. No matter what we've faced, your enthusiasm was always more than we needed to rise above our critics and drive forward with our God-sized dream. Proverbs 27:17 says, *"As iron sharpens iron, so a friend sharpens a friend."* God bless every person who has ever given even just a cup of water to us! I only hope that we are as good to you and others as you have been to us.

BECOMING YOUR OWN BEST FAN

In the fourth chapter of Philippians, Paul wrote about his early years of ministry when only *one fan church* financially supported him. Paul (who was named Saul at the time) said:

> *As you know, you Philippians were the **only ones** who gave me financial help when I first brought you the Good News and then traveled on from Macedonia. **No other church did this*** (Philippians 4:15).

Can you imagine, a man who influenced the world as much as Apostle Paul, started out with an empty stadium? He most certainly did. In the Book of Acts, we see how a man named Barnabas stuck his neck out to vouch for Saul—before anybody else trusted him. (Saul was Paul's name, prior to his God encounter.) Barnabas, whose name means son of encouragement, was Saul's first fan!

Saul's preaching became more and more powerful, and the Jews in Damascus couldn't refute his proofs that Jesus was indeed the Messiah. After a while some of the Jews plotted together to kill him. They were watching for him day and night at the city gate so they could murder him, but Saul was told about their plot. So during the night, some of the other believers lowered him in a large basket through an opening in the city wall. **When Saul arrived in Jerusalem, he tried to meet with the believers, but they were all afraid of him. They did not believe he had truly become a believer!** *Then* **Barnabas brought him to the apostles and told them how Saul had seen the Lord** *on the way to Damascus and how the Lord had spoken to Saul. He also told them that Saul had preached boldly in the name of Jesus in Damascus* (Acts 9:22-27).

Every *legend* starts with an empty stadium. Even though I have one heck of a stadium today, Emily and I did not start out with very many faithful fans—and neither will you. At least for us, we had each other. Emily was a gift from God for whom I will never stop thanking Him. She is my biggest fan, and I am hers! Many times, it was just the two of us and our two children—and our dogs, fish, birds, potbelly pigs, rabbits, chickens, squirrels, snails, snakes, frogs, chinchillas—and God!

Before the world loves you, it may loathe you for a decade or two. Before people understand you, they may misinterpret even your purest intentions. Some people may even devote the major portion of their lives to bringing you down, thinking they are doing a great service to God for shutting you up. Jesus spoke of this in John 16:2 when He said, *"For you will be expelled from the synagogues, and the time is coming when those who kill you will think they are doing a holy service for God."*

I speak from experience when I tell you that the more deeply you care about these people, the more it will hurt. Dealing with this degree of rejection will shatter your heart to tiny pieces, sending you to bed many nights feeling worthless and alone.

As soon as you start to advertise your vision, most everyone will think you have lost your mind. Even if they don't say it out loud, they may think it. Familiarity breeds contempt. Prophets are usually without honor in their hometowns (see Luke 4:24). Even some of your closest pals will not be able to wait out your long season of small beginnings. This is not brought up as a condemning verdict over your family and friends; it is just a universal glitch of humanity.

No matter how hard we try, most people have to see tangible success before they can cheer. Think about this on a personal level. I bet you didn't select your favorite sports team during a ten-year slump. No, you purchased your season tickets during the build-up of a huge winning streak. Sometimes, one good year is all it takes to get us in the stands and keep us there for life; sometimes it's not. Little by little, enduring teams inevitably recruit and retain more fans than they turn away and their stadiums get fuller and louder until there is not a single empty seat.

Anyone can succeed when all they have to do is show up and ride to glory on the dynamism of a sold-out stadium. Since it does take time to recruit frenzied fans, you will need to master the art of becoming *your own best fan*. This is where legends seem to have an edge over others. They can feel positively about what they are doing long before anyone else appreciates it. Legends look far beyond their early days of unpopularity to the time when they have blessed the earth and people have benefited from their generous bequest.

BEWARE OF THE TABLOIDS

Because I frequently pray for America's government leaders,[1] I rarely miss a key presidential appearance. I like to believe that my prayers really make a difference. To pray most effectively, it helps to discern the real condition of the leader as opposed to the media hype about the person. As I watch and pray for our presidents in real time, I focus especially on their nonverbal messages—the many great lessons often shrouded behind their well-articulated speeches.

During the aftermath of the 9-11-2001 terrorist invasion in America, I watched very closely our 43rd President George W. Bush. It did not take long before the war in Iraq became an unpopular topic among many outspoken Americans. This, combined with other national challenges, formed into the perfect political storm and forced President Bush's popularity ratings downward, making him arguably (and temporarily) the most hated president in my lifetime. No matter which direction he turned, President Bush could not shake the ever-present pack of scowling wolves. Day after day, they circled his mangled soul, salivating at the possibility of his demise. Perhaps he found comfort in the words of Jeremiah:

> I have heard the many rumors about me. They call me "The Man Who Lives in Terror." They threaten, "If you say anything, we will report it." Even my old friends are watching me, waiting for a fatal slip. "He will trap himself," they say, "and then we will get our revenge on him." But the Lord stands beside me like a great warrior... (Jeremiah 20:10-11).

We can only imagine what it would be like to get up every day knowing that our staff is reading through piles of hate mail. How many of us could remain true to our convictions and finish out a presidency like that of George W. Bush—while so many people hissed at our sacrifices with thankless evaluations.

I believe that President George W. Bush's easiest course of action would have led him to defer the conflict in Iraq under the banners of false peace and diplomatic flattery. To secure his presidential renown, he would have avoided military retaliation and forwarded the very real threat of American annihilation to a future generation—something he was not willing to do.

In the face of it all, President Bush woke up every morning and kept to the passions of his legacy-driven heart. He would not flinch, not even for one moment, valiantly confronting the heartless evils of the global terror movement, demanding that America's attackers be brought to justice. I contend that he took a deep breath, stared back into that fierce and intimidating glare of unpopularity, and ran his race like a champion—with very few claps, hugs, smiles, or high fives along the way.

Who really knows how history will end up assessing President George W. Bush. I can only speak for myself. President Bush was (during his presidency) and remains today, one of my greatest sources of inspiration. On the days when I, too, have felt like nobody in all the world—except my wife and kids and a few others—understood me or appreciated what I was trying to do for them, I found my inspiration in this modern legend. Love him or hate him, President George W. Bush showed us how to be our own best fans even during the worst of times. I can only hope that he will be able to look back

20 years from today and know that his country will finally appreciate what he did for her.

From his example, you and I can learn to stop believing all the garbage we read about ourselves, or the untrue things we overhear people saying that spread like stink through a public restroom. Even at our worst, we are still beautiful people. We are still the salt of the earth and a necessary part of tomorrow's better world. Let's believe it and celebrate it often, no matter what the rest of the world might say about us from time to time.

LOVE YOURSELF OUTRAGEOUSLY

Please consider the harsh reality of what I am about to say. Until you believe in yourself, how can you really expect others to believe in you? If you are not optimistic about your future, how will your fans envision triumph? Sure, you may sucker a small group of sympathetic supporters to take you on as their short-term benevolence project. They will prop you up as long as they can tolerate your wretched self-pity. But eventually, they will escape your prison. They will run for their lives. And who can really blame them? Most people don't have the perfect love of God needed to stand long term with an unchanging negative Nancy. Besides that, even if they did, you're trying to become a legend, remember?

If you want other people to fall in love with you, then guess what? *You* will have to fall in love with *you*. And I don't just mean a little bit. You will have to love yourself *outrageously!*

Oh please don't get shy on me now! Don't worry; I am not trying to form an elitist clique of egomaniacs. I am not shoving you headfirst into *the pride of life*. This is not about creating an obsession for reward or a demand for personal honor. Just like you, I believe we should be humble people. What I describe here is that very fine line between *humility* and *confidence*.

Life is a million times more happy and successful when you love yourself. At first, you may feel a little awkward with the change. You may think that you are not the easiest person to love, and that old destructive habit of self-degradation may put up a serious fight—but if you dedicate yourself to the transformation, it will happen.

Start by thanking God for making you exactly like you are. Focus on your positive features. Everybody is beautiful. Everybody has strengths. You just have to locate your own adorable qualities. You know what they say, "Practice makes perfect." Do you want to practice now? Then *clap out loud* to God for making *you!* Thank Him *enthusiastically,* because even though you are still very far from being perfect, you are everything you should be right now.

Believe me, it is not a sin to love yourself. God wants you to love the person He created. The psalmist David said, *"I praise You because I am fearfully and wonderfully made; Your works are wonderful, I know that full well"* (Ps. 139:14 NIV).

Throughout this life, when you find yourself standing in the arena all alone, and you're banished to silence until your heartbeat is heard with your ears—in that painful, lonely place, dare to love yourself *outrageously.*

Even after the day comes when you have so many fans that you don't have enough time to meet them all, always remember those good old days when you were your only fan, because you can be sure that the time will come when you are standing alone again.

In those moments, don't sit around wallowing in your own misery wishing for the sympathizers. Get up and shout yourself back into the game! Believe in the loving God who stands with you! Stand up tall as your own best fan! Dare to throw back your head, open wide your mouth, and rave all by yourself with the comparable force of 60,000 frenzied fans! Always love yourself—*outrageously.*

RECOGNIZE YOUR PROGRESS

After you break the habit of self-degradation, you must learn to recognize your progress—and this, for some people, is one of the most difficult skills to acquire. Here I will help you see your same old life with fresh new eyes! Even though you cannot go back and relive the concrete events of your past, you can create a superior perspective—and that can change everything for you! This is not *just* about your past. It is about learning to see your entire past, present, and future as one momentous collage of progress!

Frenzied fans are experts at recognizing progress. *Progress* is defined as "development, usually of a *gradual* kind, toward achieving a goal or reaching a higher standard."[2] In the business world, we are taught that the very best way to successfully complete a lengthy assignment is to break it down into manageable increments. The same is also true in the business of *life.*

You are today, the grand total of a thousand baby steps. So what if you are not yet influencing presidents and kings. You have *development of a gradual kind*. Look at how far you have progressed from where you began. If you take a few minutes to reminisce, surely you will see yourself raised up high on a beautiful monument of progress.

A while back, I was reading the Book of Genesis and marveled at how God created the entire universe leveraging this principle of celebrating progress.Ch11notes (See Genesis 1:10,12,18,21,25,31.) During His six days of creation, God paused at the end of each *gradual development*, assessed His own progress, told Himself how good He was doing, and continued on to the next phase. Then after God finished the entire project, He glanced over His creation and told Himself, "It is excellent in every way!" In the beginning of everything, God was His own best fan!

While He could have gotten three-fourths of the way through the process and griped about all the work still left to be done, God celebrated each of His *gradual developments*. If this is the way God conducts His epic life and work, why wouldn't we do the same?

Most people can think of lots of things they would love to change about themselves, and they can be commended for being so zealous about transformation. But we must be careful not to fall into the trap of over-managing our lives and miss the many opportunities we have to positively reinforce our amazing progress.

The rule is this: the more critical you are about your shortcomings, the more consciously you will need to celebrate your progress. Never criticize your flaws unless you simultaneously celebrate your strengths. Because no matter how flawed you stand today, you are not anything like you used to be. Really think about this! You are already a beautiful person, becoming more and more beautiful every day.

In a vast sea of setbacks and failures, it is not always easy to recognize your progress. Most of the time, real progress doesn't start out looking like progress. Even a *successful* surgery can look like murder halfway through. Oftentimes, situations have to go from bad to worse and worse to dead, on their way to better! Think about your own life. When situations go from bad to worse and worse to dead, on their way to better—when things become bloody and volatile, can you still recognize your progress?

Weak people fall to pieces at the sight of their own blood. When all hell breaks loose, weaklings throw temper tantrums. *"If you fail under pressure, your strength is too small"* (Prov. 24:10). Legends are not like this. When faced with tribulation, legends celebrate! This is because legends track a different set of variables from everyone else. They never size up situations as they first appear. Legends track progress. They see where they are going, from where they have been. To be a legend, you must be able to recognize and celebrate your progress long before anyone else envisions the victory ahead. Are you a legend? Yes, of course you are! That's because you recognize your progress!

CELEBRATE GOD'S HELP

I cannot describe to you how excited I get every time a professional football player scores a touchdown, and then kneels in the end zone, so the whole world knows, "I am only great because I kneel to my Father in Heaven." It is a beautiful thing when triumphant humans deflect their honors to God.

What does it look like when you and I score touchdowns? How do we normally handle our ten seconds of fame? Do we tend to drink down our pitchers of exaltation like we are *self-made* people? It is way too easy to feel this way, isn't it? After all, we have worked so hard and sacrificed so much, and we have earned the right to gloat—haven't we?

This is not what I meant when I asked you to love you yourself *outrageously*. While I want you to become your own best fan, love yourself *outrageously*, stay away from the tabloids, and better recognize and celebrate your incremental progress—you must remember that every good and perfect gift comes from above (see James 1:17). You are only great because you are the creation of God's great love!

In his book *Folk Psalms of Faith*, Ray Stedman tells a story that illustrates my point perfectly.

> Harry A. Ironside was a Canadian-American Bible teacher, preacher, pastor, and author in the late 19th and early 20th centuries. One day he was sitting at a table in a crowded restaurant. Just as Ironside was about to begin his meal, a man approached and asked if he could join him. Ironside invited him to have a seat. Then, as was his custom, Ironside bowed his head in prayer.

When he opened his eyes, the other man asked, "Do you have a headache?" Ironside replied, "No, I don't." The other man asked, "Well, is there something wrong with your food?" Ironside replied, "No, I was simply thanking God as I always do before I eat." The man said, "Oh, you're one of those, are you? Well, I want you to know I never give thanks. I earn my money by the sweat of my brow and I don't have to give thanks to anybody when I eat. I just start right in!" Ironside said, "Yes, you're just like my dog. That's what he does, too!"[3]

We are not self-made people. Therefore, none of us should ever give an acceptance speech without exposing the invisible cause behind our manifested effects. For the rest of our lives, we should gracefully redirect every round of applause sent our way, giving it back to the God who makes us worthy of such honors. Oh, for a new world of humble, grateful people—each one pausing, kneeling, and pointing upward in our end zones every time we score! Here is what the prophet Moses had to say about this topic:

> *When you have eaten your fill, be sure to praise the Lord your God for the good land He has given you. But that is the time to **be careful!** Beware that in your plenty you **do not forget the Lord your God** and disobey His commands, regulations, and decrees that I am giving you today. For when you have become full and prosperous and have built fine homes to live in, and when your flocks and herds have become very large and your silver and gold have multiplied along with everything else, be careful! **Do not become proud** at that time and forget the Lord your God, who rescued you from slavery in the land of Egypt. **Do not forget** that He led you through the great and terrifying wilderness with its poisonous snakes and scorpions, where it was so hot and dry. He gave you water from the rock! He fed you with manna in the wilderness, a food unknown to your ancestors. He did this to humble you and test you for your own good. He did all this so you would **never say to yourself, "I have achieved this wealth with my own strength and energy"** (Deuteronomy 8:10-17).*

When my life is over, I only desire one special designation from God. As He takes me by the hand and leads me through the highlights of my earthly pilgrimage, I want Him to nominate me for His very own "frenzied fans" hall of fame! I want my heavenly Father to look back over every era from Adam and Eve to the end of the world, and say, "That Chuck Balsamo was one of My greatest fans of all time!"

Even though we live in a world that mostly frowns on frenzied worship, I am willing to stand alone when necessary, to be for God, His one man mob of maniac fans! Without Him, I would be divorced, deadbeat, and lying desolate in the dark corner of a jail cell today—that is the truth! I want to celebrate Him with the resonance of a thousand choirs. If I thought He would appreciate it, I would gladly bare my naked belly all painted up with His favorite colors, and I would rave His name in sub-zero temperatures for the rest of my time on earth.

Just how important is celebration to God? Do you think He ever gets tired of hearing our cheering? Consider the following revealed facts about God:

1. In Revelation 4:8, He describes four massive angelic creatures that are always flying around His throne celebrating His awesomeness. They never stop flying and never stop repeating the phrase, *"Holy, holy, holy is the Lord God Almighty, who was, and is, and is to come."*

2. In Psalm 100:4, God describes exactly how He wants to be approached. He commands everyone to *"Enter His gates with **thanksgiving** and His courts with **praise**; give thanks to Him and praise His name"* (NIV).

3. In Psalm 22:3, God is described the Holy One who is *"**enthroned** on the praises of Israel."*

There are hundreds of biblical references about the subject of celebration. It seasons the Bible from cover to cover. Celebration is one of the great mysteries of God's omnipotence. Maybe God knows something about celebration that you and I have never fully understood. No wonder He is so amazing all the time!

APPRECIATE THE PAST

The word *celebrate* means to perform, honor, mark, hold up, or play up for public notice. When we celebrate something, we exhibit the outward manifestation of an inward perspective. We hold up, or play up (something of perceived value), for public notice. Every time we celebrate God, we make a public notice of our inner *appreciation* for His blessings in our past.

In order to celebrate our progress like *frenzied* fans, you and I must choose to view our past far more optimistically than others. While many people stack their past into an ugly monument of betrayals and disappointments, we must choose to build a grand memorial of breakthroughs and blessings, especially from the blessings we have picked up in hideous places.

We have far happier things to do with our time than to vomit our complaints on every undiscerning soul we can lure into our space. Legends don't become legends by grumbling about the unfair dysfunctions of their miserable childhoods. This is the 21st century. We are all dysfunctional! No matter how bad things have been for you and me, we are *legends*—remember? As children of faith, we should see God when we look back, right there in the middle of every situation *with* us. While the rest of the world cries, "Where was God?" We say, "Where would I be today if it was not for God?" Do you see the difference?

To celebrate with *appreciation* means to amplify God's assistance in each of your *gradual developments*. As you can tell, I am very extravagant about the way I celebrate God's assistance in my own life. As often as I can, I thrill to look back over my past and see all the places God laid His hand of blessing on my head. I love to lavish my gratitude on Him for looking after me. Yet, no matter how consistent I am about this, I still find quite a few uncelebrated blessings *every time* I look back. This is why I am such a big promoter of *frenzied* worship. Maybe you and I can raise the level of *appreciation* throughout the world so that no blessing will ever go uncelebrated again.

ANTICIPATE THE FUTURE

A few paragraphs ago I said, "Every time we celebrate God, we make a public notice of our inner *appreciation* for His blessings in our past." Celebrating God is not just about appreciating your past. It is more than smiling into your rear-view mirror. Sometimes when you and I celebrate God, we outwardly showcase our hidden *anticipation* of a winning future.

To celebrate your future with *anticipation* is to advance God's cheers on the premise of His faithfulness and ability. This kind of celebration is an act of faith. Instead of waiting for some tangible thing to cheer about, you go ahead and shout your lungs out over your future blessings before they show up. You look ahead with spiritual insight to a future where God has already gone before you. You do this confidently because you believe in God's track record. Your frenzied faith forces you to live and celebrate in continual *anticipation* of tomorrow. And *this* is the *funnest* way to live!

Instead of scuffing your feet through life paranoid with the likelihood of your next big hardship, you should gallop forward in a constant state of high hope. You should always dream like your Father is the God who He really is. Mark Twain once said, "I have been through some terrible things in my life, some of which *actually* happened."[4] Isn't that the truth! Oh, the times we have wasted our own opportunities to celebrate potential dreams because we dreaded the odds of some terrible thing that never actually happened. Let's not do this anymore. From now on, let's celebrate God far more excessively than we have ever done before—for our *past* and our *future*, with *appreciation* and *anticipation!*

POLICE YOUR STADIUM

How long can a would-be legend live in an empty stadium? Since you are becoming your own best fan and you are recruiting God as your biggest and most reliable Fan, maybe you should just say the heck with the hassle of a stadium. No way! Don't ever give yourself permission to think like that. Too many have gone the way of closing their stadiums. Some people do this to protect themselves against the pain of potential abandonment. Others feel like they are too holy for their fans. I suppose everyone else just thinks stadiums are too much of an initial investment.

Legendary stadiums never happen by accident. If you want one, you will have to dedicate your life to building it. You will have to know going into this venture that great stadiums demand a pile of up-front and on-going time, energy, and resources. Sometimes, stadiums seem like far more work than worth. Crowded stadiums can even be host to rivalry and rioting. But a well-policed stadium always yields far more than it ever demands.

Truly, so much rides on the quality and quantity of your fans. In fact, invite me to your stadium, introduce me to your fans—and I will predict your future! Think about that. How can a person become anything less than remarkable when they are surrounded with remarkable people? The same is true on the negative side of this equation. How can a person become anything more than pathetic when surrounded with pathetic people? If this is true, then we should be very purposeful about who we recruit and realize that our fans—when all mixed together—are the air we breathe; they are the *environment* we live in.

According to Michael Zimmerman, environment can be described as: "All of the *external factors* affecting an organism. These factors may be other living organisms (biotic factors) or nonliving variables (abiotic factors), such as temperature, rainfall, day length, wind, and ocean currents. The interactions of organisms with biotic and abiotic factors form an ecosystem. *Even minute changes* in any one factor in an ecosystem *can influence whether or not a particular plant or animal species will be successful in its environment.* Organisms and their environment constantly interact, and both are changed by this interaction."[5]

Let us consider the wonder of scuba divers for a minute. Because divers are not able to sustain life in an aquatic environment, they bottle an environment, strap it to their backs, and take it with them—into the deep. In a place where human life is not biologically sustainable, divers thrive!

Just like the scuba diver, you can bottle up your *frenzied* fans, strap them to your back, and dive to the deepest hell! You will thrive where others have failed before you, because you will draw your breaths from the environment on your back. This point can never be overstated. Lasting legends carefully and prayerfully screen for the highest-grade fans they can strap to their backs. Even though everyone is welcome to join them for a game or two, legends police their stadiums insistently.

Thanks to modern advancements in technology, sports franchises now have metal detectors, surveillance cameras, and all kinds of handy devices to help them secure their stadiums. You and I should be as serious about policing our stadiums. Since most of us still have a boatload of seats to fill, we had better figure out how to identify, recruit, and retain stadium-worthy fans. To do this, we should first create a detailed sketch of "Joe/Jane Fan." Then we will be able to identify the kinds of fans we want to keep and the ones we want to keep out. Yes, I did say that we want to keep some people out. Think about it, we don't want some psycho with a backpack bomb coming in and blowing everyone up, do we?

Sometimes that is all it takes—one heckler-antagonist to spoil the game for everyone. So please don't get desperate and start filling your stadium with suspicious persons. After all, you are not protecting only yourself; you are responsible for the safety and synergy of your entire stadium of fans. Don't worry, this does not mean you have to become an intolerable snob. It just means that you will choose to be very careful about who is offered the power to personally influence you. Certainly, you should be friendly and helpful with all humankind, and you should sincerely love everyone you meet; but when it comes to your stadium, you can and should be exceedingly selective.[6]

Consider grouping all your acquaintances into one of three specific categories:

1. The *haters*—those who bring you down like kryptonite around Superman's neck.

2. The *neutrals*—those who don't really contribute anything negative or positive to your life.

3. Your *frenzied fans!*

Once your list is completed, send a very kind letter to all the haters and neutrals, humbly encouraging them to shape up or ship out. Explain that it is nothing personal, you only have so many seats in your stadium, and you want to fill every one with a *frenzied* fan.

Actually, I'm kidding about very kind letter, but it sure does drive home my point. I am very serious about what to do with the precious souls who make it to your *frenzied* fan category. I suggest that you right away set up a dinner to honor them for their faithful frenzied support. Let each one of these people know that you are reserving them lifetime seats in your historical stadium. Don't forget to describe your pledge to make their celebration count—on every game day, without exceptions!

PLANTING FOR A HARVEST OF FANS

If you really want to have frenzied fans in your stadium, you will have to become the frenzied fan of other people—especially your dearest friends. I suggest that, starting now, you pay extra special attention to their amazing dreams. Demonstrate how deeply you care about their progress at every opportunity. Become the kind of person everyone thinks to call when they need a resurrection. The more frenzied you are in *their* stadiums, the more frenzied they will be in yours. So, don't hold anything back!

Always celebrate with people who are celebrating. Always keep your ears open and your eyes scanning for every excuse to get up on your feet, put your hands together, and cheer! Go absolutely out of your way and utterly off your rocker whenever your friends score touchdowns. I suggest applauding even when they barely make it across the line of scrimmage. Like this, you will be doing a great service for the people who mean the most to you. Your frenzied celebration will cause them to see progress they may not have recognized on their own.

Trust me, if you cheer sincerely and from the heart for enough people over enough time, you will have no vacant seats in your stadium. If you lay your life down for your trusty supporters, they will lay theirs down for you. Value celebration, recognize progress, love yourself *outrageously*, celebrate God's help, police your stadium, and plant for a harvest of fans. Over time, you will have crowds of *frenzied* fans lined up outside your gates, crossing their fingers for scalped tickets to your game. And with a stadium like this, you can be sure that your future will be nothing short of *legendary*.

COMING UP

See, just as I promised—this was a fun chapter! I had a blast writing it for you and hope you had a blast reading it. Up next, I've decided to write about the fascinating world of spirits. Because some may not be immediately attracted to the topic, I have animated my message in several layers of imagination. If given a chance, these next two chapters will blow your mind—in a very positive way.

Chapter 12, *Stop Being So Human,* is a portal to another realm. It's my Chuck-like explanation to a very complex and controversial subject matter. So please turn on all the lights in your house, turn the page, and keep reading!

Chapter 12

Stop Being So Human

Size matters not. Look at me. Judge me by my size, do you? Hmm? Hmm. And well you should not. For my ally is the Force, and a powerful ally it is.

—YODA, *Star Wars* Saga

Disclaimer: Because I fear this chapter may scare off a few of my mainstream Christian friends, I should say that for you, my thoughts here are simply suggestions intended to spark curiosity. If your group deems my propositions heretical, then please, view them as an amusing work of fanciful fiction and enjoy the dreams they will inspire. All I am borrowing here is a tiny fragment of your life, so you can contemplate my hypothesis, throw out a few "what ifs" of your own, and then move on. For everyone else who hungers for this sort of thing, put on your SD (Spirit Dimension) glasses and follow me into another realm.

WE ARE NOT ALONE

Blind to the naked eye, more permanent than this fleeting physical earth—there is something *out there!* When trying to describe the unseen realm, some people simply call it "energy."[1] Others tend to be more comprehensive with their explanation, and they use terms like "aura" or "karma." These people even claim to measure the light and dark sides of these intangible forces. In Christianity, there are certain theological differences existing between our denominations, yet most Christians will convincingly express to you a realm *of spirits* that is just as touchable as the living cells of our human bodies.

When we refer to a physical manifestation from the spirit world, we commonly use the term "supernatural." Supernatural is defined as "events that are not of the natural world, relating to or attributed to phenomena that cannot be explained by natural laws; relating to or attributed to a deity; or relating to or attributed to magic or the occult."[2]

Have you ever felt or sensed an unexplainable physical manifestation and thought, *There has to be a spiritual explanation for this!* I do not suggest that you look for a demon under every rock or an angel behind every tree. But you have to at least wonder if there is more to this remarkable cosmos than the tangible things you can reach out and touch with ease.

What if...we are really not alone? What if time and eternity share this same universe, and our physical world is actually the lesser of two or more greater dimensions? What if right now, just beyond the scope of our finite eyes, there is a mass company of angels whispering through the skies? What if God's omnipresent Spirit is with us right now, undetectable with a natural glance? What if we are being watched, even admired, as we work and play and sleep? Suppose every incautious step we take is being safeguarded by these divine and angelic influences. Do you ever wonder what this spirit world might look like if you could peel off your physical body and see it through God's eyes?

THERE *IS* SOMETHING OUT THERE

It seems that many Christians try to ignore the spirit world in fear of what they might stir up. They suppose they can just mind their own business in this physical world, and spirits will mind theirs as well. But is this possible? Are these spirits drifting through the universe, thinking nothing about you and me, unless we accidentally wander into their realm?

What if, somewhere out in this world of spirits, there is a dark swarm of demonic predators now combing this planet for the naïve victims of their next massacre? Are we being hunted? Could it be that an evil flock of disembodied assassins are right now circling our homes poised for descent? If we listen, will we hear them threatening to hurl their curses down? If we look closely, will we recognize their names and know what each one of them stands for? Have they come to us with disease, abuse, and depression? Are they here to make us prisoners of immorality, anger, and hatred? Are they holding off for the perfect moment, ready at a split-second notice to tear apart our good and blessed lives?

You can be certain that there is a dark force, gorged with evil far beyond the most horrifying narratives of Stephen King. Like foul rats in the winter pressing against the vulnerable places of your abode, scaling every wall without a moment's rest, sniffing, scratching, and gnawing a hole of access— there is something out there hell bent on getting into your life. Some critics may charge me of using fear tactics to con gullible readers into accepting my beliefs. Yet, as positively as this topic can be taught, I want to present the truth and generate a necessary awareness of the spirit world. I want you, my beloved reader, to know that you cannot make this go away by jumping into your bed and pulling the covers over your head.

TERRORS, ARROWS, DISEASE, AND DISASTER

Psalm 91 is the unofficial psalm of the United States military. It is a promise of divine intervention. There are three big reasons so many people value this psalm. First, it offers a clear and detailed portrayal of the spirit world. Second, it describes the human need for divine and angelic protection. Third, it promises this protection to all who live "in the shelter of the Most High." As you read the first seven verses, pay special attention to the way its author peels back the thin veil of humanity and offers you a look into the spirit world.

> *Those who live in the shelter of the Most High will find rest in the shadow of the Almighty. This I declare about the Lord: He alone is my refuge, my place of safety; He is my God, and I trust Him.* **For He will rescue you from every trap and protect you from deadly disease.** *He will* **cover you with His feathers.** *He will* **shelter you with His wings.** *His faithful promises are your armor and protection. Do not be afraid of* **the terrors of the night,** *nor* **the arrow that flies in the day.** *Do not dread* **the disease that stalks in darkness,** *nor* **the disaster that strikes at midday.** *Though a thousand fall at your side, though ten thousand are dying around you,* **these evils will not touch you** (Psalm 91:1-7).

From this Scripture passage we know there are *terrors* of the night, *arrows* that fly in the day, *disease* that stalks in the darkness, and *disaster* that strikes at midday. It breaks my heart to think about all those uninformed souls who play with dark things every day, never realizing how much damage will be done before they break away. They turn out the lights and turn on the horror films, and satisfy their cravings for terror, gore, and death. They have a growing attraction to paranormal activity. They ignorantly channel dark spirits on a Ouija board, and humor that intriguing, amusing fortune teller at the county fair. They phone a medium for $19.99 to connect with a deceased loved one—never realizing that each of these seemingly harmless activities rips wide-open portals to the darkness.

Then there are less obvious portals some people open when holding bitterness against a betrayer, or staring into perverted images—or toying around with alcohol and drugs, gossiping and rebelling against leaders, and acting out in anger, hatred, and rage. The entranceway to darkness is wide and very enticing; there are so many ways of falling in.

With every tick of the clock, another dark creature tears its razor sharp talons into our world to pick off another unprotected soul. Thousands are right now under assault; many of them will never rise to see the morning light of another day. In its darkest realms, the evil side of the force is petrifying to the most wicked souls. In the dark, there is no goodness at all—no love, peace, rest, hope, no inner satisfaction—only evil. These dear people cannot see how the chains have been tightening around their necks. It is only a matter of time before they will depart from this physical world, and no one can imagine what is next. After God's grace has been exhausted and His protection has been removed, the darkness will swallow them up as if they never existed. This is the desire of the dark force.

The grave is licking its lips in anticipation, opening its mouth wide... (Isaiah 5:14).

SPIRIT POWERS FOR SPIRIT WARS

I do not teach that every trial we face is the symptom of a spiritual assault. Some challenges are merely the consequences of natural interactions between our environment and us. If you get a flat tire on the way to work and your tires already have 40,000 miles of normal wear and tear, don't start looking for a spirit behind this natural circumstance. If you get behind the wheel of a car and drive like a maniac until you cause an accident, don't blame the devil for damages. If you show up 15 minutes late for work every day, and you're the laziest, sloppiest worker in your company, and you get fired, please don't tell everyone that satan stole your job. These are all the natural consequences of natural actions.

There are, however, as mentioned throughout this chapter, many circumstances we face every day that start up in the *spirit world*. No matter how carefully you go about fixing them through natural means, you must know that *spirit wars* are best waged with *spirit powers*! In fact, most of the time, you will intensify a spirit war when you try to work it out on your own.

> *We are human, but we don't wage war as humans do. We use God's mighty weapons, not worldly weapons, to knock down the strongholds of human reasoning and to destroy false arguments* (2 Corinthians 10:3-4).

How many times have you called up a hostile adversary, intending to smooth things over with your *super duper people skills*—and by the time you got finished, things were a hundred times more out of control! Whereas, I agree that time and dedicated natural effort can heal many things, and I agree that bad circumstances can eventually improve on their own, but I wonder how many of our tribulations would end faster and far more successfully if we learned how to spiritually resolve them. For instance, we could:

> *Put on all of God's armor so that you will be able to stand firm against all strategies of the devil. For we are not fighting against flesh-and-blood enemies, but against evil rulers and authorities of the unseen world, against mighty powers in this dark world, and against evil spirits in the heavenly places. Therefore, put on every piece of God's armor so you will be able to resist the enemy in the time of evil. **Then after the battle you will still be standing firm*** (Ephesians 6:11-13).

A NEW GATEWAY TO EVOLUTION

While we struggle like weaklings through the daily grind of life, hiding underneath our nerdy Clark Kent costumes, this society needs us to bare our inner legend—just like superman did it! Have you heard of that television show, *Heroes*? A few years back when *Heroes* first became popular, I watched their intro trailer on the Internet. Almost immediately, I was "in the spirit" and jaw-dropped over the sheer truth being presented in this sci-fi advertisement.

Heroes begins with a teenage boy videoing his cheerleader friend named Clair as she tumbles a few stories to the solid ground. After lying there for a few seconds apparently in serious condition, Clair climbs back to her feet, snaps her contorted shoulder back into socket, realigns her spine, and walks away unharmed! From this, we are left to assume that this teenager has some kind of healing superpower.

When you have time, search YouTube for the *Heroes* intro video I reference.[3] I am going to transcribe some of the dialog from that video for you, even though it might be difficult to follow. It's fast paced, and it hurries its viewers through a highly erratic collage of thoughts, but try to read it just the same.

[Words flash onto the screen] *In every human...*

[Dialog] "Do you ever get the feeling you were meant to do something extraordinary?"

[Words] *There exists the potential...*

[Dialog] "Yes, we are all special..."

"Why do you want to be different?"

"Why do you want to be the same?"

"Some individuals, it's true, are more special..."

"It begins with a single individual seemingly ordinary, except they're not..."

[Words] *A change is coming...*

[Dialog] "I keep having these dreams."

[Words] *Ordinary people... discovering extraordinary powers...*

[Dialog] "I'm hearing voices in my head…"

"Are you a crazy person?"

"I'm hearing people's thoughts…"

"Something is happening to me and I feel like you're the only person that's gonna understand."

[Words] *With great power… comes great danger…*

[Dialog] "Is this outside the realm of possibility or is man entering a new gateway to evolution…"

"My whole life, I have no idea what I'm supposed to do or supposed to be…"

"Do I have a destiny of my own…?"

"It's my turn to be somebody now."

[Words] *We're all connected… Do you know who you are?*

[Ending Dialog] "So what about you, Clair, did you do anything *special* today?"

Whenever possible, I like to present my teachings with far-stretched illustrations, to build bridges of hope between limited reality and boundless imagination. Whenever a natural person inserts himself into a fanciful plot, he has a chance to dream of what might be. Here I have chosen *Heroes* because it creates a tremendous degree of intrigue about superpowers. But you may say, "Come on, Chuck, you're alluding to science fiction as a basis for your whimsical suggestions, and I'm not convinced! We should just acknowledge our humanity—that we are natural creatures, period—end of story."

Don't worry, I'm not asking you to take three steps and leap into the air, and I am definitely not suggesting you hurtle from a tall building to see if you can fly. I am, however, acknowledging my vision of a far more "spiritual" civilization. I'm courageously predicting that over the next few decades, the partition between nature and spirit will become thinner than ever before.

I believe we are entering the gateway to a new evolution! In the days ahead, the children of the night will become increasingly darker and they will carry out unthinkable acts of evil; while simultaneously, the children of the light will rise like the first gleam of dawn, *"shining ever brighter till the full light of day"* (Prov. 4:18). The legends of today and tomorrow will go down in history as the greatest legends, not because we will mind and muscle our way into the records, but because we will wage our war as the most valiant spiritual warriors on the most spiritual battle field of all time! Some of us might be known in eternity as the renowned *spirit legends of the last days!*

Have you ever read the Bible with a *Heroes* paradigm? Have you ever considered God's holy servants from Biblical history and what they modeled for the rest of us? If you have, you know that my ideas are not beyond the scope of what has already been. Let's begin with the obvious.

- Moses exercised superior domination over nature when he hurled ten plagues on Egypt at God's command. During that great Exodus, Moses broke the Pharaoh's resolve and freed his people—a nation of mangled slaves—from Egypt's tyrannical chains. While Moses was leading them away, Pharaoh and his assassin warriors chased them in a fury of rage—thirsting for their Hebrew blood. Moses glanced back at the incoming army, leaned forward to the impassable barrier facing him, slammed his shepherd's staff into the Red Sea, and ordered the waters to move! Again, nature heeded this man's voice—and miraculously, Israel walked away from Egypt on dry ground. (See Exodus 3-12.)

- Elijah called fire down from the skies; he outran a speeding chariot on foot for at least 15 miles; told the skies to withhold rain for three and a half years, then commanded rains to end that drought; and he brought a dead person back to life, just to mention a few of his *Heroes*-like episodes. (See 1 Kings 18.)

- Samson is remembered as a real-life "Superman" for tearing apart a live lion's jaw with his bare hands; slaughtering 1,000 enemy warriors with the jawbone of a donkey; uprooting the gates to a city, including its posts, and carrying them to the top of a hill on his back; and wiping out thousands of enemy leaders by pushing down the mightiest building in their city! As long as Samson honored his covenant with God, he was invincible! (See Judges 13-16.)

- Shadrach, Meshach, and Abednego were three friends who were tied up and thrown into a blazing furnace—all three walked out moments later, unbound and without even the scent of smoke on their fireproofed bodies! (See Daniel 3.)

- Apostle Peter defied physical gravity and walked on water, just like Jesus. Amazing! (See Matthew 14:27-29.)

- Jesus healed every sick person He prayed for. Of course He is the Son of God. But there was *Peter, John, Paul, Luke, John Mark, Stephen, Barnabas, Silas,* and *others* too—they did it just like Jesus! (See the Book of Acts.)

- Let's not forget about Philip, the evangelist. He was teleported from Gaza to Azotus, a distance of 30 miles! Yes, just like in the Star Trek movies. (See Acts 8:39-40.)

In each of these examples, we see natural men—not legendary because of their beautiful bodies or their marvelous minds, but because of who they became when *the Spirit of God came upon them in mighty force.* These biblical examples I have mentioned are just the obvious ones. The list goes on and on and suggests to us the boundless potential of every natural person—when we also widen our influence in the spirit world.

According to the Bible, humans are given spiritual life and spiritual authority when they are born again (see John 1:12; 3:7, Rom. 10:9, Matt. 28:18; Luke 10:19). Through this hallmark experience, people are translated from a *kingdom of darkness* to a *Kingdom of light.* I believe you can bank on this happening for a number of reasons. The Bible is enduring and dependable! God's love and power can be felt just as much as any tangible thing. Billions throughout the ages have tasted this heavenly gift and testify to its authenticity. At salvation, spiritual orphans from this temporary, natural world become *"children of the light and children of the day"* and no longer *"of the night, nor of the darkness"* (1 Thess. 5:5 KJV). This is how it begins!

Yet to all who received Him, to those who believed in His name, He gave the right to become children of God—children born not of natural descent, nor of human decision or a husband's will, but born of God (John 1:12-13 NIV).

THERE IS A FORCE

Star Wars was the first movie I ever watched on the big screen. Luke Skywalker was my very first role model! I think I would have sold the family pet to get my hands on a Jedi light saber back in those days. My imagination ran wild as I fantasized about defying gravity and moving objects around with my thoughts. In my adolescent mind, the Jedi life almost seemed possible. Just like Luke, I wished for a Yoda who could teach me the ways of the Force.

During those days, I enjoyed sorting though a hundred whys and what-ifs about the universe. I spent hours in my bedroom playing with my *Star Wars* action figures reasoning away like a grey-headed philosopher, challenging my beliefs about the natural world and how those beliefs could be reducing my potential. I just knew that there had to be more to this life than the natural things I could taste, touch, hear, smell, and see.

According to an article on Wikipedia:

> One of the prominent elements of *Star Wars* is the "Force," which is presented as an omnipresent form of energy which can be harnessed by those with that ability. It is described in the first produced film as "an energy field created by all living things that surrounds us, penetrates us, and binds the galaxy together." The Force, George Lucas claimed, *allows users to perform a variety of supernatural feats* (such as telekinesis, clairvoyance, precognition, and mind control) and also *can amplify certain physical traits*, such as speed and reflexes; these abilities can vary from user to user and *can be improved through training*. While the Force *can be used for good*, it *has a dark side* that, when pursued, imbues users with hatred, aggression, and malevolence. The six films feature the *Jedi*, who use the Force for good, and the *Sith*, who use the dark side for evil in an attempt to take over the galaxy.[4]

My friend, I believe that there is a very *real* living Force that surrounds us and penetrates us, a Force that binds our galaxy together! Similar to George Lucas' conceptual force, there is a Holy Force longing to be expressed in our natural world. Here is a biblical description of the Force from Colossians 1:15-20 (MSG):

...For everything, absolutely everything, above and below, visible and invisible, rank after rank after rank of angels—everything got started in Him and finds its purpose in Him. He was there before any of it came into existence and holds it all together right up to this moment. ...Not only that, but all the broken and dislocated pieces of the universe—people and things, animals and atoms— get properly fixed and fit together in vibrant harmonies, all because of His death, His blood that poured down from the cross.

For me, I will never forget the winter of 1991 when I first encountered the Force myself. How glorious were those early days, when all my childlike curiosities were satisfied in so many irresistible and experiential evidences! And still today after two decades and thousands of additional experiences and evidences, I remain a believer and servant of the Force.

There really is more to this life than the natural things we can taste, touch, hear, smell, and see. The Force is everywhere, imploring us as a complex spiritual species, to *stop being so human!* This natural world is not going to last, and we are not going to last in it forever. Even if you and I live longer than most people, our time here is still short at best. If you and I really believe this, and we really believe we have a definite *spiritual* nature, then we should stop hesitating, and go on to learn the ways of our Force.

When I express our God as a Force of light, I do not want to make light of the personal relationship we cherish with Him. I am simply portraying to you the profound influence of His Spirit on our universe, the very same influence He longs to have in and through you and me. The Christian life is supposed to be so much more than a discipline of religion. When we become sons and daughters of God, we become citizens of His eternal Kingdom and spiritual recruits of His divine will. In His divine will, our Father has a legendary purpose for each person. Until the end of time, He is obsessed about rescuing people from the enchantments of the dark force. He wants to express Himself in this physical world through us. We should let Him do this!

"Dear God, please express Yourself through my dear reader and me. When we consider the terrors we see creeping up from the darkness and we consider how desperate our world is for Your light, we want to hurry up and learn your ways. Increase our faith, give us a far

greater revelation (and experience) of Your holy presence, and shine the fullness of Your glory through us."

COMING UP

This chapter gives me goose bumps and teary eyes. What a rush! No matter your theological position on the spirit world, there is no denying the electricity it creates. The endless wonders of this realm—the curiosity it triggers—is too wonderful for words.

What if God is really inspiring me to ask you to stop being so human? What are people so afraid of? Ahh, now that is the question! In the next chapter, I am going to neutralize your lingering inhibitions and lead you deeper!

Chapter 13

Put on Your Legends Cloak

This is your last chance. After this, there is no turning back.
You take the blue pill—story ends, you wake up in your bed
and believe whatever you want to believe. You take the red
pill—you stay in Wonderland and I show you how deep the
rabbit-hole goes.

—MORPHEUS, The Matrix Trilogy

WHAT ARE WE AFRAID OF?

It is a fact: today's doctor spends 10-12 years and a few hundred thousand dollars to become a physical healer. Why then would the average Christian go to a one-hour church service every few Sundays, reluctantly toss ten bucks into an offering plate, and then marvel over why so few of us experience any real miracles in our lives? Let's face it; we are not adequately educated in the ways of our Force. Many in this generation are biblically illiterate and spiritually malnourished. It's like starving to death in the middle of a grocery store. We are sitting on a message of *power* beyond our wildest dreams, lacking the oomph to break its ancient seal!

Why are so many highly respectable folks so ridiculously hesitant about venturing into deeper waters? Especially in the mainstream church, there is a stigma about going for a deeper spiritual experience. What are we so afraid of? Why is today's religious Christian establishment so ritualistic and lifeless, lacking even the slightest degree of spiritual power and authority? No wonder society looks elsewhere for the solutions to life's most difficult problems.

Are we afraid of overdosing on too much Bible? Do we fear that too many prayer meetings will turn us into crazy people? Do we actually believe God is going to look down on us for aiming to be more spiritually empowered? Why would He applaud people for cultivating natural talent and denounce some of us for aspiring to advance in the ways of His Spirit? Come on; let's be wiser than this.

The Bible is not vague on this topic. Here are just two of many such verses, straight from the mouths of Jesus and the apostle Paul—both verses clearly imply a far deeper spiritual experience to the child of God who desires it, and asks for it:

> So if you sinful people know how to give good gifts to your children, how much more will your heavenly Father give the Holy Spirit to those who **ask Him** (Luke 11:13).

> Follow the way of love and **eagerly desire** gifts of the Spirit, **especially** prophecy (1 Corinthians 14:1 NIV).

Back in the early '90s, we cautioned each other not to become so heavenly minded that we were no longer any earthly good. Today's Christian is just the opposite, far too earthly minded and not much heavenly good. The mainstream person claims that being a good Christian is all about manifesting the character of Jesus, while the charismatic person claims it is all about manifesting the presence and power of God. Why can't we exhibit both of these extremes in one last-day Church? Why can't we become heavenly-minded and earthly good? Isn't this really a true picture of how Jesus lived during His earthly ministry? Didn't He embody a perfect mixture of mainstream character and charismatic power? Definitely, He did.

Can a modern person tether himself to God's written Word and dive into the world as a tangible expression of God, just like the ancient prophets did? I believe we certainly can, if we can just overcome our fear of going too far. Since the creation of man, God has existed in humanity as a present God who is continually revealing Himself. He has always been a God who thrills to manifest His fathomless power.

Forget about your religious spin for a minute and answer a few common sense questions. Don't you think this world needs a surge of prophets? Can you imagine how humanity would benefit from another Moses or Elijah? Don't you at least wonder if you, me, or one of our friends can lay bare all the fullness of God for our generation—with soberness, dignity, and saintly character? I think we can! Whether you call us prophets, preachers, or Christians—God is going to break out like fire in the churches and thunder in his messengers again!

Even though it seems entirely out of reach right now, I dream of shaking up camps on both extreme sides of this issue. I dream of a glorious marriage between the mainstream and the charismatic sects of Christianity—and oh the potential gorgeousness of their offspring! I am talking about a new Christian species, walking in compelling spiritual power, built on a platform of extravagant character and integrity!

For this to happen, we must get past the false assumption that God isn't supernatural like He was in the first-century Church. Why did Jesus take the *cat o' nine tails* to His back, and why did He hang on a cross and spill out His precious blood to establish a covenant of healing—only to take it back a few decades later? Where is the logic—or love—in this kind of thinking?

In a quest for justifying our powerlessness, have we mistakenly redefined God? I think we have. Instead of contending for the faith that was given to our forefathers, Western Christianity has contrived for itself a deist religion of faithless modern doctrines. In short, we have dangerously offered our world an unconcerned God. Yet, this God clearly invited His earliest disciples all the way into His force to carry out His Great Commission (to rescue people from the darkness, alleviate human suffering, and populate the heavenly kingdom)—an assignment the church has not yet finished, by a God who is by no means, *unconcerned.*

Maybe this caring God is just waiting for another consecrated, believing generation to rise from obscurity and show the world that He is not today any less than He ever was!

REALLY, WHAT ARE WE SO AFRAID OF?

I believe the bigger reason behind our hesitation comes from the "charismatic" abuses we have all witnessed in modern history. We church people have done so many weird things in the name of being "spiritual." Does this mean we ought to cage up God's Holy Spirit and limit His influence in our lives just because a few humans have misrepresented Him from time to time?

Jesus proved that we do not have to be weird to be spiritual. Even though He put on some pretty wild spiritual demonstrations, Jesus was not seen as mentally unstable. He was well respected and highly influential. His character was impeccable. Jesus kept His emotions perfectly between the lines; He was a flawless communicator. Jesus radiated with peace and joy. To his true followers, Jesus was a very fun person to hang out with. Jesus was, and still is today, the original Yoda Jedi! There is only one Jesus. The rest of us are doing our best to learn from Him and be like Him.

I thank God for the Christian prophets of these past 50 years. I thank God for their prophetic schools, prophetic conferences, and prophetic worship music. Even though we have seen way too many embarrassing extras in the "healing" and "revival" movements, we should thank God for all those renegades who followed their spiritual curiosities—even if that meant being mistreated, misinterpreted, and misrepresented right up to the day of their deaths. I thank God for their courageous experiments and the ancient spiritual theories they have presented, and proven, as a basis for our better future.

A New Christian Era

For the past seven years, I have received visions, dreams, and prophecies about a coming mainstream revival. If this happens, millions will be positively affected by what I am predicting. This will not be limited to the free-spirited Christian population. According to my spiritual hunch, God is going to lavish Presbyterians, Lutherans, Baptists, Methodists, and all the other mainline Protestant denominations—and the Catholics and Anglicans, too! I believe we will all practice Christianity just like our founding apostles instructed when they wrote to us centuries ago.

I am predicting and praying for the dawn of a new Christian era. I am praying for something far more substantial and much longer lasting than the charismatic renewal. And one more time, we will be that city on a hill Jesus Christ talked about—the light of the world, one body united under Christ. A trumpet is going to sound in the Spirit world and millions of spiritual sleepers are going to hear it at once! Prophets will rise from the mainstream church—some of the purest and mightiest prophets of all time.

I heard this message from the Lord:

Just like the storyline in Frank Peretti's book *The Prophet*, I am recruiting influential people to speak for Me! In the near future, you will see prominent news personalities, politicians, financial leaders, and high-status entertainers—some of the foremost prevailing voices in your country coming out of a "burning bush" encounter with Me—and they will shock the world! I will change them in what seems to be a single day! I will give them a prophetic kind courage, just like Moses had. They will not hesitate to do what I say. They will smash down political correctness! They will humiliate the oppressor's of this hour! When satan unleashes his foulest hordes—I will rush at him with My brightest prophets. There is a battle on the horizon. Out of the darkness, evil will surge at my people like never before. But the darkness will never extinguish My light!

When I heard that message, I envisioned a hypothetical snapshot of many well-known influencers like Bill Gates, Donald Trump, Oprah Winfrey, Steven Spielberg, Justin Timberlake, Peyton Manning, and others from a variety of national arenas. They were changed with the snap of Gods fingers! Can you picture this? Can you imagine God appearing to people like this—and just like He did with Moses, He should say to them, "Bill, Donald, Oprah, Steven, Justin, Peyton! Take off your shoes, for you are standing on holy ground! For I have heard the cries of My people—they are crying for deliverance from their oppressors! Yes, I am aware of their suffering. So I have come to rescue them—and I have chosen *you* to lead them out!"

I am not talking about creating a new religion here. I am just saying that if you will listen, perhaps you will hear God whispering your name in the middle of the night. If you can break away from those feeble Hollywood religions, and bow low before God with all your fame, money, and power, you will hear something.

Everyone should want to be God's expression of love to the world. When He gushes out His compassion, He wants to ride on our tears. When He reaches out to a disease-infested child, He wants to use our hands. God takes pleasure in you and me every time we give His blessings to the people who need them. He loves it when His children turn out just like their Father.

This is why the Bible so proudly announces, *"...as He* [God] *is, so are we* [His beloved children] *in this world"* (1 John 4:17 KJV).

NATURAL VERSUS SPIRITUAL EXPRESSIONS

To make us like Him in this world, God gives us His compassionate heart, His flawless character, and His matchless power. As we become abundant with each of these great qualities, God then demonstrates His love through us in an endless array of *natural* and *spiritual* "God-expressions."

By *natural expressions,* I mean things like: blessing people with the five languages of love (acts of service, quality time, the giving of gifts, kind words, and loving touch); forgiving people when they hurt us; performing acts of compassion (in the form of food, shelter, medical attention, and other necessities of life); giving helpful counsel and a listening ear in times of crisis; and interceding to God, in prayer, on the behalf of others. Most of these expressions do not require a supernatural manifestation. They are the product of Christian virtue.

Spiritual expressions are a little bit more complicated. Simply stated, this is when God expresses Himself *supernaturally* through His Holy Spirit working in Christians. These expressions include, but are not limited to:

- *The gift of simple prophecy*—This spiritual gift does not necessarily predict the future. It is more of a forth-telling ability— to provide strength, encouragement, and comfort. When a person operates in this spiritual gift, he utters messages from God to other people—to create a better understanding of God's character, commands, and promises. Simple prophecy blesses its recipient with a greater awe for God, conviction of sin, fresh faith, and increased spiritual fortitude.

- *Words of wisdom and words of knowledge*—These two spiritual gifts reveal knowledge and perspective, from God's mind, about the past or present (as with the word of knowledge) and the future (as with the word of wisdom).

- *Supernatural faith*—This is different from natural faith. It is God lending us His infinite faith so that we can stand in the face of untold odds and press a miracle into existence, for ourselves or on the behalf of others.

- *The extraordinary powers of healing and the working of miracles*—These two gifts produce healings and miracles with divine power, not through natural means, or even by the faith of its recipient. When a person operates in these gifts, God makes physical contact with the sick person, through the body of His messenger.

- *The gift of discerning spirits*—This gift exposes the kind of spirit that is operating in specific people and specific situations. Through this gift we can recognize the presence or absence of angels and demons, and distinguish whether the human spirit, the Spirit of God, or a demon spirit is motivating an individual's mind and corresponding actions—so that we can know how to best help in various situations.

- *The gift of commanding nature and multiplying provision*—These spiritual abilities are seen manifested in the lives of ordinary people throughout the Bible and in Church history—when God operates through humans to demonstrate His power over weather conditions and other natural elements and when humans are given the power to multiply natural substance through faith and prayer.

- *The five supernatural ministry offices*—the apostle, prophet, evangelist, teacher, and pastor (see Eph. 4:11-13). Each of these ministry offices comes with a deeper, richer spiritual activation.

These spiritual expressions listed are only a few of the many others that are listed in the Bible and very much available to natural people for building a better tomorrow. Surely, the more you and I seek to learn God's ways, the more He will reveal Himself through us—if we can just stop getting so freaked out with our fear of the spiritual unknown.

LEARNING THE WAYS OF THIS FORCE

You may ask, how does it work? How can I deepen my faith? There is really no way to cover so vast a subject in a few paragraphs. Without getting overly theological, I will tell you how. Immediately following the born-again experience, each new Christ-ling discovers a new insatiable appetite for spiritual nourishment—just like a newborn baby craves its mother's milk.[1] Every living thing has an appetite. Without it, we would not survive. Most of us have no problem remembering to eat a few meals each day. Here, I am talking about spiritual eating.

How often should a person spiritually eat? That's up to you. Follow your own spiritual appetite and always eat at least once or twice a day—even when you are not that spiritually hungry. The Bible is the perfect spiritual food! The more of it you consume, the faster you will grow. Here is what Jesus, King David, and the prophet Isaiah had to say about spiritual food and spiritual eating.

> But Jesus told him, "No! The Scriptures say, 'People do not live by bread alone, but by every word that comes from the mouth of God'" (Matthew 4:4).

> As the deer longs for streams of water, so I long for You, O God. I thirst for God, the living God. When can I go and stand before Him? (Psalm 42:1-2)

> Is anyone thirsty? Come and drink—even if you have no money! Come, take your choice of wine or milk—it's all free! Why spend your money on food that does not give you strength? Why pay for food that does you no good? Listen to me, and you will eat what is good. You will enjoy the finest food (Isaiah 55:1-2).

> On the last and greatest day of the festival, Jesus stood and said in a loud voice, "Let anyone who is thirsty come to Me and drink" (John 7:37 NIV).

Your spiritual survival depends on a regular, healthy spiritual diet. You will never enjoy any lasting degree of spiritual growth and empowerment until you acquire a desire for God's Living Bread. Some people refer to spiritual devotions like they've offered God a sacrifice. These people should smack themselves real hard for ever letting this become a chore. Eating is the privilege of every species! We should be racing to our prayer room every early morning—just like a hungry child races to the kitchen table for breakfast. We should salivate for fresh spiritual bread, more than we hunger for any physical food. This is what Job meant when he made the following statement:

> I have not departed from His commands, but have treasured His words more than daily food (Job 23:12).

In addition to reading the Bible, you should learn how to pray. God Almighty, the Creator of everything, wants to have a relationship with you. People are fools for not spending more time with Him.[2] You should long for each private moment with God, knowing that the more time you spend with Him in prayer, the more you will become like Him in person. If you keep your prayer routines fresh enough for long enough, eventually you will feel His heartbeat within you and His desires will become your desires. I think there is no greater blessing for you as a son or daughter than to bear your Father's name and carry your Father's heart!

As you spend this quality time with God each day, ask Him to teach you. Be brave and ask the big questions! You have nothing to lose and everything to gain. Ask Him to point out anything in your life that may be holding you back. Invite God to pour Himself into you—and keep pouring until you're filled to the highest level. Surrender yourself to His will for your life. Ask Him to give you every spiritual gift you can have.

I can only imagine how ambitious this may sound to some people, but I am positive there is no other way to build a better tomorrow. None of this *Make Me a Legend* stuff is ever going to be a reality unless a lot of people are willing to go all the way—spiritually!

The more you grow, the more you will desire the company of others who are growing. The time will come when you are drawn to a prime, moving church, and you will yearn for the mentorship of a master Jedi Christian. There are many scattered throughout the earth today. Be careful how you search, though. Some are not yet leading the masses. Look for a beautiful servant leader, one who models the Force as well as he or she teaches it.

The trick in finding a good mentor is not to bypass the character test. Value character first, then talent. Don't ever forget that proverb I told you about earlier—one of my favorites, *"A righteous man falling down before the wicked is as a troubled fountain, and a corrupt spring"* (Prov. 25:26 KJV).

206 / Make Me a Legend

Always ask this question: Does this person have a private devotion strong enough to support the magnitude of his or her public mission? Can they endure the agony of setbacks and the scrutiny of haters? Can this person resist the temptations that come with fame and fortune? Don't ever compromise when choosing your mentors. There is more on this subject in Chapter 14.

The Gods Are Coming Down

I dream of the day when God fully answers a 3,400-year-old prayer of Moses—a day that Moses longed to see fulfilled in his lifetime when he prayed, *"I wish that all the Lord's people were prophets and that the Lord would put His Spirit upon them all"* (Num. 11:29). The prophet Micah hoped for the very same thing. He expressed great frustration about the prophetic deadness of his generation when he cried:

> *Then you seers will be put to shame, and you fortune-tellers will be disgraced. And you will cover your faces because there is no answer from God. But as for me, I am filled with power—with the Spirit of the Lord...* (Micah 3:7-8).

Then there is the prophet Joel—he got down on his knees and pleaded with his generation:

> *Let the priests, who minister before the Lord, weep between the temple porch and the altar. Let them say, "Spare your people, O Lord. Do not make your inheritance an object of scorn, a byword among the nations. Why should they say among the peoples, Where is their God?'"* (Joel 2:17 NIV)

These prophets were very much concerned about how God looked to the people of their ancient worlds. They were not OK with people wondering where God had gone! Throughout history, whenever a generation failed to properly represent Him, men like Moses, Micah, and Joel would blast onto the scene and say, "Wait a minute! There is still a God and He is with me! Here, let me show you what He is really like!"

To me, there seems to be little difference between their ancient worlds and our modern one. In this generation, I am equally concerned about God's great reputation. I don't want anyone wondering where He's gone!

I say we step up now, and pray like Moses did: *Dear God, please let all of Your people become prophets, and put Your spirit upon them!* Let us state our position just like Micah did: *that in a time when the seers are put to shame and the fortune tellers are disgraced because there is no answer from God—we can say, without hesitation—we are filled with God's power—with the Spirit of the Lord!* I say we get down on our knees in front of this generation and appeal to God just like Joel did: *Please God, do not make Your inheritance an object of scorn, a byword among the nations! Why should they say among the people of this 21st century world, where is their God?*

Dear reader, this is it for us—time for making history! We are capable of so much more! Just a few more training sessions to go, and we may be openly exhibiting the living Force of an all-knowing, all-seeing, and all-powerful God.

Perhaps we will represent God just like Barnabas and Paul did—so perfectly that our world also mistakes us for Zeus and Hermes, shouting, "The gods have come down to us in human form!" The essence of God flowing through our lives can become so profound until we, too, are ripping off our clothes and rushing out into the crowds shouting, "People, why are you doing this? We too are only men, human like you!" This is exactly what happened to Paul and Barnabas when they were preaching in the city of Lystra (probably the hometown of Timothy) in south central, modern-day Turkey.

> When the crowd saw what Paul had done, they shouted in the Lycaonian language, **"The gods have come down to us in human form!"** Barnabas they called Zeus, and Paul they called Hermes because he was the chief speaker. The priest of Zeus, whose temple was just outside the city, brought bulls and wreaths to the city gates because he and the crowd wanted to offer sacrifices to them. But when the apostles Barnabas and Paul heard of this, they tore their clothes and rushed out into the crowd, shouting: "Friends, why are you doing this? We too are only human, like you. We are bringing you good news, telling you to turn from these worthless

things to the living God, who made the heavens and the earth and the sea and everything in them" (Acts 14:11-15 NIV).

I don't want to force your actions. I can only tell you what I have decided to do with my life. Even though I have gone after God without hesitation, and I might already be considered a radical in many Christian circles, I am admitting it right now—I have been far too human, and I cannot keep impounding myself to a mere natural kind of existence when I was destined to run with the armies of Heaven. Call me crazy, but I have dedicated myself to master the ways of this Force, and I won't stop until I am to my generation what Moses was to his.

WHO IS THE BIG BOY NOW?

About ten years ago, I was at the gym with a very good, long-term friend of mine—Jon Higginbotham. At that time, Jon was a physical Hercules. He and his brother were exceptional body builders. Jon even won the "Mr. West Coast" title, back in 1990. The obvious problem with Jon back then was that while he was an animal in the gym, he was a spiritual weakling. A super person with a beautiful spiritual heritage—Jon just had not done much with the spiritual side of his life yet.

When Jon walked out of the locker room that afternoon, all the ladies were looking his way! Just like most men with his level of conditioning, Jon wore a tiny muscle shirt to showcase all of his muscles. I think I was wearing a sweatshirt that day! I went straight to the treadmill and then to the Nautilus weights. Of course, Jon strutted over to the free-weights—where all the goliaths lived. Little guys like me never go to the free-weight section; we don't even *glance* in that direction!

Everything was going fine that day until Jon walked over to my treadmill and asked me to spot him while he did his bench workout. I remember thinking to myself, *Ha-ha Jon, that's a good one Mr. Funny!* Reluctantly I agreed, rolling my eyes as I steadied my knees from shaking while we headed over to the stud zone. We approached the bench and Jon asked me to help him add weights to the bar. So we added weights—until the bar was filled with all the biggest ones on each side! Then Jon lay down on the bench and told me to help him if he struggles!

I remember saying, "Jon, I can't even pick up one side of this bar! If you struggle, you won't even feel the slightest relief from me!" I was really scared for Jon. More than that, I was humiliated for myself! How had I let him talk me into this?

Well, Jon started lifting—and just as I expected, people started to gather around him. And there I was with my *sweatshirt*, acting like Jon's rescue man! Thankfully, Jon finished up his reps with ease, so I didn't have to call for a crane! I admit, at first I was very proud of my buddy, for all of 15 seconds before he sprang back to his feet, looked over at me, and said, "Your turn!" What? My turn? The heat of that moment met up with the warmth of my thick sweatshirt, and I sweated like a long tailed cat in a room full of rocking chairs. He was having fun with me that day. And hey, he had earned that right—in the gym, that is. I was speechless for a second or two, but I didn't stay silent for very long.

Looking at him, I said, "Jon, the good thing for me today is that my spirit man looks like your physical body." I paused for a few seconds, just long enough for that beautiful image to pop up in Jon's mind. Then I nearly laughed myself out of a dear friendship as I continued, "And Jon, the bad news for you today is that your spirit man looks like my physical body!" Oh, I was so back in the game with that surprise cheap shot. Thankfully Jon received my sass with grace and we both had a great laugh that day!

Fortunately for Jon, he is a spiritual beast today. As for me, I'm still hanging out on the treadmills, and playing on the rest of the machines every now and then. In the natural world, I may look like a scrawny fellow; but in the spirit world, I am a force to be reckoned with!

Back in the early '90s, my training began with the diaper demons. One by one, they came at me like scrawny, little, ankle-biting Chihuahuas with all kinds of temptations and insufferable circumstances. Sometimes they knocked me down, and I would lie on the floor for days while they barked and snapped without pity—fueled with my obvious fears. Then, when I felt as if I could not handle another second of their abuse, God would reach down and pick me up—and He would doctor me back to health.

Eventually, and with plenty of experience, I started to prevail over those diaper demons. First every once in a while, then more consistently, I grew stronger in my faith and character, and I learned how to stand against all odds through the power of trust and prayer. As God worked through me, I defeated bigger and bigger spiritual opponents until finally, I prevailed over many deep-rooted family demons, and a few neighborhood and small town demons. I have warred with regional demons—and I've been exposed to a few national demons. In the Book of Daniel, I learned how there are high-ranking dark spirits fighting hard for the dominion of specific territories. I believe these spirits can be confronted and their prisoner nations can be freed!

I may never win a bodybuilding title with this frame, but maybe one day God will call me His legend. When I grow up, I will be one of God's finest generals—a front-liner on His fiercest battlefields! In recent years, I have prayed for spiritual dominion over the modern terrorist movement. Maybe I won't be able to handle that one on my own, but I am positive that if we put enough of us Spirit legends together, we can deliver a series of fatal punches to the unseen principalities behind every terror cell! There is nothing beyond our reach when we are willing to go all the way!

Prayer: Dear God, please don't give us another kiddie mission because we are still too spiritually weak for a real fight! Make us Your *legendary*, herculean warriors—Your spirit-human creatures, perfectly engineered for these perilous times. Commission us to war—against the highest dark forces of this rebelling universe. Train us and send us to hunt Your ten most wanted! And we will go, armed with record measures of Your love and power; we will race against time to free the groaning prisoners! You told Moses that the king of Egypt would not let go unless a mighty hand forced him. You promised to raise Your hand and strike the Egyptians by performing all kinds of miracles among them. And You said, *"Then at last he [Pharaoh] will let you go"* (Exod. 3:20b). You told Moses, *"Pay close attention to this. I will make you seem like God to Pharaoh, and your brother, Aaron, will be your prophet"* (Exod. 7:1). Just as Moses stood like God and punished that evil pharaoh, we want to punish the ancient spirits behind today's foremost worldwide devastations and lead entire countries back to You! This is our desire—it is our prayer.

TRAVELING THE ANCIENT PATHS

One silly man asked the apostle Peter, "Let me have this power, too…so that when I lay my hands on people, they will receive the Holy Spirit!" But Peter replied, *"May your money be destroyed with you for thinking God's gift* can be bought! You can have no part in this, for your heart is not right with God" (Acts 8:19-21).

From this we see that spiritual powers cannot be purchased with the currency of this earth. God is never going to cheapen His gifts! There is only one way, one ancient pathway mostly covered over with weeds and brush— waiting for a few courageous pioneers to open a path for everyone else! Make no mistake about it, God is right now calling to the people of this earth—in the words of Jeremiah, *"And you will seek Me and find Me, when you search for Me with all your heart!"* (Jer. 29:13 NKJV).

WINDOW SHOPPING IN A GHOST TOWN: THE VISION

Several years back, I had a remarkable vision—so real, I will never forget it! In the vision, I was window shopping in an old ghost town. I was the only person there. Just like in all the Western movies, there was one typical dirt road running through the middle of town and wooden porches on the fronts of the buildings lining both sides of the road. As I strolled past a few saloons, a hardware store, and a barbershop, there was one particular store that captured my attention. I noticed a few antique mannequins in the window display, and I leaned in for a closer look. Each mannequin wore the dusty cloak of an ancient prophet. I noticed a sign attached to the bottom of each mannequin. The first sign read, "The Cloak of Prophet Moses, 35 trillion HC (Heaven's Currency)." The second sign read, "The Cloak of Prophet Jeremiah, 31 trillion HC." The last sign read, "The Cloak of Prophet Elijah, 30 trillion HC."

As I read these prices, my head dropped and I broke down and cried. As I turned to walk away, suddenly God was standing there with me! He put His arm around me and asked me why I was crying. I replied, "I really want to have one of those cloaks but I don't have enough money." I thought for a minute and continued, "If these cloaks have been for sale for all these years and nobody's been willing to pay these prices, why don't you put them on sale?"

To that, God postured up fast, and explained, "I will never reduce the high cost of wearing a *legend's* cloak!"

Someday, in the not too distant future, a few of us are going to shop in that ghost town from my dream, and God is going to give us one of those legend's cloaks! It can be you, dear reader! Yes, it really can! But how far are you willing to go? While the rest of your world is much too content living shallow on someone else's faint description of yesterday's God, while so many smoke up their days toying around with Him as if He is little more than a momentary hobby, what are *you* going to do with the rest of your life?

As you can see from the past two chapters, anything is possible for the believing generation! We can become so much more than what we are right now—if we will stop being so darn human and accept the truth that we are far more spiritual than we are physical! We must stop waiting around for a legend-cloak inventory blowout sale! It is time we thoroughly eradicate all our fears and false assumptions, and fully surrender to God so we may hasten ourselves to the dream.

COMING UP

It has been said that a rubber band stretched never returns to its original size. Just a few more chapters and you will be stretched far beyond the possibility of returning to your original size. These remaining chapters are crucial. So, please complete your training young Jedi—or be in danger of the dark force!

Chapter 14

Get Connected: Mentors, Peers, and Apprentices

Strange is our situation here upon earth. Each of us comes for a short visit, not knowing why, yet sometimes seeming to a divine purpose...Many times a day, I realize how much my outer and inner life is built upon the labors of people, both living and dead, and how earnestly I must exert myself in order to give in return as much as I have received.

—Albert Einstein[1]

What? He Answered the Phone—Ahhh!

I still remember every vivid detail like it happened just yesterday. I had that warm feeling deep inside my heart, like this was going to be one of those standout moments of my life! As the phone was ringing, I told myself, *Calm down and breathe Chuck; he is just a man.*

And then it happened. He actually answered *my* call. I remember racing through our family room with my hand over the transmitter, asking everyone in the house to please be quiet because I was on the most important phone call *ever!*

That first conversation went very well. He must have recognized some kind of potential in me. He said I could call anytime. So I called him again—and again. He seemed to be happy when I called. After all, he could have ignored me if he didn't want to talk. Was I calling him too frequently? Was he rolling his eyes every time my number popped up on his caller ID?

A big part of me didn't want to wear out my *Obi-Wan Kenobi*, but I could not stop myself—once or twice a week, whether he was happy about it or not, I just had to make those calls! Sometimes, it was a matter of life or death for me—I hung on every word, cherished every conversation—my growth was accelerated by ten years from every ten minutes of quality time I spent with this living legend.

You must be wondering, *Who is Chuck's mystery mentor?* It is Marion Dalton, one of my earliest ministry mentors—founding pastor of Bethel Harvest Church in Lexington, Kentucky. Pastor Dalton first preached at my small town church when I was still a young Christian; and for the first time in my life up to that point, I felt like Elisha on the day he first met Elijah! After that service, we talked in the foyer, and I tried my hardest not to say anything stupid! I kept telling myself, *Be cool, Chuck—don't blow this!*

I was a new, dry sponge at its first sight of water. Marion Dalton had skillfulness in the Force like nothing I had personally experienced before. I wanted this man to teach me everything he knew. He actually gave me his home phone number that day, but I did not have the courage to call until many years later. It's OK, because timing is everything; and when the time was ripe, I made that first call. It was in the year when I transitioned from business to full-time ministry. Without a mentor, there were so many variables to that situation, so many wrong turns I could have made.

God used Marion Dalton more than he can know, not just then, but so many other times throughout the years, to help shape some of my most significant accomplishments. His brilliant, creative, and loving words have made a measurable difference in my life. Pastor Dalton has been more than a mentor to me—he and his amazing wife, Stephanie, are two of my greatest friends. I sincerely love their two sons Parker and Pearce, their two hyper Boston Terrier dogs, and Stephanie's delicious cooking. Yes, mentors can become lifelong friends—when enough love and humility is present on both sides of the relationship. Even though I still become a little like a stalker sometimes—I believe the Daltons are at least a little happy I latched on.

It is a pretty intriguing story so far, don't you think? I told it to you because everyone has had one or two of these "standout moments" in their lifetime—at least I hope *you* have! If not, I pray that it will happen very soon, a connection made in Heaven so profound it weakens your knees and soaks your cheeks!

As you consider my story, rise above your own insecurities, shatter your mental limitations, and dream big for the right relationships. God can definitely make it happen! What He has done for me, He has done for many others—it is His way of making legends. I thank God every day for pointing me out to all the right legends at all the right times—people with high love and foresight, and a rare willingness to invest in a long-shot dreamer.

THE SECRET POWER OF A LEGENDS NETWORK

Please think back to Chapter 11, *Celebrate Your Progress*, where I emphasized the high value of frenzied fans and home field advantages. There, I showed you how to recognize your incremental progress—and celebrate it like a star athlete. I said if you're ever going to play your best game, then you will need to pack out your stadium with people who really believe in you. I talked about policing your stadium—to get the right people in and keep the wrong people out. Remember?

In this chapter, "Get Connected: Mentors, Peers, and Apprentices," we are climbing down from the bleachers and stepping into the private lives of the star players—before and after game time. This is a huge revelation about the secret to their legendary strength and skill, the reason we get shivers when they race into the arena.

If you want to see it all, you will need to walk softly and be invisible—so we can study our subjects without spooking them. Watch and listen as they do life with their family, friends, fellow players, and coaches. Once you see how they interact on those unappealing practice fields during those painful, sweaty practices, and you sit in on a few of those historical, smelly pre-game, half-time, and post-game locker room speeches, you will more fully comprehend the secret power of a legends network!

Without the right *connections*, there can be no victory on the field and therefore no need for a stadium. Without a coach and his players, without the lesser leagues, middle leagues, and higher leagues—there will be no more *legends*.

In "Celebrate Your Progress" I made the following statement, "Invite me to your stadium, introduce me to your fans—and I will predict your future!" Here I will improve that statement with thoughts from this chapter: "Invite me to your stadium, introduce me to your fans, *show me your three-stranded network of mentors, peers, and apprentices*—and I will predict your future!" A three-stranded network of mentors, peers, and apprentices! Sounds intriguing, doesn't it?

I have chosen these three terms: *mentors, peers,* and *apprentices* to describe three primary categories of relationships—*above, beside,* and *beneath*—mentors (above), peers (beside), and apprentices (beneath). Mentors provide covering (over us), peers create synergy (with us), apprentices establish legacy (from us). Let's begin with mentors.

1. MENTORS PROVIDE COVERING

In today's world, *mentors* are also referred to as *fathers*, or *coaches*. Behind every aspiring apprentice is a dedicated mentor; behind every star player is a brilliant coach; behind every flourishing son and daughter is a loving father. Without these *coverings*, potential *legends* are left to themselves to struggle and fail far more than they can handle the pain. It's sad that most neglected children burn out of the race long before they have a real chance at living their dreams. I honestly believe there is a *covering* crisis in our world today. Each generation gradually worsens. We are neglecting our young, and this sin is hurting us. I believe this is a primary source of social infection in every declining civilization.

I see a vision of our young—mentor*less* apprentices, coach*less* players, and parent*less* children. They lay at the feet of the elder generation with plenty of unrefined talent, not able to turn their talents into skills, lacking the confidence that comes from being covered—they are face-down in the dirt, waiting for the people *above* them to step up and cover them!

Listen, as they pray, "Dear God, please let me stand out to someone. Please give me a mentor—a coach—a father. I'm so weak and confused, and I don't know what I'm doing, and nobody seems to care about that. Anytime someone promising comes along, all they seem to want from me is a trophy they can wave in front of their friends. Please send someone into my life who loves me like you do—someone who really wants to give their life for the acceleration of my purpose. Dear God, will you please inspire someone to cover me, before it's too late?"

OUR WARRIOR NATURE

A few years ago, I spoke about "coverings" in a zealous Father's Day message titled, *The Warrior Nature of Every Man*. In something like 45 minutes, I shined a bright light on the problem as I saw it and inspired my congregation toward an achievable solution. At the end of that message I commissioned the men of our church to fall more deeply in love with God and further develop their spiritual authority so they could rise immediately to cover their wives and children. I even spoke beyond my reach when I prayed and prophesied to the other fathers of our nation. I prayed also for leaders of companies to cover their employees, and pastors to cover their churches. The transformation that took place in that meeting is still felt today.

Even though many of the world's greatest mentors are female, there is so much for everyone to learn about mentorship from the warrior commission of a father. Every person—man and woman, young and old alike—is called to leverage our attained influence and mentor different people at different times in our lives. I speak to men *and* women throughout this chapter because both are equally gifted to be mentors.

If we will take the time to look around every once in a while, we will see someone looking up to us who is secretly praying to be covered. In the next few paragraphs, I will describe the warrior nature. Let it challenge you and change you just like it challenged and changed those Father's Day men, and continues to challenge and change me today.

The prophet Ezekiel spoke for God to the leaders of his generation when he said:

> *I looked for someone who might rebuild the wall of righteousness that guards the land. I searched for someone to stand in the gap in the wall so I wouldn't have to destroy the land, but I found no one* (Ezekiel 22:30).

During those days, God looked for someone to rebuild the crumbled wall of righteousness that guarded the country. He looked for someone to stand on the wall and fight for the citizens—and He couldn't find one such person.

Then, in tremendous contrast with those cowards, there was a different time and a different man—Nehemiah, a father with the warrior nature.

When it was suggested that he "save his own life" by hiding in the temple during conflict, Nehemiah responded, *"Should someone in my position run from danger? Should someone in my position enter the Temple to save his life? No, I won't do it!"* (Neh. 6:11).

What a perfect *covering* attitude! If that's what Nehemiah voiced aloud, can you image what he must have thought to himself? *Should someone in my position run away and save his own life, while his legacy is chewed to pieces? Absolutely not! I will not do that! I understand the responsibility of my high calling and to whom I am responsible. God has commissioned me as a covering in Israel. If there is an attack on this land, I will run to the front lines with my sword in the air. If an enemy gets to my family, he will have to go through my dead body!*

Nehemiah was a *father* to the people he led. He was a true *shepherd* to Israel. In the business of shepherding, there is one sure way to distinguish a true shepherd from a hired helper. In times of danger, the hired helper will run away to save his own life, while a true shepherd will never abandon his sheep—he will fight, even to his own death, protecting his flock from predators. Nehemiah is remembered as one of Israel's greatest (mentor, coach, and father) *coverings* of all time.

It seems like there have been more times than not, when leaders have neglected the generations they were commissioned to cover. As previously mentioned, this was especially true during Ezekiel's era. In the following prophecy, God spoke again through Ezekiel, further expressing His agitation to the heartless, self-seeking leaders of that day.

> *Son of man, prophesy against the shepherds, the leaders of Israel. Give them this message from the Sovereign Lord: What sorrow awaits you shepherds who feed yourselves instead of your flocks. Shouldn't shepherds feed their sheep? You drink the milk, wear the wool, and butcher the best animals, but you let your flocks starve. You have not taken care of the weak. You have not tended the sick or bound up the injured. You have not gone looking for those who have wandered away and are lost. Instead, you have ruled them with harshness and cruelty. So My sheep have been scattered without a shepherd, and they are easy prey for any wild animal* (Ezekiel 34:1-5).

We have this same problem today—and even worse. The floors of this earth are piled high with famished, half-devoured sheep because there is no coach to discover them, no mentor to model a better way for them, no father to love them. There is a huge gap between the generations and it's crushing me. I want to build a bridge across this gap and merge the divided generations. I want to see every orphaned reader with his or her very own loving father—and then every loving father honored like crazy by each of his loving kids. The prophet Malachi cried for this very same thing when he said:

> Look, I am sending you the prophet Elijah before the great and dreadful day of the Lord arrives. His preaching will turn the hearts of fathers to their children, and the hearts of children to their fathers. Otherwise I will come and strike the land with a curse (Malachi 4:5-6).

Since godly coverings are so rare, I want to cherish mine. I want to be a respectful and loving apprentice, player, and son to all of my mentors, coaches, and fathers. I also want to spread a safe, wide covering over my young. I want to hulk up fast in the face of danger and fight to my death if necessary, for the sake of my dear Coree and Heaven—and for the sake of my spiritual children. I have a warrior nature and I'm not afraid to use it!

Iye-yie-yie-yie-yie! Did you hear that? It's my war cry! Here, listen again—Iye-yie-yie-yie-yie! Picture this: my face is covered in war paint and I'm ready to go in a second's notice; my spiritual ears work like shortwave radio antennas—I can hear my kids cry from anywhere in this world. If devil or man tries anything with anyone under my covering, I will act like a Liam Neeson in the movie *Taken*—and it'll take more than an army to bring me down. That's my warrior nature—God forbid you should ever be within a hundred miles of me on the day when some vile beast lunges at one of mine! Now, obviously, this paragraph is written for effect. I'm not actually threatening brute physical retaliation. I'm using an image painted with words to describe the instinctive warrior nature deep inside every true mentor, coach, father, and shepherd. Do you have it?

FINDING YOUR MENTORS

To every fatherless son and daughter, mentorless apprentice, and coach-less player, I say this with tears in my eyes: It has always been in God's plan to cover you! I am so sorry for all those lonely, younger years of having to raise your siblings and suffer in private over Mom and Dad's drug-induced rages. I'm sorry for the long, dark years of secret abuse from insecure leaders. I can't imagine the pain you've endured. With God's grace, you can forgive your abusers. Free them to go find mercy and peace, and thank God for whatever value they added to your life despite themselves. Now, lift up your weary head! Pray for a covering. Wipe your teary eyes and look again—because God will answer this prayer for you; it is going to happen.

Since God already wants you covered, He will make it happen when the time is perfect. Don't get nervous, or obnoxious. Divine connections must form naturally. All you have to do is be yourself, and pay attention to the people you meet, the places you go, the friends you already have, and the friends of all your friends. Pay attention to everyone and everything. If you are yourself and pay attention long enough—before you know it, the sparks will fly!

I am not suggesting you sit at home and wait for your mentor to levitate his awesome self onto your front porch! Go ahead, be brave and test the waters. Put yourself out there, be vulnerable, and take a risk. Get out of the house, secretly interview people, hand out a few applications, and see what happens. Be very careful not to cave under the pressures of your unresolved insecurities and force yourself on the wrong person. Of course, you can always hire a life coach if you can afford it. Under the right circumstances, this is a very good option.

Whether your mentor is paid or volunteer, still you must wait for a chemical—better yet, a spiritual—reaction if you expect the relationship to last. Don't ever settle for anything less than God's mentor for your life. Don't ever settle for anything less than a mentor who will love you with a father's heart. You deserve it.

HONOR YOUR MENTORS

When the day comes and you find yourself in one of those mentor relationships set in Heaven—guard it with your life! Lavish your good mentors honor.

Don't hold anything back. Bless your mentors with encouraging words, extravagant service, and material gifts as often as you can. *"Giving a gift can open doors; it gives access to important people!"* (Prov. 18:16). When your mentors are thanking God for *you* more than everyone else, you are on your way up!

Think about the prophet Elisha. He started as the devoted apprentice of a powerful mentor—Elijah, the prophet of fire. Elisha served his master Elijah so passionately; people called him the man who *"poured water on the hands of Elijah"* (see 2 Kings 3:11 KJV). Elisha did this for ten years prior to having his own national ministry. Then there was Joshua, the man who conquered 31 cities with an army of freed slaves. He too began as the honorable servant of a world-class mentor—Moses, the prophet and deliverer of Israel. He served Moses for 40 years prior to his promotion.

Are you seeing the pattern? Honor always precedes promotion. This is a true and proven biblical principle. Jesus said:

> *Give, and you will receive. Your gift will return to you in full— pressed down, shaken together to make room for more, running over, and poured into your lap. The amount you give will determine the amount you get back!* (Luke 6:38)

God will make happen for you whatever you make happen for others. In this case, the things you make happen for your mentor leaders will return to you pressed down, shaken together to make room for more, running over, and poured back into your lap!

Honor your mentors with personal space. Don't wear out your welcome! Honor your mentors with mercy. Don't require perfection! Be selective, yes, but perfection is out of the question; so don't move from mentor to mentor in haste just because nobody seems "good enough" to cover you. This is especially a challenge as you get to know people well enough to see their flaws. Familiarly often breeds contempt, which is the certain death of countless divine connections. Apprentices beware.

MY SHORT LIST OF MENTORS (FATHERS AND COACHES)

Mentors don't come to us bundled in a multi-pack starter kit. You can't just log on to a mentor warehouse website, click through a few hundred profiles, proceed to check out, and wait three to five business days for their arrival. Mentors show up one at a time, from different parts of the world, with different backgrounds and belief systems, different social standings, races, ages, etc. Your mentors don't have to know each other or even like each other. Variety is good. For some of my mentors, the only thing they have in common among themselves is me. I would love to gather them into the same room someday!

I've had mentors in parenting, character, business, money, and ministry. Here is my (short list) mentors hall of fame: my mother, Barbara Lynn Balsamo; father-in-law Merle Wall; grandfather Adam Paul Dobzeniecki; track coach Ron Wilkerson; real estate gurus Mike Ferry and Tom Ferry; Pastor Marion Dalton; real estate coach Ren Jones; Real estate brokers Donald Sheets and Melvin Sweeney; Evangelist Gerald Mayhan; Gaines and Sandy Dittrich; Dr. Tim Bagwell; worship *legend* Kent Henry; Pastor Lindell Cooley; Pastor David Frech; Prophet Arvind D'Silva; Pastor Ronnie Harris; Pastor Jeffery Myers; Author Achim Zahren; Pastor Roy Bickford; Pastor Tony Hiles; Pastor Steve Dodson; Pastor Jeff Ferguson; Pastor Bill Roberts; Pastor Ken Burtram, Dr. Bob Rhoden, and a few others. Each of these *legends* poured their lives into me—so much, that I am today a monument of their compiled strengths. Besides these, I've always had the loving influence of a devoted family.

Some of my mentor relationships have been long term, others short term. I have learned from experience that no matter how hard we try to hold on, some mentors flash through our lives just to help us over an obstacle, and then are gone to their next assignment. Therefore, you and should cherish the special people we have today and pay attention. We should learn everything there is to learn from them and fully absorb their dear hearts, because we never really know when something unexpected may go down.

As you can imagine, some of my mentors are now remembered as the unfortunate casualties of war. Some of them fought a very good fight, for a very long time, under incomprehensible conditions, until they could not stay upright for one more second. Eventually, something impeded their path and they tripped and collapsed right in front of me! This is one of the saddest and most unnatural things to go through in this life—to watch a cherished mentor stripped of honor right in front of you. Whenever this happens, you must never play the expert in someone else's life. No matter how much you think you know, you will never fully understand the spiritual warfare behind another person's demise.

Pray and fast for your fallen mentors. When it is possible, reach down with a humble hand. Before you ever think about sitting in the judge's chair, remember this: apart from God's grace you will collapse someday.

I have fallen out of closeness with a few of my past mentors, though I still honor them as much as it is possible. Three of my mentors have passed into Heaven. As you grow and succeed, keep on respecting your mentors. Sometimes, this will be difficult. There is no easy way of saying this: don't be surprised if a mentor turns against you. Sometimes, just like King Saul caved under the pressures of his insecurities and he turned on his young apprentice David, one or two of your mentors may also snap on the inside. Their love for you may turn to hate so fast you are just barely able to run away fast enough! When this happens, pray for God to give you the heart and humility of David, who would not dishonor his mentor—even when the man sought to kill him! For a whole lot more on this subject, I recommend *A Tale of Three Kings*, by Gene Edwards, and two great John Bevere books: *Under Cover* and *Honor's Reward*.

Wherever my past mentors are today, whatever they are doing with their lives, they will never fully know the difference they each made in my life. Dear God, please bless these men and their families, businesses, and ministries—bless them with greater influence, perfect health, and long and happy lives. Show them a lifetime of kindness for the kindness they have shown to me. Move their mountains, calm their storms, wipe away their secret tears, and answer their deepest prayers.

2. PEERS CREATE SYNERGY

Just as we need a covering, we also need the companionship of an equal—a peer. A peer is "one who is of equal standing with another."[2] Your peers are the people who are standing in the same spot you are right now. They feel what you are feeling most of the time. When you talk to them about your dreams, they get where you are coming from, because they have similar sized dreams—and an equal degree of progress toward those dreams. Peers have an equal level of skill and experience. When you look into the heart of a peer, it is like looking at your face in the mirror.

I like to compare peer relationships to the synergy generated between two competitively matched running partners. *Synergy* is defined as "the interaction of two or more agents or forces so that their combined effect is greater than the sum of their individual effects."[3] Synergy is the opposite of *antagonism*, which is "a phenomenon where two or more agents in combination have an overall effect which is less than the sum of their individual effects."[4]

A good example of peer synergy for me is my friendship with Chris Whetzel. He and I are perfectly, competitively matched—both running neck and neck, as fast as two men with our age and experience are capable of running! Chris leads the thriving church he founded some years ago, Believers Victory Center in Moorefield, West Virginia.

Chris is a ministerial prodigy! His pace is supersonic—sometimes a little bit slower than mine, and sometimes a whole lot faster. Every now and then, Chris increases the pace so much, I'm tempted to make him go on without me. Even on our very worse days, we inspire each other to get up and run like the wind—even through hurricanes, blizzards, and tornadoes! Sometimes, there is not another runner within a few hundred miles of us, outrageous enough to turn down some of the trails my peer Chris and I have chosen to trek! We thoroughly enjoy one another's families. We share similar aspirations. We laugh out loud every time we connect. Our friendship is perfectly synergistic. I would not be anywhere close to where I am today without him.

FINDING YOUR PEER PACE

Successful peer relationships require huge amounts of give and take. They never last long when one person does all the giving while the other person does all the taking. Therefore, whenever I am not able to keep pace with the other runners, I either shape up fast, or drop back into another, slower peer circle.

I have been privileged to run with a few much faster runners from time to time. Just like so many insecure people do, I could have smothered these guys until I killed their race. One perfect example is my peer relationship with international worship leader, Jason Upton. I will never forget how excited I was the first time he and I talked on the phone. I got off that call and told my wife, "I think Jason likes me! I can see us becoming best friends!"

Although I had a very successful contemporary Christian singer-song-writer, composer, and recording artist's cell number, and he actually answered when I called, and I was so honored to tell everyone that I was becoming friends with "Jason Upton"—it didn't take me long to see how much faster Jason was running.

I wanted to get closer to Jason for two primary reasons—first, because he was a living *legend* with a profound degree of spiritual influence, and second, because Jason Upton was one of the most fascinating human beings I had ever met. He made me feel like he wanted me around. He even invited my family and me to his house. There seemed to be a real friendship forming between us and I so could have taken advantage of it. Yet I knew in my heart, I had to let Jason Upton run his faster race. Perhaps one day, after I have mastered a few more of these medium levels, he and I will connect again—next time, in an equivalent arena. Maybe then we will be able to synergize for something big—if that's in the Master's plan.

I am not saying that every person you relate with has to be running at your pace. Some enduring friendships definitely transcend commonality of purpose. I am not suggesting you call all of your friends and tell them to eat your dust because you're *moving on!* I am just saying that you should look for peers with similar aims and convictions—people who are naturally running in your same direction. Then, you have to know when and how to make a peer change. You have to pay attention to your ever-shifting circumstances and the remarkable evolution of each person's unique destiny and when peer realignment is necessary.

I guess I'm being so passionate about this because we all have a race to run—a race that matters in the face of eternity. What we do with our time and with whom we spend our lives greatly affects the outcome of these races. When I talk about peer bond, I am highlighting those specific peer bonds we form on the track—while we run! Hopefully, more and more people will more fully understand what is at stake, and a huge wave of synergistic realignment will take place.

Sad to say, there are times when one peer falls down so hard, he threatens to drag another down with him. Herein is a benefit of peer relationship—to have a strong hand up on a real bad day. When one is down, the other is usually up. Even when both peers fall down on the same week, there is safety.

Amazingly, as God engineered it to be, synergy still works in the valley! Rightly matched peers always find a way to rise together in victory.

If two peers are falling back more than they are going forward, there is a mismatched pace. This means that one peer is trying to run much faster than he can, while the other faster peer is holding back. The slower one eventually burns out, striving to perform way over his head. The faster runner may have patience and humility, but eventually he becomes frustrated, knowing he is built for a faster pace. Can you feel the antagonism here? When this happens, necessary adjustments must be made.

ADJUSTING YOUR PEER PACE

Here is my advice: Run your race as fast as you can run it. Make sure you're adding tremendous value to each of your peers. Give more than you take, as often as you can. Give as much as you take, most of the time. And never take more than you give, longer than you have to.

Please don't get upset when one of your faster peers wants to run ahead. Have the guts to admit when you're temporarily out of your league. Don't ever become that insecure small-town boy who ruins his own life trying to sabotage his little brother's bigger dream! Trust me, your time will come. So shed your tears, pat your brother's back, and cheer loudly as he races off into the horizon. It is a whole lot better to release people than to smother them, and it frees you to run with peers more perfectly matched for your current race.

If you are the faster runner, do your best to encourage the slower runners. When the opportunity presents itself and you perceive a certain level of teachability, look deep into the slower runner's life and point out few ways he might pick up his pace. Be humble; don't ever forget those days when you were the slower person holding up the faster traffic.

Give everyone the opportunity to run with you as long as they can keep up. Yet, in all your humility, never let a stubborn, slower runner control your race. Don't fall into manipulation and run slowly all your life just because you are afraid of offending people with your success. Dream big, Joseph (and Josephine)! Those legs were born for running and you will never be happy until you are running like you know you can!

*Therefore, since we are surrounded by such a great cloud of witnesses, let us throw off everything that hinders and the sin that so easily entangles. And let us **run** with perseverance **the race** marked out for us* (Hebrews 12:1 NIV).

3. APPRENTICES ESTABLISH LEGACY

Do you remember the great mentor I talked about during the opening of this chapter—Marion Dalton? As we talked on the phone one day, I realized he actually benefitted from having this apprentice! Of course, I was still the obvious pupil in our relationship, but I felt there were moments that he learned as much (or more) from me as I learned from him. My progress gave him the honor of seeing his legacy carried out!

When I first noticed this, it blew me away. Never before that day did I fully comprehend the inner cry of aging mentors—their dire want for legacy. For every genuine mentor, coach, father, and shepherd, this is the truest meaning of life! They wake up every day, longing to give away something of great value, to anyone who recognizes the great value of that something. Every time an eager young apprentice jettisons across the universe to meet up with his mentor—the culmination of youthful zeal and humble admiration together with ripe old wisdom and protective vigilance—cause the fireworks to explode!

THE SILENT CRY OF A MENTOR

I know a man named Danny who is a hardworking older fellow, crazy in love with his wife and family. Danny is always telling funny jokes and happy phrases—and every time he introduces his wife to a new friend, he says, "I prayed for God to send me a decent woman—and he sent me an angel!" He has certainly become a very good friend of mine over the past few years.

Through his remarkable daughter, our dear friend Tammy, Danny heard about my growing fascination for gardens. During those days, Emily and I were two struggling apprentice gardeners eager for an education. The timing was perfect. One early summer afternoon, Danny invited us to his house for lunch—and to our sheer astonishment, Danny and Dolly led us around their front, back, and side yards, and through their greenhouse—and introduced us to more than 250 species of plants. Our search was over, our prayers were answered—there was no doubt about it, we had found our gardening mentor!

Since that day, Danny has spent quite a few hours at our house—very patiently instructing Emily and me in the ways of the gardening force. Since then he has given us loads of plants—too many to count. Thanks to Danny Leslie, we have become two fine master gardeners! Well, not really—we still have a very long way to go, but we're learning fast.

Danny and I have spent quite a few spring and summer days laboring together for the better good of our beloved plants. While all the neighborhood birds, frogs, fish, and squirrels frolicked about thanking God for the beautiful habitation we were creating for them, Danny and I talked about everything under the sun. I've learned many interesting things about this man. For example, Danny is one of the greatest master bakers of all time! I wish you could have the pleasure of experiencing one or two of his scrumptious signature food creations. Mmmm!

One day, Danny took my family through his house and showed us his many awards and trophies. There is no end to learning all he knows. Thirty minutes with Danny is like a three-credit-hour college course. He talks faster than most people can comprehend, gives away more information than most of us can process, and he loves to teach more than anyone I've ever met.

Sometimes I watch Danny move, and I'm tempted to offer him a chair. Sometimes I hear him talk and I am tempted to slow him down—until I realize he is aging fast, and his time is running out. You can see it in his eyes; Danny is deeply concerned that he wont be able to pass it all down before his time runs out. This is the silent cry of every good mentor. I imagine that every night they climb onto their knees, bend their elbows, cross their hands, and pray:

> *Please God, give me at least one eager apprentice! Please, bring someone into my life with a desire for my craft! Give me at least one humble, loyal apprentice, and I will give the rest of my life to teach that person everything I know. Dear God, I have lived my best days and I have achieved so much—and today none of this means anything if I cannot give it to someone else. Please God, before I leave this earth, please answer one last prayer—establish my legacy.*

When Danny found out my daughter Heaven was going to culinary school to be a baking and pastry chef—he reverse-aged by 40 years! "A baking and pastry chef, did you say she was going to become a baking and pastry chef? Well, that just so happens to be my specialty!" Danny must have called our house every day for several weeks! "When can I meet with Heaven? There's so much I need to teach her before she starts school this fall! Oh, and I have a few very valuable items I want to give her! Oh my, there's so much we have to do! This is *great!* I'm so proud of Heaven for going this direction with her life!"

Just as soon as our schedules allowed it, we finally accepted Danny's kind invitation—and let me tell you—He gave Heaven a knife set, special cookbooks, an oven thermometer, and other valuable items, including a very sentimental professional garnishing kit given to him by his beautiful Dolly. What a difference this man has made in our daughter's life—and what a difference she has made in his.

There are so many Dannys in our world. They have a lifetime of experience and skill, and a strong desire to pass it down, but every day, they awake to another pointless agenda. Please don't misunderstand me. This is not to downplay their enjoyment of friends and family and the satisfaction they find in work, church, and play. I am just saying what nobody wants to say. They may stare into the bathroom mirror to find a few more wrinkles and a little less hair. They may have strange cramps and aching bones and a few chest pains every once in a while—and they wonder, *How much more time do I have? When I die, this all dies with me unless I find an apprentice.*

Dear God, awaken the apprentice generation! Give us a desire for the real inheritance of our mentors. Let us see past their money and material possessions, to the heart and spirit they long to give us. May we comprehend the value of our mentors before the opportunity for impartation is gone!

Again, I will refer to the well-known mentor/apprentice bond between Elijah and Elisha. On the final day of Elijah's life, when he realized that his brief but full life was nearly up—he set his eyes on his young apprentice Elisha. Elijah asked Elisha, "Tell me what I can do for you before I am taken away." From Elisha's immediate reply, we can assume that he had already thought about what he really wanted and he was just waiting for the question. Surprisingly, he did not ask for Elijah's mansion, or any of his earthly possessions—without hesitation, Elisha responded, *"Please let me inherit a double share of your spirit and become your successor"* (2 Kings 2:9).

I can hear Elisha thinking to himself, *Everyone else can spend the next ten years fighting over my master's material estate—I want the thing nobody else will even think to ask for. Um, master Elijah, I know what I want—a double share of your spirit! Please, make me your successor!* Brilliant, Elisha! There is no better way to honor a mentor, then to ask for his spirit. Apprentices establish legacy! Because of the apprentice, the mentor can rest in peace, knowing that his legacy will endure.

BUILD YOUR NETWORK

Someone might be able to beat up one of you, but not both of you. As the saying goes, "A rope made from three strands of cord is hard to break" (Ecclesiastes 4:12 CEV).

I have found this to be true in my own life. One person, standing alone, *is* easily overpowered. Two people, standing back to back, *can* defend themselves. A rope made from three strands is very hard to break! For the purposes of this teaching, I have labeled the three strands—mentors, peers, and apprentices. If you want to be a *legend* in tomorrow's better world, you need to braid your rope—a strand of mentor *legends*, a strand of peer *legends*, and a strand of apprentice *legends*. Mentors provide covering, peers create synergy, apprentices establish legacy.

Hopefully, because of this chapter, you will be closer than ever to braiding your network. In the future, spend more time concentrating on all three strands—your mentors, peers, and apprentices. Pray for God to bring the right people into your life. Believe that God's favor is starting to increase in your life—that from now on, you will stand out to the right people at the right time, and that they stand out to you.

At the time of this writing, I have an amazing strand of mentors. I also have many great peers, and a few great apprentices. Over time, the lineup will change. Some old mentors will pass into eternity where they will cheer me from the heavens. New mentors will come into my life for each next level of my journey. My peer circle will always be changing. As I mature in my calling, perhaps someday I will have a million apprentices or more. This is my dream. It's also my dream for you.

Coming Up

I bet you've read a few stinky books in your lifetime. Am I right? You know, those ones where it seemed like the author ran out of things to say and only wrote the last 50 pages to fluff up a skinny message. Well, that's not the way this book was written. I've saved my very best thoughts for right now!

To be a *legend*, you need a heart—a beautiful, loving, caring heart! The following two chapters will be some of the most introspective content you have ever read.

Chapter 15

Bow Lower as You Climb Higher

I've had just enough of the spotlight when it burns bright to see how it gets in the blood. ...I've had just enough of the quick bites of the best lies to know how prodigals can be drawn away. I know how I can stray and how fast my heart could change.

—CHRIS SLIGH, *American Idol* sixth season finalist,
"Empty Me" lyrics

SOMETIMES I FEAR SUCCESS

This is not my final topic, but it is the topic I saved to write after finishing the rest of this book—because I felt like God needed to create a deep metamorphosis in my own heart before I could really say this like it needs to be said. I never want to be a hypocrite on purpose or in ignorance, so I have to be honest with you—I am still working very hard to walk out so many of the things I am about to lead you through. Please pray for me that I will become everything I am asking you to be. Just like you, I want to be so much more like Jesus—and sometimes I still fall way short of that.

I often think of all the men and women who once stood where I am standing right now—all the beautiful Christian people who started out with a similar degree of humility toward others and a perfect dependence on God. I think of all the men who once loved their wives, cherished their families, and desired nothing in life except to run a faithful race. I think about the times they must have prayed, "Please God, don't let anything in this whole universe ever drag me away from You. Please, don't ever let me forget where I came from. Don't let me fall down and make a fool of You in front of everyone. Keep me pure and humble as I ascend the ladders of success." Then, after five or ten years of being worn down and trodden over, they wake up to an entirely different, far more evil version of themselves. In outright perplexity, they are left to wonder, "What happened to my heart? Dear God, how I have lost myself!" This is why I fear success sometimes.

Remember the title of this book, *Make Me a Legend?* It's all about becoming powerful, aiming big, taking risks, and changing the world. I am not writing this chapter to fill your mind with fear. No way! On the contrary, I am simply asking you to consider the risks and prepare for them—you know, to count the cost. Jesus said:

> But don't begin until **you count the cost.** For who would begin construction of a building without first calculating the cost to see if there is enough money to finish it? Otherwise, you might complete only the foundation before running out of money, and then everyone would laugh at you. They would say, "There's the person who started that building and couldn't afford to finish it!" (Luke 14:28-30)

SAVING MY FUTURE—AND YOURS

Of all the chapters in this book, this is the one I send ahead of us—to save our future! It is the chapter I hope you will read once or twice a year for the rest of your life. I feel such a pressing obligation to get this out of me, I don't even want to walk out of my office one more time or lay my head down one more night before this is penned. This is the message we could forget as we succeed, the one I am writing before my own heart has a chance to harden.

BEWARE, THE ANGRY MOBS

Every time a high profile person collapses, I feel their pain like it is happening to my family and me. I am not one to churn out the jokes, or shove the strugglers down to hell. While the newscasters, talk show hosts, and self-righteous church folks mock and jeer and hiss and boo for months to years, I fall down on my face in intercession for these humiliated people and their suffering families. I pray for fallen people, no matter how hideously they have transgressed, oftentimes with a river of tears, that God will bend down in His great mercy and nurse them back to life. In what is thought to be the oldest book of the New Testament, James recorded:

> *Speak and act as those who are going to be judged by the law that gives freedom, because judgment without mercy will be shown to anyone who has not been merciful. **Mercy triumphs over judgment*** (James 2:12-13 NIV).

Merciless people outrage me, when they so arrogantly sidestep their own failures to "expose" a broken person. One self-righteous person gets a taste of blood, then another, and a few more—and in a matter of seconds, a mob is formed. It is one of my highest life goals: to never lead an angry mob or join one. I never want there to be any mistake about my position. I will never endorse a mob with my spineless neutrality. If you're a bully, you'll be no friend of mine.

I never want to point my finger in judgment when someone is failing. I never want to kick a knocked down person. If I can't help, then I will pray. I will search the depths of my own heart. In the fear of God, I will keep on telling myself, *Chuck, you have no idea what kind of pressure that person was under that led to such a failure. And Chuck, if you even think for a minute this could never happen to you, then think again; you have never known that degree of satanic solicitation, the kind of pressure and erosion that person has faced these past years. Someday, soon enough, you will have your shot. Someday, you will stand on their mountain. In that day, you will see how much more violently the wind blows up there. So, don't brag because you are doing so well these days. You are just facing a few diaper demons, and look at how easily they still slap you around at times.*

God told Jeremiah, *"If racing against mere men makes you tired, how will you race against horses? If you stumble and fall on open ground, what will you do in the thickets near the Jordan?"* (Jer. 12:5). This is why I hope you will read and re-read *Make Me a Legend* Chapters 9 and 10 and build your extravagant foundation. This is why you need to grow slowly. You have to master the footmen before graduating to the horses. You have to crawl to each next level on your knees, knowing that it's violent at the top. If you do not ascend in grace and humility, then you will be crushed with what lies ahead.

THE HEART IS EVERYTHING

King Solomon, who is remembered for his wisdom, talked about the heart when he said, *"Keep and guard your heart with all vigilance and above all that you guard, for out of it flow the springs of life"* (Prov. 4:23 AMP). From the advice given in this verse, we can say that even with a good foundation, and even with a sold-out stadium of frenzied fans, and all the best mentors, peers, and apprentices—even then, we must always keep and guard our hearts above all that we guard, because the springs of life flow from them. If we ever lose our hearts, we lose everything!

It is terrifying to think of how fast a heart can harden. It happens to the best people all the time. One day we are full of God's love and compassion, and one year later we can become an entirely different person. We have to pay very careful attention to the way real life affects us. I have learned that my own heart is most endangered during times of great change, during times of severe pain and suffering, and during times of great success.

For example:

- A sheltered young man heads for college with no concept about the potential deadliness of sudden freedom. This time of great change endangers his fragile heart.

- A kind and innocent young lady is forced into her boyfriend's back seat where she is raped and physically assaulted. What she doesn't understand at first is that the damage to her heart is far more deadly than the abuse inflicted on her body.

- A trusting and loyal person is betrayed and humiliated all over town by his very best friend. He may never be able to trust or love on that level again. This time of severe pain and suffering endangers his injured heart.

- A hardworking new employee gets promoted to manager over his tenured peers, not realizing the hazards of sudden exaltation. This time of great success endangers the promoted employee's uplifted heart.

Whether it is because of great change, a moment of severe pain and suffering, or a time of great success, we have to fight for our hearts! When our heart is bruised, we have to nurse it back to health as quickly as possible. If not, we might lose ourselves—for a few years to a few decades, or even for the rest of our lives!

THE 12/17 WINDOW

One of the best ways to illustrate an endangered heart is to look at a child between the ages of 12 and 17, when they are standing on the threshold between adolescence and adulthood. Look around at your circle of family and friends, and pick out one of their preteens. Take a very close look into his or her eyes and notice the humble soul; this young person is still innocent and respectful, still tender and compassionate, and has morals. Now, move forward five years and re-interview this same child. Take another very close look into his or her eyes; take a second inventory of the maturing, hardening soul. More often than not, now this child is obsessed with outer appearance, not as respectful toward authority figures, is sitting on a mound of secrets, and cares far less for the needs of others. This young person may be guarded, bitter, self-centered, unhappy with what he or she is becoming, and thinks that nothing can be done about it.

There may not be another time in the human journey more threatening to the heart than 12/17. This is when parents and those responsible for children really need to be pay attention. We have to help our children and grandchildren, nephews and nieces, and everyone else's kids—safely to 17 and beyond without spilling a single drop of their inner beauty.

Sadly, this isn't the only time the heart is threatened. Understanding 12/17, helps us identify other times in our lives when we are repeatedly endangered with great change, severe pain and suffering, and great success. Always guard your heart!

WHAT IF I FALL?

Sometimes I think that my dreams may actually happen, and in a single day I will rocket into the public eye as the next high-profile Christian leader. This great success will usher me into the biggest change of my entire life. Right now, I feel like I am 12 going on 17 again! The thought of bringing hope to millions and leading many of them to my Savior is too wonderful for words. Then I think about how quickly money, fame, and the exaggerated praise of others could go entirely out of control.

What if I can't handle success? What if I can't assemble the correct team for properly managing the millions of dollars God may lay at our disposal? What if I am pulled under by the seductiveness of women who prey on popular men? I feel strong right now, but I have no idea what that kind of life would be like. What if I become arrogant, impatient, and mean-spirited—or I burn out and lose my willingness to sacrifice? I would rather turn back now than to gain this whole world and lose my heart! The following two Scripture passages speak directly to such concerns:

For the love of money is the root of all kinds of evil. And some people, craving money, have wandered from the true faith and pierced themselves with many sorrows. But you, Timothy, are a man of God; so run from all these evil things. Pursue righteousness and a godly life, along with faith, love, perseverance, and gentleness (1 Timothy 6:10-11).

*While I was at the window of my house, looking through the curtain, I saw some naive young men, and one in particular who lacked common sense. He was crossing the street near the house of an immoral woman, strolling down the path by her house. So she seduced him with her pretty speech and enticed him with her flattery. He followed her at once, like an ox going to the slaughter. He was like a stag caught in a trap, awaiting the arrow that would **pierce its heart**. He was like a bird flying into a snare, little knowing it would cost him his life. So listen to me, my sons, and pay attention to my words. **Don't let your hearts stray** away toward her. Don't wander down her wayward path. For she has* *been the ruin of many; many men have been her victims. Her house is the road to the grave. Her bedroom is the den of death* (Proverbs 7:6-8,21-27).

BALANCE IS DIFFICULT

So far, I've been able to juggle my fruitful life pretty well—on these lower levels, that is! For the past two decades, I have consciously dedicated a proportionate degree of time to each of my nine life equities. Today, my family thrives under the blessing of a balanced husband and father. My church enjoys the fruitfulness of a balanced pastor. I feel like my moderate universe is at least adequately balanced today. Certainly, there is always room for improvement. I love everything about my current life, and I do not want to let anything or anyone throw it out of symmetry. Balance is difficult. It doesn't happen by chance. To have it, we must manage our lives on purpose. In the professional world, people hire life management coaches to help them create and follow a life plan. Life coaches divide the human existence into subcategories commonly referred to as "life equities."

Here is a list of nine life equities, taken from my daily blog site, chuckbalsamo.com. Maybe you'll want to create more balance in your own expanding universe with this inspirational exercise. All you have to do is answer the following five questions for each of your nine life equities:

1. What about _____ am I currently dissatisfied with? (Brutal honesty required)

2. If life were perfect, how would my life look in the area of _____? (Dream without limits)

3. Who can I apprentice myself under for _____?

4. What are my top three goals for _____?

5. What is my specific plan of action and completion deadline for _____?[1]

YOUR NINE LIFE EQUITIES

1. Spiritual (your relationship with God)

2. Family (your inner circle)

3. Character (managing the real you)

4. Career and Calling (career—your occupation, calling—your divine purpose)

5. Contribution (management of your time, talents, and resources)

6. Physical (your health)

7. Financial (your money management)

8. Education (new information, impartation, and experience)

9. Experiences (exposure—visiting new places, trying new things)

Soooo Much to Risk!

God has shown me so much love, especially over the past 20 years. He has held me closer than anyone can fathom. Right now, I am still absolutely obsessed with Him. At this exact moment, I am listening to *Arms Wide Open* sung by Misty Edwards and tears are streaming down my face. There is a wind of God rushing through my (completed) sunroom—it's too wonderful for words. When I look at a cross, I still see Jesus hanging there for me. When I pray, several times each day, I still pray like I did when He first saved me. I still cry during a good worship song, and I am not ashamed to bow on my knees in front of any audience. I feel like my heart is in the right place. Even though there is still so much more I want to change about myself, I love the person He has turned me into.

Please do not mistake my gratitude for conceit. I am a very thankful man. God has blessed me with twenty years of marriage to the greatest wife in the world. Emily is my very best friend. I cannot even describe to you how much I love her and how much she loves me. And my kids, dear God I love them too—and now, while they are young adults, I think we are all still best friends. Speaking of friends—God has enriched me there too. The exchange of love between my special buds and me is hard for some people to believe.

God has given me a high degree of compassion for destitute people everywhere; I still cry for them! It eats me alive. Anyone who really knows me will tell you that as of today, there is nothing more important than preserving this heart. Just like the apostle Paul wrote to Timothy in the following verses, I see my conversion as a prime example of God's great patience with even the worse of sinners. I want my testimony to keep affecting people in a positive way for the rest of my life. To do this, I must find a way to carry this heart up with me.

> This is a trustworthy saying, and everyone should accept it: "Christ Jesus came into the world to save sinners"—and I am the worst of them all. But God had mercy on me so that Christ Jesus could use me as a prime example of His great patience with even the worst sinners. Then others will realize that they, too, can believe in Him and receive eternal life (1 Timothy 1:15-16).

HUMILITY IS SIMPLE FOR THE HUMILIATED PERSON

Up to this point, I have had an equal share of high successes and low failures. Since going into full-time ministry ten-plus years ago, I have been hunted, humiliated, and smashed to pieces. Believe me, I have died a thousand deaths to remain in my calling—that's not an exaggeration.

In May 2009, I was two months into the worst betrayal of my life. There has never been a close second. From my perspective, that situation was on a biblical scale much like the stories of Absalom betraying David, or Judas Iscariot betraying Jesus Christ. I was running through a tunnel of horror without a single glimmer of light. There was one particular day during that unbearable time, when I had been hiding under the sheets of my bed, crying for most of the morning. Around noon, I fumbled my way into the bathroom, fell to my knees, then down to my face—and all alone on my bathroom floor, I wailed like a dying animal.

Somehow, I wound up in fetal position; the room was spinning in circles and I felt like I was having a massive heart attack. The pain was so intense; I hurled my puke onto the floor because I could not make it to the toilet. If I could have gotten to the phone, I would have called for an ambulance. During that time, I told my wife one night, "Honey, I'm losing my mind! This pressure is so intense, I'm scared I might just flip out, strip down naked, run out into the road, and dance around like a chicken until the police pick me up." Have you ever known this kind of pain before?

Oh, please don't feel bad for me. I didn't die that day. Just when I thought I would never see the outside of that master bathroom again, God knelt down in my vomit, took me into His arms, and held me close until that storm passed. Just like the poem, "Footprints in the Sand," I look back now, and all I can see is one set of footprints.

I am writing to you from the blessing side of that trial. The pain that came to kill me definitely made me better! Not just once, but every time in my life when it seemed like I was kicked down so low that I would never be able to rise from the ashes of my destruction—by an act of God, I lived to see a better day. Rejection produces humility, and humility arouses grace. "...God opposes the proud but gives grace to the humble" (James 4:6 NIV). God does give grace to the humble—and there is nothing like a vicious betrayal to humble a person!

Humility is simple for a humiliated person. Every time we rise from the ashes with a new heart, we more fully appreciate the value of brokenness. We see that God is drawn to us when we are humbled! Whatever we lost in the trial, we didn't really need anyway. Apostle Paul wrote about the hidden value of painful circumstances. He said:

> That is why we never give up. Though our bodies are dying, our spirits are being renewed every day. For our present troubles are small and won't last very long. Yet they produce for us a glory that vastly outweighs them and will last forever! So we don't look at the troubles we can see now; rather, we fix our gaze on things that cannot be seen. For the things we see now will soon be gone, but the things we cannot see will last forever (2 Corinthians 4:16-18)

BEWARE, THE FEAR OF SUCCESS

As we learn to appreciate deep humiliation, we tend to feel safe in our brokenness. If we are not very careful, we may find ourselves preferring a life of continual suffering. We may shun success through the fear of pride. This is the anti-biblical belief that says: As long as we are always in some kind of unbearable conflict and so messed up that nobody else will have us, then we will always be perfectly united with Christ. Believe it or not, many people fear success more than they fear failure.

Give a person a huge success—challenge the person with power and decorate him or her with honor—then we shall see what that person is really made of! I think everyone knows this and it is a very big reason too many goodhearted people settle with a safe and manageable dream. We are not afraid that God might think too little of us, but that He may be counting on us to step up and save the world! We hope that we are called to be legends, and we spend years dreaming of a legend's future—but when God says "now," we run away and hide.

A few years ago, when I was about halfway through this book, I went through several months of hating myself for the filthy sins of my dark past life. I glanced forward with prophetic eyes and sensed that I was racing forward too fast to stop. It hit me like a ton of bricks when I heard God say to me, "Chuck, this is going to happen! Your future is not a far-fetched dream anymore. That future is now! Over the next few years, I am going point you out—and the whole world is going to feel the warmth of your light."

Instead of being excited with this reality, I fell into a miserable depression. I stopped writing, toned down my preaching gift, and stopped doing anything powerful that might further expand my influence. I told God I had changed my mind because I no longer felt worthy of His high calling. I asked Him to remove His power from my heart and leave me to an average future. I told Him that I would certainly fail, so He better give my dream to someone else.

God was gracious to me during that breakdown. He gave me plenty of time to pray, meditate on His Word, and rest. Then, finally, when I was in a position to hear from Him again, I received a mysterious phone call from an old real estate partner and friend—Robert Michon. He asked me what I was doing those days, and he said he wanted the whole truth; so I held nothing back.

Thank God, Rob listened to me cry for an hour or more and then he spoke. His brilliant words and persuasive attitude rescued my dying dream that day. He said to me, "Chuck, God has given you a gift—a wonderful, beautiful gift! The Big Guy has chosen you to rescue people out of this suffering world. You cannot hide your light under a bushel just because you're scared of all that power. People are right now crying out for your book and everything else you're called to give them. I know you're afraid of what might happen, and you're afraid of failing, but those people deserve your blessing. So get back in the race, run as fast as you can, and don't look back again!"

Rob will never know how much that one phone call changed my life. Still, the fear of success creeps up every now and then. When it does, I think back to that conversation, and I stare fear in the face—and I lay everything on the line again for my dream of a better tomorrow. You can do the same!

> Our deepest fear is not that we are inadequate. Our deepest fear is that we are powerful beyond measure. It is our light, not our darkness that frightens us most. We ask ourselves, "Who am I to be brilliant, gorgeous, talented, and famous?" Actually, who are you not to be? You are a child of God. *Your playing small does not serve the world.* There is nothing enlightened about shrinking so that people won't feel insecure around you. We were born to make manifest the glory of God that is within us. It's not just in some of us; it's in all of us. And when we let our own light shine, we unconsciously give other people permission to do the same. As we are liberated from our own fear, our presence automatically liberates others.[2]

Until you overcome this "deepest fear," you will always unconsciously assassinate your God-sized dream in the hopes of preserving your humility. You will keep shunning high success and wishing instead for a lowly life of poverty and rejection. I call this the trap of playing it safe!

THE TRAP OF PLAYING IT SAFE

All this talk about fear, angry mobs, and "What if I fall?" There is so much to risk—and yet, you and I are stuck with this tameless passion in our sacred hearts! We want to run away to the safety of a no-challenge life and yet we are driven with a dream that matters! We are positive there is a way to change the world and not lose ourselves doing it. There has to be a way of holding on to love. There has to be a way of catapulting today's humble posture forward—even into the most prominent earthly arenas.

Heck yeah, we can succeed without becoming the biggest jerk in town! We can head our billion-dollar companies, sit in high political seats, and even run for president or prime minister—all without having to forfeit our values. I just know there is a way to shrug off the bloodthirsty mobs and every lurking, loathsome temptation. I just know there is a way to manage millions of dollars without making it lord. I honestly believe that we can change the world!

Either we stay right here try our best to play it safe, and we hurry up and burn this *legend* book and turn down our beauty so we never have to worry about standing out. Or, we can take a holy risk—and if we fall, then at least we will never be like the "man who points out how the strong man stumbles, or where the doer of deeds could have done them better."

We will know that:

> *The credit belongs to the man who is actually in the arena* (and we will be that person in the arena), whose face is marred by dust and sweat and blood, who strives valiantly; who errs and comes short again and again; because there is not effort without error and shortcomings; but who does actually strive to do the deed; who knows the great enthusiasm, the great devotion, *who spends himself in a worthy cause,* who at best knows in the end the triumph of high achievement and who at worse, if he fails, at least he fails while daring greatly. So that his place shall never be with those cold timid souls who know neither victory nor defeat.[3]

As for me, I cannot bear the thought of living little when I was born to stand out! Can you? We should not think up a run-of-the-mill dream for ourselves, because we fear potential failure! If you and I were created for something big, then we should never duck away from God when He smiles in our direction. Instead, we should do everything we can to run our best race with honor, endurance, and a very impressive finish!

We must never forget that even at our very best, we are still just a men or women. Yes, we definitely want to feel the pressure of accountability to God for the way we represent Him. We just have to keep on reminding ourselves that we are not God, and we will never be big enough to shoulder His

Kingdom. We are mortal. We are weak. But still, we are called for big things! Knowing this frees us to try and fail, and try and fail again—as people stepping out for God.

A few years ago, my dear friend Jason Upton challenged my ego with the following statement. It was right after the shocking collapse of a major, national Christian leader. As I remember, Jason said something like, "One of the biggest flaws I see with modern Christianity is the way we are all fighting to build our own kingdoms. We worship our fellow mortals too excessively—and when they fall, we are smashed to pieces with them." I agree; somehow, we need to learn how to esteem great people without elevating them above Christ.

I hope and pray that none of my friends will ever stumble and fall on the more difficult path. But if that happens, at least everyone will know they had the guts to blaze a trail. If that day should ever come, and you find yourself too broken for human intervention, you will have trust your loving and merciful Father to bend down, wipe up your tears, and put your broken life back together again. Remember my alternative ending to the *Humpty Dumpty* rhyme in Chapter 6? It's not over even when it's over! God can bring you back from the dead. There is always another new life waiting to be lived, just beyond your biggest losses—new successes beyond your temporary failures. God always loves His children, even when the rest of the world damns one of us to hell with their self-righteous judgments. God is not like arrogant people. He always forgives, always heals, and always restores.

NO SAFETY IN PLAYING IT SAFE

There is really no safety in playing it safe. No one wins a gold medal in life with a perfect, simple routine. Think about the Olympic games—scoring perfectly with simple tricks (playing it safe) never produces a winning score. Take figure skating, for example. Can you image a person winning the gold for executing five or six single Axel jumps? Absolutely not! Championship competitors are judged on execution *and* difficulty. In my humble opinion, playing it safe is the surest way of failing big. Playing it safe is a false hope, the most dangerous path a person can take.

Remember when Jesus told His parable of the three servants? He talked about a man who gathered his three servants together before taking a long journey. This man gave five bags of silver to one of his servants, two bags of silver to another servant, and one bag of silver to the other. When the man returned from his long journey, he gathered his servants to find out what they had done with his money. The servant who started with five bags of silver invested the money well and doubled his master's silver. The servant who started with two bags of silver also invested the money well and doubled his master's silver. The servant who started with one bag of silver submitted to his fears, and instead of taking a risk, he played it safe—and all he had to give his master was the one bag he started with.

> Then the servant with the one bag of silver came and said, "Master, I knew you were a harsh man, harvesting crops you didn't plant and gathering crops you didn't cultivate. I was afraid I would lose your money, so I hid it in the earth. Look, here is your money back." But the master replied, "You wicked and lazy servant! If you knew I harvested crops I didn't plant and gathered crops I didn't cultivate, why didn't you deposit my money in the bank? At least I could have gotten some interest on it." Then he ordered, "Take the money from this servant, and give it to the one with the ten bags of silver. To those who use well what they are given, even more will be given, and they will have an abundance. But from those who do nothing, even what little they have will be taken away. Now throw this useless servant into outer darkness, where there will be weeping and gnashing of teeth" (Matthew 25:24-30).

Does it seem to you like God frowns on the low-risk life?

Let me tell you a story. Every summer, my family vacations on Hatteras Island in North Carolina. In the late '90s, there was an island-wide outrage over the proposed new location for the Hatteras Lighthouse. I have to admit it was amusing for we vacationers to watch some of the locals go wild with their "save the lighthouse" campaigns. These people were serious; that lighthouse is to those Hatteras Island locals what the Statue of Liberty is to every devoted New Yorker. They didn't want to risk the potential collapse of their 1.25 million brick, 4800-ton defining landmark, while the government attempted to move her across 2,900 feet of sand.[4]

It was a highly controversial undertaking and the entire island was ener-gized on one side of this fence or the other. During that time, I was speaking at a local church and I used their lighthouse relocation to explain a power-ful spiritual principle. I remember fearing how they would react, but com-pelled by the Holy Spirit to speak the following message, "Beloved locals of Hatteras Island, the risk of leaving your lighthouse in her current location is far greater than the risk of moving her inland. The risk of doing nothing is far greater than the potential high risk of collapsing on the move. For if you do nothing, your legendary monument is only a few hurricanes away from falling into the ocean." Despite the opposition, she remains upright to this day, in her new inland location.

The spiritual principle: In real life, the risk of playing it safe is always far greater than the potential high risk of collapsing on the move. If you do nothing, you can be certain that natural erosion and future storms will inevi-tably bring you down. There is no doubt about it; *humility is far simpler for the humiliated person.* There is an apparent safety in the whipped down, low-risk life. But, you don't have to avoid success to keep that beautiful heart. You can definitely take it to the top with you! That is what I mean when I say, "Bow lower as you climb higher."

COMING UP

I have to admit, when I wrote this next chapter, I spent hours crying through most of the thoughts. I suffered with painful memories of past evils and visions of a hundred dreadful future scenarios. It wasn't easy for me to be this transparent. I wrote and deleted, and rewrote and deleted again—finally deciding to put myself out there and leave it. I am very serious about preserv-ing my own heart and helping you preserve your heart, too. After this, you will be ready for the wildest, hyperest, and final chapter of our great adventure!

Chapter 16

Take Your Heart Up With You

Above all else, guard your heart, for everything you do flows from it.

—GOD[1]

OH LORD, IT'S HARD TO BE HUMBLE...

I had a friend in high school who was an exceptional singer. Really, he sounded just like country music singer Randy Travis, and the crowds went wild every time he stepped up to a microphone. If we had the *American Idol* competition back then, Brian Supinger would have been the 1989 American Idol! He used to prank me with a Mac Davis song because he knew how much it made me want to bang my head against a wall. Every time Brian got into my truck, he adjusted my rear-view mirror toward his passenger's seat, then he would make the biggest cheese-smile you can imagine, point into the mirror, wink at himself, and sing:

> *Oh Lord it's hard to be humble*
> *When you're perfect in every way*
> *I can't wait to look in the mirror*
> *'Cause I get better lookin' each day*
> *To know me is to love me*
> *I must be a hell of a man*
> *Oh Lord, it's hard to be humble*
> *But I'm doin' the best that I can.*[2]

Have you ever pointed at yourself in the mirror and sang a piece of this song to your cheesy reflection? It can be very hilarious to smile at your reflection and say something that conceited every once in a while—as long as you don't really mean it! However, Mac Davis is correct. It really is hard to be humble when we feel as though we are becoming "perfect in so many ways." This is the deadly sin of self-righteousness, or pride—the enemy of humble!

It is easy to be humble before you have something to brag about. Once you have tasted a little success and you start to feel like you are getting your life together, and once you no longer feel like you need that much help from others and you start to feel invincible, that is when it is hard to be humble!

It took nineteen years before I finally came to my senses and gave my life to Christ. Then it took another ten years before Christian character really started to show up in my life. And here I am today, after such a long and dedicated journey, still with so many underdeveloped places in my character. How can I ever look down on the failures of other people when I still fail so often myself? Even though I've made tremendous progress, I am still so much less than I know I can be. I mustn't forget this and neither must you!

This is the paradox of spiritual maturity and the biggest challenge for a maturing Christian. On the one hand, you want to grow immensely in your faith and bear much fruit. On the other hand, you don't want to become arrogant about it. The threat you're facing in this chapter is the camouflaged deadliness of *fruitful* Christianity, the unconscious development of a "spiritual" ego. I think this must have been what Jesus was cautioning against when He told the parable of the unforgiving debtor.

> *Therefore, the Kingdom of Heaven can be compared to a king who decided to bring his accounts up to date with servants who had borrowed money from him. In the process, one of his debtors was brought in who owed him millions of dollars. He couldn't pay, so his master ordered that he be sold—along with his wife, his children, and everything he owned—to pay the debt. But the man fell down before his master and begged him, "Please, be patient with me, and I will pay it all." Then his master was filled with pity for him, and he released him and forgave his debt. But when the man left the king, he went to a fellow servant who owed him a few thousand dollars. He grabbed him by the throat and demanded instant payment. His fellow servant fell down before him and begged for a little more time. "Be patient with me, and I will pay it," he*

pleaded. But his creditor wouldn't wait. He had the man arrested and put in prison until the debt could be paid in full. When some of the other servants saw this, they were very upset. They went to the king and told him everything that had happened.

Then the king called in the man he had forgiven and said, "You evil servant! I forgave you that tremendous debt because you pleaded with me. Shouldn't you have mercy on your fellow servant, just as I had mercy on you?" Then the angry king sent the man to prison to be tortured until he had paid his entire debt.

That's what My heavenly Father will do to you if you refuse to forgive your brothers and sisters from your heart (Matthew 18:23-35).

This evil servant forgot where he came from. He forgot about the time when he was desperate for a pardon. We cannot let this same thing happen to us. We have to be the fastest people in all the earth at letting others off the hook for their few thousand-dollar sins against us—considering how fast God lets us off the hook, for our multimillion-dollar sins against Him. We have to maintain a humble attitude and posture, especially as we feel like we are becoming good people, because we are simply the product of God's love and grace. He is the real reason behind every good deed. If God ever lets go of us, we will fall straight back down to rock bottom and stay there for the rest of our lives.

Do Not Become an Elitist

It is not wise (or Christ-like) to shun the people with whom we no longer have anything in common. Whenever our Christian maturity becomes a hindrance to the Great Commission of Jesus, then our apparent progress is really no progress at all. We should care *more* about broken people as we climb, not less. Real Christian maturity is about loving, serving, and sacrificing, not about strutting through our world with a golden crown.

As I look into the future, I'm afraid that we may gradually forget what hopelessness feels like. I am scared we may become impatient with slow movers and demand them to grow a hundred times faster than we were permitted to grow. God was very patient with us! And now that we are becoming somewhat righteous, will we turn our noses up at the more sinful person who is just beginning the journey? Isaiah prophesied against the people who say, *"Stand by thyself, come not near to me; for I am holier than thou."* Isaiah continued, *"These are a smoke in my nose, a fire that burneth all the day"* (Isa. 65:5 KJV). Please God, don't let this happen to us.

I don't want to let my heart grow cold, not even a little bit. I don't want to become so comfortable with all of my maturing friends that I only desire their company. I can't imagine spending my whole future in a moderately perfected elitist alliance. If I ever found out that a lowly person was shamed in my "exalted" presence—it would crush me to the floor. God forbid that I should ever despise the strugglers. I never want to lose my passion for reaching them, never want to forget my tears when praying for them, never want to cease to honor them with sincere humble service.

I often wonder, *Wouldn't it be a shame if the compassionate person who knelt down in my gutter had become an elitist just a few months before the two of us intersected?* Where would you and I be today if someone hadn't taken their *heart* up with them? We should thank God often for the humble people in our past who kept the gap closed in humility, between what they had become and what we were not yet.

Let's never consider ourselves too clean for a dirty assignment. Let's never become so comfortable in our five-star hotels that we are no longer willing to bed down in the slums. Let's not become so addicted to the chanting crowds that we are no longer thrilled to help one person. Let's not choose the cleanest, easiest people and missions just because we have the power to do so—and leave the filthiest people for "Mother Teresa." Every person matters to God, and every person should matter to us—always!

BE HUMBLE AND COURAGEOUS

As I talk so much about humility and heart, someone might think I'm trying to raise a generation of cowards. Humility is not passivity. On the contrary, humility is a rare and powerful force. At first, the truly humble person assumes himself to be weak, common, and barely noticeable as he decorates others with his selfless service and honor. Then one day he realizes, "Wait a minute, my humility has earned me the high respect of others. My influence is huge because my love is deep. Now, if I had just had some courage, I could really change the world."

At first, most humble people refuse to leverage their attained influence in the fear of becoming a perceived aggressor. Yet, a humble coward is no better to the world than a courageous dictator. *Legends* learn how to combine the best of both extremes and live in the power of courageous humility.

Once we have developed a truly humble posture, we can say just about anything to just about anyone and they will take radical actions based on our suggestions—even when those suggestions rub them the wrong way. If we use this power for good, we will create positive change for many people.

In March 2010, a very kind lady complimented me on Facebook for being uncommonly gentle with an aggressive critic. She was right; I had perfectly handled a potentially hostile situation, and I was very proud of myself. Even before she posted the compliment, I felt like I was graduating into another level of communication. Really, I haven't always been known for communicating my truths in courageous humility. My past is filled with a long strand of botched confrontations. I'll bet yours is too.

I used say, "I would rather not talk about this disagreement because I'm just not a confrontational kind of person." I was the person who ran away from conflict as long as I could, as often as I could, until I was chased into a corner. And once I wasn't able to sidestep the situation a second longer, I would close my eyes and run out swinging! Some of my oldest close friends still remember those days. I thank God things have changed. I am still no expert, but I am not the serious pushover that I once was.

To act with courageous humility, we must develop a deep inner security. It is only when we really know who we are and how much God loves us, and we don't feel the need to protect ourselves from rejection or abuse that we are freed to present pure truth—without manipulating a desired response. As I have matured in my own character, this is one of the areas in which I have invested quite a bit of my time. I want to be so entirely secure in my relationship with God that I can bow low before loftiest people and lay myself out there in the perfect love of God. I don't want to just be the kind man weeping on the sidewalk with "kick me" signs all over my back. I want to be respected and heard, because I love! I want to model a difference, preach that difference with high volume, and see it manifested everywhere I go.

COURAGEOUS HUMILITY VERSUS TRASHY ARROGANCE

As some people become powerful, they often turn into control freaks. The challenge is to be courageous without becoming a butt face. It seems that as people climb, they become less and less fearful of others. They usually stop obsessing over who likes them and who doesn't because, after all, they made it to the top despite the resistance!

If we are not careful, we might fall into the trap of feeling like we have so much power that we no longer need to humor our irritating antagonists. We may even be tempted to "accidentally" kick a few of them in the face during our victory dance! Just kidding; but remember, the kind of courage I am calling for comes from humility, not pride. There is a very big difference between *trashy arrogance* and *courageous humility*.

Apostle Paul could see that Timothy was climbing much faster than all the other average younger Christians. Knowing that Timothy would outlive him by many years, Paul admonished him concerning matters of the heart. In the following verses, Paul explains to Timothy, the fine line between courageous humility and trashy arrogance. It is the perfect amen to this segment.

> *A servant of the Lord must not quarrel but must be kind to everyone, be able to teach, and be patient with difficult people. Gently instruct those who oppose the truth. Perhaps God will change those people's hearts, and they will learn the truth. Then they will come to their senses and escape from the devil's trap. For they have been held captive by him to do whatever he wants* (2 Timothy 2:24-26).

THE KISSES OF BETRAYAL

In theory, taking your heart up with you may seem like an easy thing to do. You may think to yourself, *OK, I get where Chuck is coming from. All I really need to do is keep on caring about people as I become powerful. How hard can this be if I really put my mind to it?* In a perfect world, you are right; it would be an easy undertaking. Yet, in the real world, there are a million hardening agents all fighting for the death of your good heart.

Let's take "betrayal" for example. In my opinion, there are few things more dangerous to your heart than betrayal. I can think of no better example of betrayal than the one found in the story of Judas Iscariot betraying his dearest friend Jesus—the most caring Person of all time.

> *While He [Jesus] was still speaking a crowd came up [the angry mob], and the man who was called Judas, one of the Twelve [one of Jesus' best friends], was leading them. He approached Jesus to kiss Him, but Jesus asked him, "Judas, are you betraying the Son of Man with a kiss?"* (Luke 22:47-48 NIV)

Through Judas, evil mobsters captured, tortured, and slaughtered an innocent Man. Have you ever been kissed like that?

Humans can be cruel and heartless. Even the very best of us—every person is capable of anything under the right amount of pressure or with enough temptation. You may have been cruel and heartless a whole lot more than you've convinced yourself. Please admit it. You have gossiped about a dear friend or two. You have betrayed someone's confidence. You have lied. No one stands perfect before God—not even close to perfect. The people who feel most perfect are oftentimes the most imperfect of all.

King Solomon said:

> *There is not a righteous man on earth who does what is right and never sins. Do not pay attention to every word people say, or you may hear your servant cursing you—**for you know in your heart that many times you yourself have cursed others*** (Ecclesiastes 7:20-22 NIV).

When I first understood the meaning of those verses many years ago, I stopped listening to the whisperers. I simply accepted the fact that even my closest friends are going to curse me every once in a while. I hate this, just like I am sure that everyone does. But it's a fact. Thank God I seem to be surrounded with loyal friends today. Perhaps one of them is puckering up in secret places for my next shocking betrayal. If I live long enough, it is certain to happen a few more times. Yet, I am not going to live in a state of constant paranoia over the hidden identity of my next Judas Iscariot. Neither should you.

Betrayal is a poison in the heart of its victim. If we are not very careful, the more we are neglected, abandoned, abused, and betrayed, the less we will trust. Little by little, our love will become hate, our faith will become fear, our optimism will turn into cynicism—and our trusting, caring, loving heart will be hardened.

SPIDERMAN 3: VENOM SYMBIOTE

In the movie, *Spiderman 3*, an extraterrestrial organism descends into the Earth and attaches itself to Peter Parker (Spiderman), which turns him into a psychotic villain. They refer to this symbiotic organism as the *Venom Symbiote*—an evil sentient alien with a black, gooey, almost liquid-like form. Venom requires a host, usually human, to bond around for its survival. In return, Venom enhances the powers of its host.

While Venom was attached to Peter Parker, it heightened Peter's hatred for his uncle's killer. His family and friends grieved to witness the evil in Peter's heart, but they couldn't do anything to help him. In a matter of days, Peter's trashy attitude destroyed his relationship with everyone dear to him, especially with his girlfriend, Mary Jane. Peter lost everything right down to his reason for being and his flawless Spiderman reputation!

The most revelatory scene in the whole movie for me was when Spiderman Tarzaned his way to the tower of a Catholic church. This was a do or die moment for Peter Parker. He was smothering to death inside of his jet-black Spiderman-Venom suit. Not too much longer, and he would be trapped in the darkness forever—or so it seemed to me.

Unlike each of Spiderman's previous villain battles, the enemy of this episode was the man in the mirror. Peter flayed and tussled, he embedded his fingers into the torturing symbiote and he flexed and pulled, revealing his bare skin at various places.

Venom waged a furious war! It seemed undefeatable—defiant about retaining its stronghold in Peter Parker. This is exactly how betrayal darkens the hearts and minds of every careless host. Once it roots in, it is very difficult to get rid of.

The church bell gonged as Peter's loud groans echoed down into the empty stone church below. While the struggle ensued, Eddie Brock (who was offended with Peter Parker over an unresolved work-related situation) happened into this same Catholic church. Brock walked down the aisle, sat down in front of the crucifix, and prayed, *"It's Brock, Sir. Edward Brock, Junior. I come before You today, humbled and humiliated, to ask You for one thing. I want You to kill Peter Parker."* Can you feel the hate?

Suddenly, the scene shifts back to the tower, where Peter is shrieking and throwing himself all over the place, still struggling to overthrow the symbiote. Brock beholds the struggle, and Venom beholds Brock—and at last, Venom leaves Peter Parker for its new host! Venom then feeds and thrives on Brock's hatred for Parker, and transmogrifies him into Spiderman's next villain enemy!

THE SYMBIOTE-FREE LIFE

In the real world, you and I have to be very serious about the potential deadliness of each betrayal. Just as Venom Symbiote searched for its human host, hate is always searching for its next host. Once it spreads over us, it dims our eyes and suffocates our passion—until the day we struggle it down and rip it from our lives. If you ever get the chance to see the *Spiderman 3* Parker/Venom/Brock struggle scene with this paradigm, it will blow your mind![3]

As wrong as this sounds, some people will hate you just because you are a good person. They will hate your smile, your dreams, your happy family, and your fruitful deeds. You must be able to withstand their hate without hating back. Never fall into the trap of thinking you can sector off one small block of your heart and secretly despise one person without infecting the rest of your relationships. Eventually, if even one microscopic hate cell lives in you for very long, it will metastasize throughout your entire soul, just like the cancer that it is.

For me, getting to the top as a fouled-up person is even worse than not getting there at all. To host the symbiote of hate, until there is nothing left of the good person I once was—it is my biggest nightmare, and it should be yours, too! We must flee to the high tower every time our affectionate heart is tested with the agony of rejection, abuse, and neglect—especially when we are betrayed with a kiss. Just as soon as we realize that something evil is shrouding our love and compassion, we should eradicate it! Because we never know how long it will be until we are lost forever.

In May 2009, I told my wife, "I am so scared of people right now. I feel like a kid who is afraid of the dark. It seems like the shadows are stalking me. I am paralyzed with the fear of who is going to stab me next! And you know what scares me even more than that? I am terrified to think about how this betrayal might be permanently damaging my heart. I don't want to hate people. I don't want to wish for the early death of my enemies. This is not a little thing. I really feel like I am fighting for my life right now. Please help."

Emily gave me a long, sincere hug and told me it was going to be all right. She prayed for me. Then I continued, "Emily, if I live another ten years on the other side of this betrayal, I will become one of two people. Ten years from today, I might be the person with "no trespassing" signs all over his yard, and when a zealous Christian couple knocks on our front door, I will greet them with my shot gun and tell them I no longer believe in organized religion! If God does not help me now, I will become that person. Or, somehow, God will answer my prayers and restore my love, and I will come out of this decade knowing what it means to love on a Jesus level. Maybe, this pain will show me how much more desperately this human race needs Jesus. Maybe I will understand that church leaders are imperfect people just like everyone else in the world and they need Jesus, too. If I make it out of this alive, maybe I will find a way to love people more than I did before it happened. I sure hope so."

THE MIRACLE OF FORGIVENESS

Prayer: Dear God, we really want Your help! Please help us to always forgive the people who hurt us, no matter how deeply they hurt us— not just on the surface, but all the way to the center of our hearts. No matter how much they take from us, and how often they slander our good name, please help us to love them—even while they are still beating us! We don't want to keep a record of wrongs anymore. Heal us from the humiliation of having our faces ground into the dirt by enemies, friends, and even our closest friends. Help us to be kind toward our betrayers just like Jesus was kind to His. Even though we hurt and we are very tempted to destroy the people who are trying to destroy us, we do not want to give in to such temptations. Please, Good Father, produce within us the miracle of forgiveness.

We cannot truly forgive a betrayer apart from God's amazing grace. People don't usually feel like forgiving when they first realize they need to forgive. The Bible says, *"Do not judge others, and you will not be judged. Do not condemn others, or it will all come back against you. Forgive others, and you will be forgiven"* (Luke 6:37).

In faith, we have to act on the command to forgive long before we actually receive the miracle of forgiveness. Eventually, if we pray for our enemies long enough and if we stand in the grace of forgiveness long enough—our feelings will unite with our spiritual position. This is how grace works!

Do you really want the miracle of forgiveness? Yes? Then, you will need to do several things between the time you first pray for it and the time it is fully manifested in your heart. First, you have to police your thoughts and words. Whenever you feel like you are being attacked for unjustified reasons and nothing prevents your angry mobs, try not to say much. Remember this formula: *More pressure—less mouth!* Trust me, I know from experience: when the attacks are on, surging at you like one murderous tsunami after another, it is very hard not to take matters into your own hands. Oftentimes your enemy will taunt you to the verge of insanity. But if you want to see a miracle, you have to carefully govern your thoughts, words, and actions—and pray for endurance. Sometimes the miracle of forgiveness, and genuine reconciliation, takes so much longer than we want it to take.

While you are waiting for God to "bring your betrayers to repentance," also search your own heart. Accept full responsibility for your own wrong actions. Become better, not bitter—every time! Remember, even when you are slapped around without mercy, there is a little truth in every complaint. Don't ever feel like you're too big for correction. Always appreciate the value of wise counsel—and the potential value of harsh criticism. I know it is not supposed to work this way, but I have learned just as much from my betrayers as I have from my loving mentors, peers, and apprentices!

A kind note to my remaining enemies: Maybe you think I am the real betrayer of our conflict and just as I am trying to forgive you—you are trying to forgive me. Satan has a way of twisting, manipulating, and exaggerating a conflict until the best of friends are the worst of enemies. I sincerely apologize for everything I have done in the past, intentionally and unintentionally, to break your heart. I hope that someday you will know how much I tried to love you the very best I knew how to love at the time. While we walked together, I woke up every day with a desire for blessing you to the fullest of my ability. If we had not cared about each other so much, it would not have hurt us so badly. King David knew this kind of pain. He wrote about it more than once:

> It is not an enemy who taunts me—I could bear that. It is not my foes who so arrogantly insult me—I could have hidden from them. Instead, it is you—my equal, my companion and close friend. What good fellowship we once enjoyed as we walked together to the house of God (Psalm 55:12-14).

> Even my best friend, the one I trusted completely, the one who shared my food, has turned against me (Psalm 41:9).

The closer a person is to us, the more of our hearts they occupy. The more we love them, the more it hurts when they turn on us. Casual acquaintances only attack us on the surface because they only have limited access. When an outsider attacks us, we usually shrug it off—with the help of our close friends. But when a close friend violates us, it takes an act of God. Most of my own past conflicts have already been brought to a happy ending. I hope yours have too! Thank God, for the conflicts that remain, we can always hope in the miracle of forgiveness.

ONE MAN WHO TOOK HIS HEART UP WITH HIM

Now let me illustrate the miracle of forgiveness with one man who took his heart up with him. In the Book of Genesis, Joseph dreamed he was going to save the world. In his dream, everyone was bowing to Joseph—even his parents and brothers. As you can imagine, things did not turn out very well when Joseph described his dream to the family. Joseph's older brothers were especially furious with him. Furious is an understatement—murderous is more like it! They all felt like the dream was a reflection of Joseph's arrogant fantasies.

You see, most people are not going to celebrate with you as long as they see themselves as lowly servants in your God-sized dream. Everybody wants to be king of the mountain, until they realize that the biggest leader is also the biggest servant and the biggest target. If everyone really trusted God with their own futures, there would be far less striving and far less persecution for the big dreamers. People would be happy about the dreams of others. But sadly, that's not always the case.

Whether this is your time for a big promotion or not, you should be faithful with your current assignment. The biggest betrayals come from insecure and jealous people struggling to become the king of another person's mountain. Just as soon as some people fail to see themselves ruling over your dream, they will do everything in their power to take you down, even to the point of wishing you dead or leaving you for dead, if necessary.

This is exactly what happened to Joseph. His jealous brothers sold him to a slave trader and then told their father he had been killed. Every time I read this story, I just can't believe it actually happened! These young men betrayed their own flesh and blood brother with no remorse, just like psychopaths. They said, *"Come on, let's kill him and throw him into one of these cisterns. We can tell our father, 'A wild animal has eaten him.' Then we'll see what becomes of his dreams!"* (Gen. 37:20).

> *Then they grabbed him and threw him into the cistern. Now the cistern was empty; there was no water in it. Then, just as they were sitting down to eat, they looked up and saw a caravan of camels in the distance coming toward them. It was a group of Ishmaelite traders taking a load of gum, balm, and aromatic resin from Gilead down to Egypt. Judah said to his brothers, "What will we gain by killing our brother? His blood would just give us a guilty conscience. Instead of hurting him, let's sell him to those Ishmaelite traders. After all, he is our brother—our own flesh and blood!" And his brothers agreed* (Genesis 37:24-27).

Joseph spent the next 13 years of his life suffering in slavery, and then in jail—left without a single friend in the entire world—to fight his way through one of the most classic stories of betrayal ever whispered. While Joseph was in jail, he interpreted prophetic dreams for two servants to the king of Egypt. Both dreams turned out just as Joseph predicted. One man was executed three days later, and the other, the king's cupbearer, was restored to his position three days later, just like Joseph called it!

A few years later, while Joseph was still in jail, the king of Egypt had a troubling dream. After no wise person in the entire kingdom could interpret his dream, the cupbearer remembered Joseph and recommended him to the king. Joseph was discharged from jail, he correctly interpreted the king's dream, and he was promoted as prime minister of Egypt, the most powerful nation in the world at that time.

Seven years later, just like Joseph prophesied it to the king, a famine swept all over the face of the earth. Because of Joseph's prophetic forecasting and his recommended survival strategy, all was well for Egypt. With the king's approval, Joseph had headed a seven-year emergency food project in Egypt and *"piled up huge amounts of grain like sand on the seashore. Finally, he stopped keeping records because there was too much to measure"* (Gen. 41:49). As you can imagine, it did not take long before every nation was forced to come purchase grain from Egypt's storehouse.

Among those affected by the famine were Joseph's biological relatives. Remember those guys? They are the ones who said, *"Come on, let's kill him [our brother] and throw him into one of these cisterns. We can tell our father, 'A wild animal has eaten him.' Then we'll see what becomes of his dreams!"* (Gen. 37:20).

Can you imagine this happening to you? Here you are still becoming acclimated to palace life, shocked that you are still alive after spending 13 years in slavery and prison—all because of the insecurity-driven hate crime of your closest allies. Can you fathom betrayal on a grand scale like this? How much pain would you have endured for all of those humiliating, lonely years?

You have to wonder how many times Joseph must have told himself, *One of these days, I will get my chance! Those guys are going to pay big for the pain they have caused me! They had no right to attack me like that. I was such a good brother to them. I wasn't perfect, but I never did anything to merit that degree of hatred. Nobody will ever know how much pain they have caused me. And when my time comes, I am going to laugh my head off watching them suffer for trying to kill me. One of these days they are going to need me—and when that day comes, I will spit in their faces. Or even better—maybe God has already paid them back by now! Maybe they are childless, crippled, and divorced, or maybe they are even dead—and look at me, sitting in the palace as prime minister. Ha-ha brothers, let's see what's become of my dreams now!*

In the process of time, God's highest blessing manifested in Joseph's life while simultaneously, judgment caught up to his betrayers. We should never assess a high-level betrayal by the progression of one or two years, because most of the time big purposes take ten or more years to reveal where God stood all along. We cannot always see God working when we are engulfed with the sadness of momentary rejection. Be patient! Trust God and watch how your life turns out. God has a way of righting every wrong and working everything out for everybody. It is amazing to me how much good God brings, especially out of the most awful situations.

Angry mobs will never prevent God's eternal plan. Remember, what is happening *in* you—in your heart and character—is always far more important than anything that is happening *to* you. With your natural eyes, things might be horrible for you while the bully prospers without a care in the world. But you must know this: nothing in this entire universe can permanently curse what God has decided to bless! The time will certainly come when all will know every hidden motive. Justice delayed is not justice denied. In the end, the offender will have the penalty and the good guy the honor.

It did not take long (two years) before Joseph's brothers ran out of food. After they had exhausted every other option, Jacob sent his humbled, starving sons to Egypt's prime minister for help. My, how things can change! With the mere nod of his head, Joseph now had enough authority to execute his betrayers at will.

Here they were—Reuben, Simeon, Levi, Judah, Issachar, Zebulun, Dan, Naphtali, Gad, and Asher—all bowing low before Joseph's royal authority with their faces to the ground, begging for Egypt's second most powerful man to spare their lives and give them food—not realizing that this acclaimed dignitary was the very same younger brother they sold into slavery many years ago.

Do you know what Joseph did? At first, he seemed to toy with his brothers for a few days, accusing them of being spies and thieves. But Joseph's wise actions were not a merciless display of reckoning. What he did was entirely insightful. He tested their hearts to find out if they had truly repented for what they had done to him years ago.

The revealing moment came when Joseph accused, and then sentenced, Benjamin (the youngest brother he had not met until then) to remain in Egypt as his slave. Just as Joseph had hoped, Judah stepped forward, risking his life to plead for the release of his younger brother. Here is a summary of that conversation.

> Then Judah stepped forward and said, "Please, my lord, let your servant say just one word to you. Please, do not be angry with me, even though you are as powerful as Pharaoh himself. And now, my lord, I cannot go back to my father without the boy. Our father's life is bound up in the boy's life. If he sees that the boy is not with us, our father will die. We, your servants, will indeed be responsible for sending that grieving, white-haired man to his grave. My lord, I guaranteed to my father that I would take care of the boy. I told him, 'If I don't bring him back to you, I will bear the blame forever.' So please, my lord, let me stay here as a slave instead of the boy, and let the boy return with his brothers. For how can I return to my father if the boy is not with me? I couldn't bear to see the anguish this would cause my father!" (Genesis 44:18,30-34 NLT)

It had to be in that moment when everything suddenly made sense to Joseph—his childhood dream, the betrayal, the slavery, and the unjust imprisonment; the interpretation of the cupbearer's dream and his predicted reinstatement; the king's dream and Joseph's opportunity for interpreting that dream; Joseph's far-fetched exaltation from jail to second in charge of the mightiest kingdom in the world; the terrible famine, his brother's destitution and their necessitated journey to Egypt—and his freakish opportunity to save his family and preserve the new nation God was establishing through them. If everything had not happened just the way it did, there might not be a nation of Israel today.

This story of Joseph and his brothers has to be one of the most emotional narratives in the entire Bible! Thank God, Joseph did not become bitter along the way. What happens next is too beautiful for words! When Joseph could not handle his feelings a second longer, he cried out to his attendants to leave. He wanted to be alone with his brothers when he revealed to them his true identity. After his attendants left the room, Joseph fell to pieces and started weeping so loudly that his sobs could be heard throughout the entire palace.

*"I am Joseph!" he said to his brothers. "Is my father still alive?"
But his brothers were speechless! They were stunned to realize that
Joseph was standing there in front of them. "Please, come closer,"
he said to them. So they came closer. And he said again, "I am
Joseph, your brother, whom you sold into slavery in Egypt. But
don't be upset, and don't be angry with yourselves for selling me to
this place. It was God who sent me here ahead of you to preserve
your lives. This famine that has ravaged the land for two years
will last five more years, and there will be neither plowing nor
harvesting. God has sent me ahead of you to keep you and your
families alive and to preserve many survivors. So it was God who
sent me here, not you! And He is the One who made me an adviser
to Pharaoh—the manager of his entire palace and the governor
of all Egypt. Now hurry back to my father and tell him, 'This is
what your son Joseph says: God has made me master over all the
land of Egypt. So come down to me immediately! You can live in
the region of Goshen, where you can be near me with all your children and grandchildren, your flocks and herds, and everything you
own. I will take care of you there, for there are still five years of
famine ahead of us. Otherwise you, your household, and all your
animals will starve.'"*

*Then Joseph added, "Look! You can see for yourselves, and so can
my brother Benjamin, that I really am Joseph! Go tell my father
of my honored position here in Egypt. Describe for him everything
you have seen, and then bring my father here quickly." Weeping
with joy, he embraced Benjamin, and Benjamin did the same.
Then Joseph kissed each of his brothers and wept over them, and
after that they began talking freely with him* (Genesis 45:3-15).

I cannot imagine how terrified these brothers must have felt when Joseph
started wailing. When he said, "I am Joseph!" Shivers must have gone all over
their bodies! They had to feel absolutely hopeless, like their lives were certainly over. Any normal person would have taken his revenge—every bit of
it and so much more. Yet, instead of paying them back for his many years
of abandonment, affliction, and disgrace—Joseph broke down and wept like

266 / MAKE ME A LEGEND

the tender person he still was. He folded up his royal power and presented it as a gift of full pardon to his betrayers. This is the miracle of forgiveness! Thank God for everyone, Joseph had taken his humble heart up with him!

Who can forgive like this without help from God? Who can say, "Don't be upset, and don't be angry with yourselves for selling me to this place. It was God who sent me here ahead of you to preserve your lives!" Can you believe Joseph's love for his betrayers? He went way beyond mere forgiveness when he bent down, embraced his brothers, and wept with them! Then, he counseled them through the guilt of betraying him. Here is what I believe Joseph was really saying to his remorseful brothers:

> "Dear brothers, please don't carry the guilt of what you did to me! Please, don't even feel bad about the way I have suffered. Instead, let's thank God together, because He always works everything out for the good of His children. He knew about this famine 22 years ago (Joseph's 13 years of captivity plus 7 years of plenty and the first 2 years of famine) and He sent me on a journey to this palace through your betrayal so that I could save your lives. Everything that was meant for my harm has now been turned around—and look at all of us together celebrating this blessing today. You have no idea how much God has worked in my life through all of this pain—how the rejection kept driving me closer and closer to Him and how He kept me alive with His grace. Please, do not feel bad for another second about what you did to me. You guys have suffered with this guilt long enough! I can see that you have truly repented. God has forgiven you, and I have forgiven you—so please, forgive yourselves!"

THE HIGHEST LEVEL OF LOVE

As twisted as this might sound—I am starting to feel like excessive betrayal is a secret stairway to the highest level of love. I am not sure if we can ever fully understand God's love for us until we have had the opportunity to forgive somebody on that level. Not until we have been betrayed so violently that everything inside of us screams for the death of our betrayer—and then out of nowhere, the love of God and the miracle of forgiveness graces our souls. There we will behold a portrait of God known only to a very small band of betrayal survivors.

I suppose you may have started out seeing yourself as the Joseph figure in this story. If this is true, then you might be psyched up right now—thinking about how God is going to humble your betrayers, and slap them down at your exalted feet—humiliated, apologetic, and desperate for your help. Am I right? Or maybe you are just excited about how fast the tide is getting ready to shift in your favor. How do I know this? Because that's what I thought. But like a cruel prank, suddenly it hit me, *Wait a minute; I've been more like Joseph's brothers than I have been like Joseph! I have played the betrayer far more than I've ever played the forgiver.* And the paradigm shifts! And the revelation you were supposed to be getting suddenly comes to light.

We try to imagine that if we had been one of the Lord's twelve disciples, we would have been like John—the one who stood with Jesus right up to his last breath. But the truth is that we have often played the roles of Judas Iscariot (the betrayer) and Simon Peter (the denier). Our sins did to Jesus exactly what Reuben, Simeon, Levi, Judah, Issachar, Zebulun, Dan, Naphtali, Gad, and Asher did to Joseph.

Do you remember when Mel Gibson released his movie, *The Passion of Christ?* Initially, there was an outcry from the Jewish community because it seemed as if Gibson was charging them with the crucifixion of Christ. Did you ever hear Mel Gibson's response to those accusations? As I remember, he said, "No, it was not the Jewish people who crucified Christ. It was the sinful human nature. It was my [Mel Gibson's] sins that hung Jesus on the cross—it was the sins of us all!"

Sure, you and I may pride ourselves at being good Christian people—but at best, we have been sinful at times. We have denied and betrayed our Lord more times than we can remember. Jesus died for us while we were sinners! We rejected Him, we sentenced Him, and we crucified Him. And still, He loves us! This is exactly what the prophet Isaiah meant when he said:

> He [Jesus] was despised and rejected—a Man of sorrows, acquainted with deepest grief. We turned our backs on Him and looked the other way. He was despised, and we did not care! Yet it was our weaknesses He carried; it was our sorrows that weighed Him down. And we thought His troubles were a punishment from

God, a punishment for His own sins! But He was pierced for our rebellion, crushed for our sins. He was beaten so we could be whole. He was whipped so we could be healed. All of us, like sheep, have strayed away. We have left God's paths to follow our own. Yet the Lord laid on Him the sins of us all (Isaiah 53:3-6).

Can you see the obvious parallel between Joseph and Jesus? Just like Joseph, when Jesus could have wiped us from the face of the earth, He bowed down before us with all of His exalted power—showing us mercy instead of the judgment we deserved! And that, to me, is too wonderful for words!

Would you like to love like Jesus loves? Yes? Then there is a path. It is not a pretty path. You will have to drink down the most nauseating chalice of betrayal you have ever imagined, and feel a hatred you've never known running through your poisoned veins—until your desperate, sickly heart gasps out to God for the miracle of God's forgiveness! You will have to carry your cross, just like Christ carried His. You may even have to hang there naked in front of the whole world in public humiliation, all the way to the point of breathing your last breath—the last breath of that lesser person you used to be.

If you really want this kind of love, then you will have to feel what it is like for your betrayers to rip into the meat of your back with sharp objects, bathe themselves gleefully in your blood, and shove you down into a grave like a man or woman forsaken of God. There you will need to feel what it's like to be lifted from the farthest brink of annihilation—as God finally delivers His justice. You will have to watch your enemies closely as they are brought to the point of genuine, heartfelt repentance—and experience what it's like to see your betrayers broken at your feet, and you in all of that power!

Only then can you possibly comprehend the highest level of love, and the sweetness of what it means to bow low with all of your exalted power—to forgive, and even elevate your betrayers. Every person should be so fortunate to know the feeling of giving and receiving unmerited forgiveness with other people. Then, we will comprehend the highest level of love and God's great salvation. It is a love that bows on the lowest level and saves to the utmost. The Apostle Paul explained it best in the following hallmark verses:

You should think in the same way Christ Jesus does. In His very nature He was God. But He did not think that being equal with God was something He should hold on to. Instead, He made Himself nothing. He took on the very nature of a servant. He was made in human form. He appeared as a man. He came down to the lowest level. He obeyed God completely, even though it led to His death. In fact, He died on a cross. So God lifted him up to the highest place. He gave Him the name that is above every name. When the name of Jesus is spoken, everyone's knee will bow to worship Him. Every knee in heaven and on earth and under the earth will bow to worship Him. Everyone's mouth will say that Jesus Christ is Lord. And God the Father will receive the glory (Philippians 2:5-11 NIRV).

I never want to hate my abusers just because I have so much power; I no longer have to pass their way. As I climb higher, I want to forgive people faster and more often than before. Anyone can forgive after enough time passes. In Joseph's situation, 22 years and a very nice exaltation can certainly downplay the sting of a past betrayal. I wonder how this story would have ended if Joseph's brothers had visited him in jail? Hopefully, Joseph would have been just as humble, no matter how things had turned out for him.

Taking your heart up with you is about sacrificing your life for the cruel people who spit in your face, pluck out your beard, and shred the skin off your back. It's about loving your betrayers at the very core of your being, even before they stop abusing you. The journey is difficult, but so worth it! Someday, when you reach the pinnacle, and you are bowing the lowest you've ever bowed—that will be the highest level of success!

In that moment you will understand God the most—just before you go to see Him! I am not there yet, but this is where I want end up. See you at the top!

Coming Up

Next is the final quest to your new legendary life! One of my dear friends was so moved by what you are about to read that he suggested this last chapter be moved to the front of the book. I considered that, until I realized that this is my last impression—the closing message I want you to be left with. Over the past 16 chapters, you have learned about the skills, the attitudes, and the disciplines of a *legend*. You might not know it yet, but you have changed! You are not the same person you were at the beginning of this quest. The only thing you need now is a trigger chapter—a message that will launch you into the *legend* realm. Here it is!

Chapter 17

Untame Yourself

Even now I can feel it, buried somewhere deep inside, watching me, waiting—but you know what scares me the most? When I can't fight it anymore, when it takes over, when I totally lose control…I like it!

—BRUCE BANNER, The Hulk, 2003[1]

STAND BACK AND SHUT UP

We are powerful, yes. We have something to say, yes we do. Our lives should be modeled and our words should be followed. We are not perfect, but there is something about us that makes us special. Jesus said that we are the light of the world! He called us the salt of this earth and a city on a hill that should not be hidden.

Every once in a while, we are provoked just about to the point of radical action, but we never actually make a stand. It has been too long since Christians have stood up, made a real stand, and had a real voice in our society. We've been talked down, mocked down, and beaten down. We hide in our safe havens, sweltering in silent frustration, resisting the evilness of our day, but only through non-participation. Although the numbers are on our side, we are slaves to a wicked minority simply because we fear them. The whole universe watches and wonders how much longer we will stand back and shut up.

Long after the Civil War, equal rights were still nothing more than a nice fantasy for most African Americans. All the way into the 1950s, segregation was still rampant across the United States. Who could have predicted the coming of one tiny spark, Rosa Parks, and how she would set the whole forest ablaze.

On December 1, 1955, Rosa refused to tolerate the segregation that demanded she yield her bus seat to a white man. News of Rosa's legendary stand inspired a sudden and swift upheaval that prepared the way for Dr. Martin Luther King, Jr. and the beginning of the end of segregation. Rosa Parks is remembered for saying, "People always say that I didn't give up my seat because I was tired, but that isn't true. I was not tired physically, or no more tired than I usually was at the end of a working day. I was not old, although some people have an image of me as being old then. I was forty-two. No, the only tired I was, was tired of giving in!"[2]

Just like Rosa Parks, it seems that Christians—you and I—have taken one too many walks to the back of the bus. Something has to change! In silent frustration, our fears are starting to shrivel before the magnitude of our God-sized dreams. The fire *inside* us is just about greater than the fire that rages *against* us. We are sick and we are tired of being dominated by this godless culture. We are tired of giving in! No sir, we will not stand back and shut up! Not today, or any other day. With one small spark we will set the forest ablaze—for our cause!

SKILLET—MONSTER

Just recently, I watched a fanatical music video[3] from the hard-rock Christian band, Skillet. By the time I was 30 seconds into this video, my eyes were tearing up so much that I could no longer see the screen just one foot in front of my face. Since I was listening to it for the very first time, I did not know what songwriter John Cooper could have been trying to say with his aggressive lyrics.

I formed my own opinion first, then I read the following explanation from its author: "Sometimes when you look deep into yourself, you can feel weighed down by sin and the 'Monster' that lives inside us all. But the more you realize your need for Christ, the less you focus on that, and on Him instead."[4]

After reading this and after searching the Internet for everybody else's explanation, I realized that to me, this song spoke something very different. I was shocked that nobody else had seen "Monster" through the lens I could not remove.

What if the raging monster of John Cooper's song could be redefined as the omnipotent *Monster* nature of God's Holy Spirit raging to be freed within us? Yes, I do realize the danger in my substitution—the wrongness in depicting God as a Monster. Endure my madness for a minute; think back to the ancient prophets, and then to the radical men and women of the first-century Church. Behold the faces of those wilder, undomesticated sons and daughters of God—during the age when God's children charged straight at the evils of their day, demonstrated an irresistible kind of love, and flipped their worlds upside down—in a good way! The writer of Hebrews said it like this:

And what more shall I say? I do not have time to tell about Gideon, Barak, Samson, Jephthah, David, Samuel and the prophets, who through faith conquered kingdoms, administered justice, and gained what was promised; who shut the mouths of lions, quenched the fury of the flames, and escaped the edge of the sword; whose weakness was turned to strength; and who became powerful in battle and routed foreign armies. Women received back their dead, raised to life again. Others were tortured and refused to be released, so that they might gain a better resurrection. Some faced jeers and flogging, while still others were chained and put in prison. They were stoned; they were sawed in two; they were put to death by the sword. They went about in sheepskins and goatskins, destitute, persecuted and mistreated—the world was not worthy of them. They wandered in deserts and mountains, and in caves and holes in the ground (Hebrews 11:32-38 NIV).

Now envision a time progression from then all the way until now. Watch very closely as God's influence in this world is wickedly suppressed with each successive generation. Behold, the mighty Lion of the universe—sedated, chained, and taunted until, like a *monster*, He rages against the madness! Envision Him reacting to the oppression. He pulls away the tape that muffles His voice. He cannot lay in silence for any longer—like a *monster*, He is breaking out!

The more I listened and watched the music video, the more I felt the pressure of God's Holy Spirit building deep within me. He asked for His freedom! My heart rate started to escalate! I found myself suddenly praying more passionately than I had before! My physical muscles started hulking, my lungs were panting! I looked around my office to make sure I was alone.

Something very good, but very radical was happening to me, and I didn't know how much longer I could calm it down!

Please read the following lyrics very slowly, and try to imagine John Cooper's song through the paradigm I have created here.

MONSTER

The secret side of me, I never let you see
I keep it caged but I can't control it.
So stay away from me, the beast is ugly
I feel the rage and I just can't hold it.

It's scratching on the walls, in the closet, in the halls
It comes awake and I can't control it.
Hiding under the bed, in my body, in my head
Why won't somebody come and save me from this, make it end?

I feel it deep within, it's just beneath the skin
I must confess that I feel like a monster.
I hate what I've become, the nightmare's just begun
I must confess that I feel like a monster.

I, I feel like a monster.
I, I feel like a monster.

My secret side I keep hid under lock and key
I keep it caged but I can't control it.
'Cause if I let him out he'll tear me up, break me down
Why won't somebody come and save me from this, make it end?

I feel it deep within, it's just beneath the skin
I must confess that I feel like a monster.
I hate what I've become, the nightmare's just begun
I must confess that I feel like a monster.

I feel it deep within, it's just beneath the skin
I must confess that I feel like a monster.
I, I feel like a monster.
I, I feel like a monster.

It's hiding in the dark, it's teeth are razor sharp.
There's no escape for me, it wants my soul, it wants my heart.
No one can hear me scream, maybe it's just a dream
Maybe it's inside of me, stop this monster.

I feel it deep within, it's just beneath the skin
I must confess that I feel like a monster.
I hate what I've become, the nightmare's just begun
I must confess that I feel like a monster.

I feel it deep within, it's just beneath the skin
I must confess that I feel like a monster.
I've gotta lose control, he's something radical
I must confess that I feel like a monster.

I, I feel like a monster.
I, I feel like a monster.
I, I feel like a monster.
I, I feel like a monster.[5]

These lyrics alone are compelling! But watching the video adds even more to the experience. It begins in a hospital operating room, where a man is being strapped to an operating table. Right away it seems that the doctors and nurses are working to surgically extract something from him—probably the *Monster*. As the video progresses, the resistant patient escapes from the operating room and runs desperately through the hospital halls, while being chased by a posse of police officers each wearing full biohazard containment suits. Finally, he breaks through an unguarded door and into the open air (with another escapee), and runs off into the sunlight. After the music fades, a voice on the police radio is heard broadcasting these words: "Sir, we have a containment breach, we lost them. They're out in the open!"

What a powerful visual! Do you ever feel like the person in this video? Do you feel like just beneath your skin, in that secret side you keep, hidden under lock and key, there is a monster force of God's Holy Spirit trapped in the closet of your heart? Do you ever feel like you want to escape with Him to the life He really wants you to have, but you fear that He might tear you up, and break you down—as the song suggests? Does it seem that every time you come close to liberating the *Monster*, a biohazard safety crew will show up with their stun guns and smoke bombs, and force you down onto an oper-ating table so they can surgically remove your *fire*?

HE BURNS LIKE A FIRE!

Come on! This is the final chapter. Now is the time; this is it! Just a few pages to go and my first chance for significantly impacting your life will be over. Hurry up, come with me the rest of the way! Rip off the straight jacket, shove away the hands that are pushing you down, spring up from the table, and follow me through the hallways to the sunlight! Stop toning down your life and message so low that you are not really living or saying anything. This is when you overcome your fear of people—godless people, faithless people, and intimidating, self-righteous people! You must know how extreme and forceful this seems, but this is God's desire. He is living inside of you right now—burning like a fire! Don't take my word for it—listen to Jeremiah describe God's influence in his life as the *monster of fire* he couldn't tame:

> When I speak, the words burst out. "Violence and destruction!" I shout. So these messages from the Lord have made me a household joke. But if I say I'll never mention the Lord or speak in His name, His word burns in my heart like a **fire**. It's like a **fire** in my bones! I am worn out trying to hold it in! I can't do it! I have heard the many rumors about me. They call me "The Man Who Lives in Terror." They threaten, "If you say anything, we will report it." Even my old friends are watching me, waiting for a fatal slip. "He will trap himself," they say, "and then we will get our revenge on him." **But the Lord stands beside me** like a great warrior..." (Jeremiah 20:8-11).

SAMSON: THE ORIGINAL HULK

Jeremiah wasn't the only one who felt this amazing God-force. I'm sure you've heard about Samson, Israel's deliverer during the time of the Judges. According to biblical history, there is no sign that Samson was a powerfully built man. Besides his unique spiritual vow to God, he was just a regular physical person, and not a big deal compared to any other man of his day.

But at intermittent times, like a *monster*, the Spirit of the Lord would rush upon the young man. During these surges, he was absolutely indestructible. Samson was the original Incredible Hulk!

"*And the Spirit of the Lord began to stir him* [Samson] *while he lived in Mahaneh-dan...*" (Judg. 13:25). One time:

> *As Samson and his parents were going down to Timnah, a young lion suddenly attacked Samson near the vineyards of Timnah. At that moment* **the Spirit of the Lord came powerfully upon him,** *and he ripped the lion's jaws apart with his bare hands. He did it as easily as if it were a young goat...* (Judges 14:5-6).

Another time:

> *As Samson arrived at Lehi, the Philistines came shouting in triumph. But* **the Spirit of the Lord** *came powerfully upon Samson, and he snapped the ropes on his arms as if they were burnt strands of flax, and they fell from his wrists* (Judges 15:14).

WE CALL HIM THE MONSTER

With all I've said about the monster you may be wondering, does God ever really take over a person and force an action against one's free will? No, I don't think so. In referring to God's Spirit as the *Monster* of our story, I am not trying to represent Him as rude or violent. I do not suggest we plunge in to a panic-induced hunt for perceived wrongdoers, like the horrendous witch hunters of the 1500s and 1600s. I do *not* approve of the anti-Jesus practices of blowing up abortion clinics or bashing homosexuals in back alleys. The Holy Spirit does not possess people in the same way that demon spirits possess their victims. The Holy Spirit moves inside of us with permission. He strongly urges us to radical *positive* actions, and expresses Himself through us only with our willful cooperation.

The Holy Spirit wants to lead us so much more than He already does, but the truth is that so many of us really don't want to be led. We don't want to be "controlled" by anything or anybody. I think we have an inborn rebellious demand for independence and a dreadful fear of the unknown. Sometimes we love our current earthly lives too much! We dread what God might have us forfeit and what He might ask us to do for Him. We fear how society might perceive us if we ever really did give God the full reins to our hearts. We want to live *our own* lives and do *our own* things, and only go so far at forgiving, loving, serving, and sacrificing. Because of this, every time God's Holy Spirit tries to rise, we call Him the Monster.

Have we hushed God's Spirit within us so much that we have asphyxiated Him to sleep? And are we doing everything we can to make sure He stays asleep? Shhh! Are we petrified that we may accidentally awaken the *Monster*? Even right now, are you at least a little bit anxious over the new spiritual fire this book has generated? Are you scared you might just flip out and go stand on a street corner with a Bible and a megaphone? Don't worry; the Holy Spirit really is a Gentleman. You can shut Him down, if you concentrate! Just close the book right here and don't read another line. Quickly, go do something loud; distract yourself from whatever's coming over you. My guess is that you can't really do that. You have permitted Him too much access, you've bent your will, and you've come too close. The *Monster* is awake and becoming active in you; and after this, you may never get Him to sleep again!

TOLERANCE + TIME = TORMENT

In the opening chapter of Exodus, the people of Israel lived peacefully in the land of Egypt. In the process of time, an evil Pharaoh rose to power, and even though the land was filled with Israelites and they were *"more and mightier"* than the Egyptians, tolerance eventually led to oppression. Pharaoh reasoned that Israel would not resist his abuse, and he was right! The Bible says:

> *And they* [Pharaoh and his slave masters] *made their lives* [the Israelites] *bitter with hard bondage—in mortar, in brick, and in all manner of service in the field. All their service in which they made them serve was with rigor* (Exodus 1:14 NKJV).

The Hebrew word for rigor in that verse is *perek* and it means to serve with *oppression and tyranny, from the signification of crushing.* In the Bible, *perek* is translated with three English words: *harshness, severity, and cruelty.*[6] Just as Lot was "tormented in his righteous soul" as he lived oppressively in

Sodom and Gomorrah without a voice of moral influence, Israel's tolerance of the growing oppression ebbed away at her influence, until she was enslaved in a country where she once thrived. Israel was first lulled into complacency, and then beaten into submission, until she was crushed with oppression and tyranny and breaking apart from harshness, severity, and cruelty.

Merriam-Webster defines tolerance as "the capacity of the body to endure or become less responsive to a substance (e.g., a drug) or to a psychological insult, with repeated use or exposure."[7] As we see it so clearly manifested in the pre-exodus Israel: tolerance + time = torment. The children of *El Shaddai*, the all-sufficient One, were weak and broken down. The people of *Jehovah Jireh*, the Lord who Provides, were living in unimaginable poverty. The people of *Jehovah Rapha*, the Lord our Healer, were sickly and suffering. The servants of *Jehovah Shalom*, the Lord our Peace, were stressed, anxious, and confused. The citizens of *El Elyon*, the Most High God, were subservient to an ancient Hitler. This should not have been. It was unnatural. But tolerance + time = torment.

Just like ancient Israel, modern Christians have become less and less responsive to the moral and spiritual deterioration in our nation and world. For more than 50 years, we have hidden behind a gutless banner of passive resistance. Instead of overcoming the evil in our government—and our educational system, economy, entertainment industry, etc.—we have become less responsive, almost *unresponsive* with *repeated use* and *exposure*. This didn't happen overnight. We have been trained to submit. Instead of transforming our culture, we are conforming to it. We should be fighting hard to save our cities, holding up a flag of enduring standard, and facing a little persecution along the way. Instead, we have relinquished our influence to the louder, eviler voices.

Here in the United States, many have abandoned our cities, run away from politics, and fled from the battlefront against every godless agenda. Our major cities have been taken—and as go the cities, inevitably so goes the rest of the nation. For the past several decades, masses of Christian people have escaped the cities to resettle their families in the sheltered townships. This seemed to be working for a little while—safer schools, less drugs and crime, traditional values. But then the city demons dispatched their troops to the hills and the valleys—even to the remotest places. There is almost nowhere else for the passive resistant people to settle. We are cornered with nowhere else to turn. Maybe, soon, we will rise.

Please don't label me an *America basher*, and please, please don't call me a *gloom and doomer*. That would really hurt my feelings! I have tried very hard to write a message of hope. I love the USA and I thank God that we are not as bad as other more evil countries, but I know how much a part of our history He has been, and how we have denied Him and betrayed Him in recent years. I believe that we are starting to suffer from the consequences of our backsliding. I know that we can become so much better than we have been. That is why I am writing so passionately right now. That's why I have to say some of these difficult things with so much boldness.

This country is becoming a modern-day Sodom and Gomorrah. You and I are becoming the *Lot* figures in our land—tormented in our righteous souls, often wondering how much longer before judgment comes. How are we ever going to become the legends of a better tomorrow unless we face the reality of where we are and what must be done to turn things around?

THE COUNTER-CULTURE REVOLUTION

Almost 50 years ago, a counterculture revolution ripped through this nation! In *The Jesus Manifesto—A Call to Revolution*, Dr. Michael Brown writes:

> "In 1962, the Supreme Court outlawed organized, public prayer in our schools (without citing a single historic precedent to back its decision), and we complied with that ruling.
>
> "In 1963, the Supreme Court banned required reading of the Scriptures from our schools, and once again, we complied with the ruling."[8]

Also, on January 22, 1973, in Roe v. Wade, we legalized what has become the American Holocaust. A holocaust is a thorough destruction involving the extensive loss of life. Hitler's holocaust was responsible for the annihilation of *six million Jews*. Since 1973, America's holocaust now carries the blood of more than *fifty million babies*! An entire generation has been wiped off the face of the earth. The only difference between Hitler's holocaust and ours is that we have annihilated *our own* children, and made *billions of dollars* doing it!

> "By 1980, the Court had ordered the removal of the Ten Commandments from public view in our schools and by 1985, it outlawed benedictions or invocations in formal school activities. Some lower courts even ruled against students praying out loud over their cafeteria meals.
>
> "In the year 2000, the [Supreme] Court has banned voluntary public prayer in our schools."[9]

What have been the consequences of these things? Since the early 1960s, America has experienced a steep moral decline. As Dr. Brown argues, we have:

- "highest percentage of single-parent families in the industrialized world.
- highest abortion rate in the industrialized world.
- highest rate of sexually transmitted diseases in the industrialized world (the rates of syphilis and gonorrhea transmission are almost 500 percent higher than the highest rates in the other industrialized nations).
- The highest teenage birth rate in the industrialized world (by far!)
- The highest rate of teen drug use in the industrialized world."[10]

Author David G. Myers says, "Had you fallen asleep in 1960 and awakened today...you would be awakening to a:

- doubled divorce rate
- tripled teen suicide rate
- quadrupled rate of reported violent crime
- quintupled prison population
- sextupled percentage of babies being born to unmarried parents

- sevenfold increase in cohabitation (a predictor of future divorce)
- soaring rate of depression—to ten times the pre-World War II level, by one estimate."[11]

In 1900 there were 28 churches for every 10,000 Americans. In 2004 there were 11 churches for every 10,000 Americans.[12] According to these numbers, we currently have 61 percent fewer churches per capita than in 1900! Four thousand churches close each year in the U.S., only 3 percent are growing by conversion growth. Today, "167 to 187 million non-Christians live in America, making us the fourth largest mission field in the world. "The Church is growing on every continent except North America."[13] Dear God, save us!

Ron Luce, in his book *Battle Cry for a Generation,* says that, "…88 percent of kids raised in Christian homes do not continue to follow the Lord after they graduate from high school."[14] This means that 9 out of 10 of our children do not see any value in what we are doing.

THIS IS JUST THE WAY IT IS?

This is the condition of our nation—this is our world! Our youngest generations have never seen a better way. They are born into the earth during a time of terrible Christian repression. This is not anywhere close to how our founders wanted things to turn out. Our young people hear us talk of yesterday's awakenings as though we have crafted a fairy tale of something that can never really happen now. Many of today's kids don't understand what is wrong with same sex relationships. Or what is wrong with sex outside of marriage. They live in a world lacking a moral compass and a spiritual conviction—a world where self is god, and anything that feels right is fine.

Until now, many Christians, you and I included, have reasoned that to rise and dissent would be far too costly. So we have chained our passions and toned down our standards. We have silenced the *John the Baptists* among us. We have chosen rather to coexist in unevangelistic compromise with Islam and the other false religions of our era. If Jesus had lived like most of us live, He would have never been nailed to a cross.

Political correctness is killing us! Cowardice has deluded us in every way, until our Good News is no news at all. Unlike Jesus, we seem to need our world to like us, enjoy us, approve us, and celebrate us! We cower in the face of radical liberal agendas. We tolerate the gross immoralities of our day, even as we are increasingly agitated in our righteous souls as we switch through the channels on our televisions and move about in public places. Somehow, we just know that tomorrow's better world is a very real possibility, but we just don't see how it can happen—because followers of Christ have become the only people in today's culture without a backbone and a voice.

WHY DID YOU OBEY?

In his book, *Revolution! A Call to Holy War*, Dr. Michael Brown wrote:

> I remember how embarrassed many of us felt as American be-
> lievers when Richard Wurmbrand—a Jewish Christian brutally
> tortured for his faith during 14 years in Romanian prisons—
> asked us one time at a meeting: "When the Supreme Court
> banned public prayer in your schools, why did you obey?" His
> gentle words were stinging! Here's a brother who was impris-
> oned three separate times for preaching the gospel. He was kept
> in solitary confinement for three years, beaten continuously on
> the soles of his feet, carved with knives and red hot fire pokers,
> frozen to the brink of death, snapped in two like a broken doll—
> and still, upon his release from prison, he went back to preach-
> ing, not once, but twice. He could do no other. Why? Because
> Jesus was his life!"[15]

DEFINING MOMENTS

Most people only rise when they reach a breaking point! The defining moment comes when one renegade clambers up to his feet, stills his shaking knees, and heralds his brave rally cry, "That's it! I will not live like this anymore! Life doesn't have to be this way! There is a better way! I know it's out there and I'm going after it! Who wants to join my movement?"

And that one audacious renegade inspires a thousand more, then thousands. At some point in this progression, enough people are willing to die to see things changed, rather than live with the shame of doing nothing. Before you know it, there is a very legitimate, newly-formed *legend tribe* standing on their feet like an army, promising to change the world forever! With the mere announcement of their intent, momentum swings in their direction, and a full-blown revolution is for certain! It always starts with that fearless, catalytic person in that defining moment.

For Israel during her time of Egyptian slavery, the defining moment came when one man had enough! That man, of course, was Moses. His rally cry resonated deep in the hearts of a few million praying slaves.[16] Once he had provoked them, there was no stopping the movement that followed. The events that led up to that moment are constant reminders to all generations of what can happen every time a prophet breaks his chain. As you process the following story, see today's Christian Church as the Israel figure—at her breaking point and longing for "Exodus!" See yourself as the Moses figure, fighting to be undomesticated. Consider that you could be the catalytic person in this defining moment.

DOMESTICATED PROPHETS

As I established a few pages back, Israel was in a very bad place. She was lulled into complacency, and then beaten into submission until she was (*perek*) crushed with oppression and tyranny and breaking apart from harshness, severity, and cruelty. While this was happening, Moses, who was also an Israelite by birth, suffered from another less obvious form of slavery. God's mightiest would-be prophet of all time was growing up in the royal palace where he was constantly lured, lavished, kissed, and cuddled with high pleasures—a wild prophetic animal by birth, tamed and fattened on the delicacies of his royal uprising. Moses was a prophet not yet aware of his destiny. He was chained up tight in the warm embrace of a very wrong, default alliance. It is believed by some historians that Moses was the likely successor to his stepfather's legacy. He might have become Egypt's next Pharaoh! It would have been so personally beneficial for Moses to cover his ears to the crying slaves.

Similar to this situation with Moses, today's would-be prophets have also been wholly domesticated. We preach what this world tells us to preach. We give them the messages we think they *want* to hear instead of the messages we know they *need* to hear. We stand on our hind legs in a pathetic begging posture hoping that perhaps, if we are good little doggies, they will fill our bowls with water and throw us a nice little treat every once in a while. We have swallowed down the pill of political correctness and it's killing us! This godless world owns us right now. We have lost the wilder edge that founded and fueled our movement throughout history. Just like that famous movie boxer Rocky Balboa, we have lost our "eye of the tiger" and we're fighting scared! We've been chained up for so many years that we no longer bark.

MOSES — UNTAMED!

Something incredible happened to Moses at the age of 40. We don't have the meticulous details of how it happened, but somehow Moses became suddenly and perfectly aware of his Jewish roots. This shocking revelation triggered a monsoon of rage within him. All it took was one fresh look at the ghastly mistreatment of his "biological kinfolk" and Moses snapped. How would he reel back the empathy that was now spreading through his tendered heart? Could he go on living in all of that luxury as if he didn't have a blood connection with his father's slaves? Moses could do no such thing, because his lavished life came at the cost of God's suffering children.

Moses must have thought he was having some kind of mental breakdown. Everything in his entire life up to that point must have seemed like one great big distraction from the *real* legacy he was created for. I can see him running to his palace bedroom and collapsing facedown onto the marble floors beneath him, and crying out, "Oh God, help me. Every time I close my eyes, I see a vision of myself walking away from all of this—my fame, my luxury, and my royal future. I envision the entire royal court banishing me to the wilderness where I will face the uncertainty of survival. If I should go to the wilderness, will You strip away my royal acclaim and turn me into a wild animal? I admit it this scares me! When I look forty years into the future, I see a vision of myself returning to Egypt and facing Pharaoh, and delivering my Jewish family. A big part of me wants to ignore these premonitions, but no matter how hard I try to distract myself, I cannot erase them out of my mind! Dear God, Your strong hand is upon me, and I am afraid there is no other option but to go with this! Everyone will say I have lost my mind, but my faith is calling me to something greater than this delusional life I have been living." The author of Hebrews tells the story like this:

> It was by faith that Moses, when he grew up, refused to be called the son of Pharaoh's daughter. He chose to share the oppression of God's people instead of enjoying the fleeting pleasures of sin. He thought it was better to suffer for the sake of Christ than to own the treasures of Egypt, for he was looking ahead to his great reward. It was by faith that Moses left the land of Egypt, not fearing the king's anger. He kept right on going because he kept his eyes on the One who is invisible (Hebrews 11:24-27).

If you have ever watched Paramount Pictures' *The Ten Commandments,* or DreamWorks Animations' *The Prince of Egypt,* then you know what happened next. Moses walked away from everything! He spent the next 40 years of his life as a comparative nobody, in the middle of nowhere. He married, started a family, and became a sheepherder. It must have seemed like God was never going to visit him again, until one day, when Moses was caring for his father-in-law's sheep, he wandered deep into the wilderness, near Sinai—the mountain of God. Suddenly, God appeared to Moses *"in a blazing fire from the middle of a bush"* (Exod. 3:2) and Moses turned aside with amazement and curiosity, to get a closer look. When the Lord saw that He had caught Moses' attention, He called out his name from the bush, "Moses, Moses!"
God told Moses:

> I have certainly seen the oppression of My people...I have heard their cries of distress...I am aware of their suffering. So I have come down to rescue them from the power of the Egyptians and lead them out of Egypt into their own fertile and spacious land... Now go, for I am sending you to Pharaoh. You must lead my people Israel out of Egypt (Exodus 3:7-8,10).

Moses was 40, a regular guy with the perfect average life! Forty years of hard labor and living in the sandy cocoon of Midian's desert wilderness—the perfect combination of elements for the *untaming* of Egypt's prince. During those four long decades, when it seemed that Moses had been forgotten, God was doing His greatest work. None of this was lost time, for God was rearing one of His top three greatest *legends* of all time! Forty years of uprooting, tearing down, destroying, and overthrowing every weak and vulnerable place in Moses. Forty years of welding and banging and forging into creation the amazing instrument of God's epic reprisal on the destroyer of His beloved children.

When Pharaoh and Moses were finally re-introduced, Pharaoh learned that this was not the same Moses he once knew. This Moses was far less domesticated. This Moses didn't need the approval of man. He was not attracted to the temporary pleasures of his world. "Hey Pharaoh, this is judgment day! Think about what you have done to God's people and tremble in horror, because I am your worst nightmare—*Moses untamed!*"

Ten plagues later, and Moses led his two million member family out of Egyptian slavery forever. Perhaps, just like Moses, you and I need a wilderness metamorphosis and one undeniable mountaintop encounter with the God of our ancestors! Yes? What Moses heard from God was not just for him—it has been for all legends throughout history, and it is for us today.

THE WILD IS CALLING

One evening I was in my office rushing through a last-minute phone call. I was already 20 minutes late for our Thursday night prayer meeting, and feeling slightly stressed about it. Since I didn't want to be rude, I tried to bring the call to an end by using the typical, "Well, I'm glad you're doing OK and we had this opportunity to chat...." But this kind fellow kept on talking like the rest of his life was reserved for me!

Then, the strangest thing happened. You need to know that our church sanctuary is located directly on the other side of my office wall. As the phone conversation continued, I suddenly heard the prayer meeting worship music and a few of our prayer team members in the sanctuary, praying out loud and with great intensity. Several of them were clapping as if the President of the United States had come for a surprise visit.

The more they celebrated, the more I wanted to be with them—they were making me jealous! This went on for a few minutes until I finally interrupted my caller and said, "I am so sorry to do this, but I have to end this call right now, something urgent has come up!"

I ripped off my headset, raced around my desk, and charged into the sanctuary with such abruptness that everyone looked back at me as if I had lost my mind. I explained, "I heard you out here worshiping and praying, and it felt to me like *The Call of the Wild!*"

I reared back my head and let out a loud and undignified sound like the howling of a wolf! *Aaaooowwwww!* We all had a very good laugh and then proceeded with our prayer meeting—and from that experience I recorded in my journal the basis for this chapter, *Untame Yourself!*

The following is a shortsummary[17] of the 1903 Jack London classic, *The Call of the Wild*. Please read it with your own spiritual imagination and watch what happens....

Buck is a half Saint Bernard and half Sheepdog that lives on Judge Miller's estate in California's Santa Clara Valley. His comfortable life ends when gold is discovered in the Klondike region of Canada and Buck is kidnapped and sold to dog traders who ship him north.

Upon arriving at the Klondike, Buck is met with the harsh reality of life as a sled dog. Before long Buck recovers the instincts of his wild ancestors: he learns to fight, scavenge for food, and sleep beneath the snow on winter nights.

Eventually, Buck's abusive gold miner master dies by breaking through some ice while sledding, and a good man named Thornton becomes his new master. Buck is devoted to him. He saves Thornton from drowning in a river, attacks a man who tries to start a fight with Thornton in a bar, and wins a large wager by pulling a thousand-pound load.

Buck's love for Thornton progressively conflicts with his growing attraction to the wild, and he feels pulled away from civilization to the wilderness. He hears a pack of wolves howling in the distance. He wants to go but he wants to stay. No matter how hard Buck resists this new attraction for the wild, something deep inside the animal is tearing off his restraints, ripping him away from the domesticated life.

According to SparkNotes, author Jack London talks about the power of ancestral and primitive instincts in *The Call of the Wild*, suggesting that:

> His success in the frozen North is not merely a matter of learning the ways of the wild; rather, Buck gradually recovers primitive instincts and memories that his wild ancestors

possessed, which have been buried as dogs have become civilized creatures.

The technical term for what happens to Buck is atavism—the reappearance in a modern creature of traits that defined its remote forebears. London returns to this theme again and again, constantly reminding us that Buck is "retrogressing," as the novel puts it, into a wilder way of life that all dogs once shared.

He was older than the days he had seen and the breaths he had drawn," we are told. "He linked the past with the present, and the eternity behind him throbbed through him in a mighty rhythm to which he swayed as the tides and seasons swayed." Buck even has occasional visions of this older world, when humans wore animal skins and lived in caves, and when wild dogs hunted their prey in the primeval forests.

The civilized world, which seems so strong, turns out to be nothing more than a thin veneer, which is quickly worn away to reveal the ancient instincts lying dormant underneath. Buck hears the call of the wild, and London implies that, in the right circumstances, we might hear it too![18]

While I'm not making a statement about whether all (or any) of London's assertions are scriptural, he does have some critical insights that apply so much to the lives of *legends*. Every time I think about this Jack London classic, I think about two very specific verses from the Bible, and I burst into heavenly flames about it!

For the truth about God is known to them **instinctively**. *God has put His knowledge in their hearts* (Romans 1:19).

Therefore we also, since **we are surrounded** *by so great a cloud of witnesses, let us lay aside every weight, and the sin which so easily ensnares us, and let us run with endurance the race that is set before us* (Hebrews 12:1 NKJV).

A HOWLING IN THE DISTANCE

Can you hear that *howling* in the distance? The civilized world of today, which seems so real, is nothing more than a thin veneer, which is gradually being torn away. You and I are so much older than the days we have seen and the breaths we have drawn. *Eternity* is throbbing behind us like a mighty rhythm—as the tides and seasons sway. We cannot hesitate! The God of our ancestors is waking up the ancient instincts lying dormant underneath the layers of our modern domestication. There is a howling in the distance!

Just like Buck, I am seeing visions of an *older world*—the first century, when my spiritual ancestors shook the planet for Jesus Christ. Every time I read from the Bible and pray in seclusion, and when I assemble with other Christians, I hear the sound of howling in the distance. It is so obvious to me that over the past few years, our species—that is, strongly committed, Spirit-filled, Bible-believing Christians—has been *retrogressing* into a wilder way of life that all Christians once shared. We've have been gradually recovering the primitive instincts and memories that our wild ancestors once possessed—instincts lulled to sleep as we've been civilized.

*Prayer: Dear God, I pray for every one of my readers, that they are so far beyond wherever they were when they started this book! It was my strong desire to give them the necessary tools for building a better tomorrow. Now may they hear that howling in the distance. As they proceed through these final pages, may something happen in the deepest places of their hearts! Will You divide their lives into a very clear before and after? Manifest Your fire within them so much that they are brought to the breaking point—until they are screaming inside for the real and lasting freedom You have promised them through me. Right here Good Father, as I have assembled my new friends to the farthest edge between a great life and a legendary one—**untame** them! Eradicate their fear of people and demons. Give them Your character, passion for hard work, and a clear life dream. Give them a sold out stadium of frenzied fans, unparalleled spiritual authority, and the highest level of love. May they become infinitely more effective than they previously imagined, even in their* *sweetest dreams. Make them Your greatest **legends** of all time! In Jesus' name, amen.*

Did you hear that? "Aaaoooowwwww!" There it is again! "Aaaoooowwwww" It never seems to stop! "Aaaoooowwwww. Aaaoooowwwww. Aaaoooowwwww!" It is a startling, fascinating, insistent howling in the distance. It rips and it rolls; it shrills and echoes, a perpetual thunder booming from the everlasting, *great cloud of witnesses!* Look up with eyes of faith and you will see your ancestors gathered in the skies. Listen and you will certainly hear them howling in the distance.

From the Old Testament era there is *Noah, Abraham, Isaac, Jacob, Joseph, Job, Moses, Joshua, Ruth, Deborah, Samuel, David, Solomon, Elijah, Elisha, Jehoshaphat, Isaiah, Jeremiah, Ezekiel, Esther, Daniel, Hosea, Joel, Amos, Obadiah, Jonah, Micah, Nahum, Habakkuk, Zephaniah, Haggai, Zechariah, and Malachi!* From the Early Church era there is *Matthew, Mark, Luke, and John; and Peter, Paul, Barnabas, James, Silas, Pricilla and Aquila, Timothy, Jude, and Philemon!* Then there is the howling of every saint and martyr; the howling of every great awakening revivalist; the howling of all your family and friends who died in faith. Eventually, Billy Graham will be there too!

A Closing Word From God

Right now, I hear God saying, "Look around and you will see how weak and domesticated My people have become over this past century. It would seem that this world has already known My Church's finest days. To this I say, don't count My people out yet! Don't assume that everything will continue to be as it has been in recent years. Everything is about to change! I am calling out to My *legends* and, just like Moses, they are turning to Me for a closer look. I'm instigating another Exodus! My children will worship Me on the mountain again. Just watch and you will see. There are people from this last-hour Church who will merit the respect of My greatest generals. Don't let anything ground you to this earth. Keep looking up to the great cloud of witnesses and run your fastest race! From time to time, you will feel them standing at your attention. Make no mistake about it, the people in Heaven are on their feet and they are cheering loudly! It's getting wild up here! Anticipation is building, the plan of the ages if reaching fruition! My greatest empowerment is reserved for the last awakening. Let it begin today. Let it begin with you. Now, I say now! What are you waiting for? Come out from the world and live like Nazarites before Me! Be My legends, build the better tomorrow—have no regrets when you cross over. This short life is for eternity. So, do not hesitate to sacrifice everything for the God-sized dream. Just a little bit longer and you will be collecting your reward."

Thank you for reading my book. Dream big, live bold, make a difference—and leave a legacy!

The End, *for now...*

Endnotes

Chapter 1

1. "As of May 1, 2008 the United Nations had 192 members; many sources include Kosovo, which brings the total to 193." Worldatlas.com, "How Many Countries?" World Atlas, accessed January 26, 2011, http://www .worldatlas.com/nations.htm.

2. Statistics projected by International Programs Center, "World POPClock Projection," U.S. Census Bureau, accessed January 26, 2011, http://www .census.gov/ipc/www/popclockworld.html.

3. "Languages of the World," Ethnologue, 2009, accessed January 26, 2011, http://www.ethnologue.com/.

4. John Mark Mcmillan, "How He Loves," Lyricstime, accessed May 31, 2011, http://www.lyricstime.com/john-mark-mcmillan-how-he-loves -lyrics.html.

5. Amy Lee and Ben Moody, "Bring Me to Life," by David Hodges, in *Fallen*, Evanescence, 2003, CD.

6. Amy Lee, "Bring Me to Life," Lyrics.com, accessed January 27, 2011, http://www.lyrics.com/bring-me-to-life-album-version-lyrics -evanescence.html.

Chapter 2

1. ThinkExist.com, Jim McCrossin, accessed March 29, 2011, http:// thinkexist.com/quotation/is-there-a-chance-obviously-there-s-a-chance -you/1504737.html.

2. David Wilkerson, "The Last Revival," World Challenge Pulpit Series, accessed January 27, 2011, http://www.tscpulpitseries.org/english/1980s/ts880411.html.

3. This section is a mixture of thoughts extracted from Winkie Pratney's book, *Revival,* and my own personal revisions and additions added over ten years of research and study. Winkie Pratney, *Revival: Principles to Change the World* (Charleston, SC: CreateSpace, 2010).

4. Ibid., 63-64.

5. R. L. Hymers, "Comments on the First Great Awakening" (sermon, Lord's Day Evening, Baptist Tabernacle, Los Angeles, CA, April 26, 2009), accessed March 31, 2011, http://www.rlhymersjr.com/Online _Sermons/2009/042609PM_FirstGreatAwakening.html.

6. Tony Cauchi, "The First Great Awakening—Jonathan Edwards," Revival Library, May 2006, The State of the Church, accessed March 31, 2011, http://www.revival-library.org/pensketches/revivals/1st_edwards.html.

7. John Jackman, "Count Zinzendorf," Zinzendorf Jubilee Homepage, accessed January 27, 2011, http://www.zinzendorf.com/countz.htm.

8. David Legge, "The Never-Ceasing Flame of Intercession," Preach the Word, accessed January 27, 2011, http://www.preachtheword.com/sermon/misc0040-neverceasingflame.shtml.

9. Nita Johnson, "The First Great Global Awakening of the 1700s: On the Blood of the Martyrs," The World for Jesus Ministries, accessed March 31, 2011, http://www.worldforjesus.org/articles-print.php?ID=36.

10. "The First Great Awakening Quotes," The Great Awakening, accessed January 27, 2011, http://www.freewebs.com/firstgreatawakening/quotes .htm.

11. "Old Time Revivals: Pray for Another One," Gateway Christian Coalition, accessed March 31, 2011, http://users.mikrotec.com/~dcgay/revivals.htm.

12. Pratney, *Revival*, and Rev. Oliver W. Price, "The Layman's Prayer Revival of 1857-1858," Bible Prayer Fellowship, accessed January 27, 2011, http://www.praywithchrist.org/prayer/layman.php.

13. James Edwin Orr, "Prayer and Revival," accessed January 27, 2011, http://www.jedwinorr.com/prayer_revival.htm.

14. Ibid.

15. Ibid.

16. Ibid.

17. Alice Smith, *Beyond the Veil* (Ventura, CA: Renew, 1997), 24.

18. John T. Christian, "A History of the Baptists: The Great Revival of 1800," Providence Baptist Ministries, accessed March 31, 2011, http://www.pbministries.org/History/John T. Christian/vol2/history2_part3_04.htm.

19. Peter Marshall and David Manual, *From Sea to Shining Sea* (Tappan, NJ: Revell, 1986), 62.

20. Smith, *Beyond the Veil*, 24.

21. Lewis A. Drummond, *The Awakening Must Come* (Nashville, TN: Broadman Press, 1978), 15-16.

22. Pratney, *Revival*, 105-106.

23. John F. Thornbury, "Interpreting the Great Awakening," *Reformation and Revival* 1, no. 2 (Spring 1992): 65-66.

24. Rev. Oliver W. Price, "The Layman's Prayer Revival of 1857-1858," Bible Prayer Fellowship, accessed January 27, 2011, http://www.praywithchrist.org/prayer/layman.php.

25. Ibid.

26. Pratney, *Revival*, 129.

27. Price, "The Layman's Prayer Revival."

28. Ibid.

29. James Edwin Orr, *A Call for the Re-study of Revival and Revivalism* (Los Angeles, CA: Oxford Association for Research in Revival or Evangelical Awakening, 1981), 27.

30. Orr, "Prayer and Revival," http://www.jedwinorr.com/prayer_revival.htm.

31. "Edmund Burke," Wikiquote, Disputed, accessed March 31, 2011, http://en.wikiquote.org/wiki/Edmund_Burke.

Chapter 3

1. The American Heritage Dictionary of the English Language, *The Free Dictionary*, s.v. "Legend," Usage Note, accessed January 28, 2011, http://www.thefreedictionary.com/legend.

2. Studio of the South, "Michelangelo Sculptures: David, Pieta," Michelangelo Buonarotti Paintings and Biography, accessed January 28, 2011, http://www.michelangelo-gallery.com/sculptures.aspx.

3. Steve Amoia, "I Live in Hell and Paint Its Pictures: Michelangelo Buonarroti," American Chronicle, September 21, 2008, Early Years in Renaissance Florence, accessed January 28, 2011, http://www.americanchronicle.com/articles/view/74960.

4. "Apollo Moon Landing 35th Anniversary," NASA Home, July 15, 2004, accessed March 31, 2011, http://www.nasa.gov/audience/forstudents/5-8/features/F_Apollo_35th_Anniversary.html.

5. Carpe Noctem, "George Washington," Seize the Night, November 2010, accessed March 31, 2011, http://www.carpenoctem.tv/military/wash.html.

6. "Sir Alexander Fleming: Biography," Nobelprize.org, accessed March 31, 2011, http://nobelprize.org/nobel_prizes/medicine/laureates/1945/fleming-bio.html.

7. "Alexander Graham Bell," PBS: Public Broadcasting Service, accessed March 31, 2011, http://www.pbs.org/transistor/album1/addlbios/bellag.html.

8. "Pasteur, Louis," New World Encyclopedia, April 2, 2008, accessed March 31, 2011, http://www.newworldencyclopedia.org/entry/Louis_Pasteur.

9. "Florence Nightingale Biography," Encyclopedia of World Biography, accessed March 31, 2011, http://www.notablebiographies.com/Mo-Ni/Nightingale-Florence.html. See also Jillian Gill, "Florence: The Light That Shines Through," Camden New Journal, accessed March 31, 2011, http://www.camdennewjournal.co.uk/2004 archive/300904/r300904_4.htm.

10. "Thomas Jefferson Biography," Biography.com, accessed March 31, 2011, http://www.biography.com/articles/Thomas-Jefferson-9353715.

11. Mary Bellis, "The Inventions of Thomas Edison," About.com, accessed March 31, 2011, http://inventors.about.com/library/inventors/bledison.htm. See also Thomas A. Edison, "Thomas Alva Edison Quotes," ThinkExist.com, accessed March 31, 2011, http://thinkexist.com/quotes/thomas_alva_edison/.

12. Mary Bellis, "The History of the Airplane: Orville and Wilbur Wright," About.com, accessed March 31, 2011, http://inventors.about.com/library/inventors/blairplane.htm.

13. "St. Frances Xavier Cabrini," Catholic Online, accessed March 31, 2011, http://www.catholic.org/saints/saint.php?saint_id=278.

14. Hannah Salter, "Biography: Ludwig Van Beethoven," Ludwig Van Beethoven, accessed March 31, 2011, http://www.lvbeethoven.com/Bio/BiographyLudwig.html.

15. The Henry Ford, "The Life of Henry Ford," America's Greatest History Attraction Home Page, 2003, accessed March 31, 2011, http://www.hfmgv.org/exhibits/hf/.

16. NBA Encyclopedia, "Michael Jordan Bio," NBA.com, accessed March 31, 2011, http://www.nba.com/history/players/jordan_bio.html.

17. The Holy Bible.

18. *Merriam-Webster,* s.v. "Challenge," definition 2, accessed March 31, 2011, http://www.merriam-webster.com/dictionary/challenge.

19. National Science Foundation, "Study Confirms: Whatever Doesn't Kill Us Can Make Us Stronger," U.S. News and World Report, October 19, 2010, accessed March 31, 2011, http://www.usnews.com/science/articles/2010/10/19/study-confirms-whatever-doesnt-kill-us-can-make-us-stronger.

20. "C.T. Studd: Echoes from Glory," Wholesome Words Christian Website, accessed March 31, 2011, http://wholesomewords.org/echoes/studd.html.

Chapter 4

1. Ronald Reagan, from his first inaugural speech as governor of California, 1967.

2. Ruben N. Lubowski et al., "Major Uses of Land in the United States," USDA Economic Research Service, May 31, 2006, accessed March 31, 2011, http://www.ers.usda.gov/Publications/EIB14/.

3. "John Quincy Adams," The Free Library, Famous Quotations, accessed March 31, 2011, http://adams.thefreelibrary.com/.

4. Adapted from Deuteronomy 32:35 (KJV), which says, *"To Me belongeth vengeance and recompence; their foot shall slide in due time: for the day of their calamity is at hand, and the things that shall come upon them make haste."* Also, Jonathan Edwards preached his classic message, *Sinners in the Hands of an Angry God* from this text.

5. Glenn Beck, "Is American History Repeating?" FoxNews.com March 11, 2010, accessed January 28, 2011, http://www.foxnews.com/story/0,2933,588989,00.html.

6. Theodore Roosevelt, "Citizenship in a Republic" (speech, The Sorbonne, Paris, April 23, 1910), accessed March 31, 2011, http://www.theodoreroosevelt.org/life/quotes.htm.

7.   Samuel was a prophet of ancient Israel, known for reestablishing the true worship of God.

Chapter 5

1.   Leonard Ravenhill, "Quotes," Samuelkordik.com, June 21, 2008, Our Crusade, accessed March 31, 2011, http://samuelkordik.com/category/quotes/page/2/.

2.   John Maxwell, "John Maxwell Leadership Quotes," SermonCentral.com, Teamwork, accessed March 31, 2011, http://www.sermoncentral.com/articleb.asp?article=John-Maxwell-94-Leadership-Quotes&ac=true.

3.   "City of David," City of David: Ancient Jerusalem, accessed January 28, 2011, http://www.cityofdavid.co.il/about_eng.asp.

4.   John C. Maxwell, *The 21 Irrefutable Laws of Leadership: 10th Anniversary Edition* (Nashville, TN: Thomas Nelson, 2007), 103.

5.   Seth Godin, *Tribes: We Need You to Lead Us* (New York, NY: Portfolio Hardcover, Penguin Books, 2008).

Chapter 6

1.   Price Pritchett, *You²: A High Velocity Formula for Multiplying Your Personal Effectiveness in Quantum Leaps* (Dallas, TX: Pritchett & Associates, 2007).

2.   Johnny Lee, "Lookin' for Love," in *Urban Cowboy*, EMI Music Publishing, 1980, accessed April 7, 2011, http://www.lyricsmode.com/lyrics/j/johnny_lee/lookin_for_love.html.

Chapter 7

1.   Walt Disney, *The Princess and the Frog*, 2010.

2.   Pratney, *Revival*, 67-69.

3.   "Helen Keller," American Foundation for the Blind, accessed January 29, 2011, http://www.afb.org/Section.asp?SectionID=1.

4.   Helen Keller, "Helen Keller Quotes," ThinkExist.com, accessed January 29, 2011, http://thinkexist.com/quotation/i_am_only_one-but_still_i_am_one-i_cannot_do/10674.html. Emphasis added.

5.   Ibid., http://thinkexist.com/quotation/it_is_for_us_to_pray_not_for_tasks_equal_to_our/13587.html. Emphasis added.

6.   Jeanne Sahadi, "Being a Mom Could Be a 6-figure Job," CNNMoney.com, May 03, 2006, accessed January 29, 2011, http://money.cnn.com/2006/05/03/pf/mothers_work/.

7.   Office of Information Services, "Life Expectancy," Centers for Disease Control and Prevention, February 18, 2011, accessed April 07, 2011, http://www.cdc.gov/nchs/fastats/lifexpec.htm.

Chapter 8

1.   Comfort Care Women's Health, formerly The Pregnancy Help Center. http://www.ccwomenshealth.org/

Chapter 9

1.   Edward Judson, "Quotations Book," Quotations Book: The Home of Famous Quotes, accessed April 07, 2011, http://quotationsbook.com/quote/37686/.

2.   Chandramita Bora, "Chinese Bamboo Tree," Buzzle Web Portal: Intelligent Life on the Web, February 15, 2010, Chinese Bamboo Tree Facts, accessed April 09, 2011, http://www.buzzle.com/articles/chinese-bamboo-tree.html.

Chapter 10

1.   Daniel Defoe, "The Education of Women," Qtd. in Richard Nordquist, "Classic British Essaays," About.com, accessed April 09, 2011, http://grammar.about.com/od/classicessays/a/educwomendefoe.htm.

2.   Julie Jordan, "Most Beautiful," *People Magazine*, May 12, 2008, Vol. 69, No. 18.

3.   *Merriam-Webster,* s.v. "Attentive," accessed January 30, 2011, http://www.merriam-webster.com/dictionary/attentive.

4.   "Major Religions Ranked by Size," Adherents.com, August 9, 2007, accessed April 09, 2011, http://www.adherents.com/Religions_By_Adherents.html.

5.   Wayne Cordeiro, "Sticky Quotes," Growing Healthy Churches Network, November 2, 2010, From Wayne Cordeiro, accessed April 09, 2011, http://www.ghcnetwork.org/page29/files/0bb0214530a9cbaf3c862676cb19c779-26.html.

6.   Stephen R. Covey, *The Seven Habits of Highly Effective People* (New York, NY: Free Press/Simon and Shuster, 2004).

7.   Shelley Esaak, "Michelangelo: The Sistine Chapel Ceiling," Art History Resources, accessed April 09, 2011, http://arthistory.about.com/od/famous_paintings/a/sischap_ceiling.htm.

8.   "Sistine Chapel Has Too Many Visitors," Catholic News Agency, accessed April 09, 2011, http://www.catholicnewsagency.com/news/sistine-chapel-has-too-many-visitors-warns-vatican-museums-director/.

9.   "Sistine Chapel Ceiling," Wikipedia, the Free Encyclopedia, accessed April 09, 2011, http://en.wikipedia.org/wiki/Sistine_Chapel_ceiling.

Chapter 11

1.   *"I urge, then, first of all, that requests, prayers, intercession and thanksgiving be made for everyone—for kings and all those in authority, that we may live peaceful and quiet lives in all godliness and holiness"* (1 Timothy 2:1-2 NIV).

2.   *Bing Dictionary,* s.v. "Progress," accessed April 11, 2011, http://www.bing.com/Dictionary/search?q=define+progress&form=DTPDIO.

3.   Ray Stedman, "Thanksgiving," Sermon Illustrations, accessed April 11, 2011, http://www.sermonillustrations.com/a-z/t/thanksgiving.htm.

4.   Mark Twain, "Mark Twain Quotes," The Quotations Page, accessed April 11, 2011, http://www.quotationspage.com/quotes/Mark_Twain.

5. Michael Zimmerman, "Environment," Microsoft Corporation, accessed April 11, 2011, http://sphseloliman2003.tripod.com/sitebuildercontent/sitebuilderfiles/environment.doc.

6. In Psalm 101, David posted his "Joe/Jane Fan" profile.

Chapter 12

1. "Energy (esotericism)," Wikipedia, the Free Encyclopedia, accessed April 12, 2011, http://en.wikipedia.org/wiki/Energy_(esotericism).

2. World English Dictionary, *MSN Encarta,* s.v. "Supernatural," 2009, accessed April 12, 2011, http://encarta.msn.com/dictionary_/supernatural.html.

3. "Heroes Season 1 Trailer," YouTube, May 5, 2008, 4:25 minutes, accessed April 12, 2011, http://www.youtube.com/watch?v=FpegMy8DDzY.

4. "Star Wars," Wikipedia, the Free Encyclopedia, Setting, accessed April 12, 2011, http://en.wikipedia.org/wiki/Star_Wars.

Chapter 13

1. First Peter 2:2-3 says, *"Like newborn babies, **crave pure spiritual milk,** so that by it you may **grow up in your salvation,** now that you have tasted that the Lord is good!"*

2. I owe this thought originally to Bill Bright, founder of Campus Crusade for Christ.

Chapter 14

1. Albert Einstein, "Albert Einstein Quotes," ThinkExist.com, accessed March 31, 2011, http://thinkexist.com/quotation/strange_is_our_situation_here_upon_earth-each_of/8534.html.

2. *Merriam-Webster,* s.v. "Peer," accessed January 30, 2011, http://mw1.merriam-webster.com/dictionary/peer.

3. "Synergy," Answers.com, accessed April 12, 2011, http://www.answers.com/topic/synergy.

4. "Antagonism," Answers.com, accessed April 12, 2011, http://www.answers.com/topic/antagonism-chemistry.

Chapter 15

1. My current life management system was built from a Tom Ferry teaching I heard at a seminar 12 years ago. Thank you Tom for teaching me how to manage my life!

2. Maryanne Williamson, *A Return to Love: Reflections on the Principles of a Course in Miracles* (New York, NY: Harper Collins, 1992), 190-191. Emphasis added.

3. Theodore Roosevelt, "Citizenship in a Republic," speech at the Sorbonne, Paris, April 23, 1910; accessed January 28, 2011, http://www.theodoreroosevelt.org/life/quotes.htm.

4. Alec M. Bodzin, "Cape Hatteras Lighthouse," North Carolina State University, June 17, 1999, accessed April 12, 2011, http://www.ncsu.edu/coast/chl/article15.html.

Chapter 16

1. See Proverbs 4:23 NIV.

2. Mac Davis, "It's Hard to Be Humble," recorded 1980, in *It's Hard to Be Humble*, Casablanca Records, audio.

3. *Spiderman 3*, dir. Sam Raimi, perf. Tobey Maguire, Kirsten Dunst (Sony Pictures, 2007), DVD.

Chapter 17

1. Bruce Banner, "Hulk Memorable Quotes," The Internet Movie Database, accessed April 14, 2011, http://www.imdb.com/title/tt0286716/quotes.

2. Athena Goodlight, "The Legacy of Rosa Parks," Factoidz.com, January 26, 2011, accessed April 14, 2011, http://factoidz.com/the-legacy-of-rosa-parks/.

3. "Skillet: Monster," YouTube, October 2, 2009, 3:07 minutes, accessed April 12, 2011, http://www.youtube.com/watch?v=1mjlM_RnsVE.

4. "Awake (Skillet Album)," Wikipedia, the Free Encyclopedia, Background, accessed April 14, 2011, http://en.wikipedia.org/wiki/Awake_(Skillet_album).

5. Gavin Brown and John Cooper, "Monster," in *Awake*, Skillet, Howard Benson, 2009, CD.

6. *Blue Letter Bible Lexicon*, s.v. "Rigor," Blue Letter Bible, accessed April 14, 2011, http://www.blueletterbible.org/lang/lexicon/lexicon.cfm?Strongs=H6531.

7. *Merriam-Webster*, s.v. "Tolerance," accessed January 30, 2011, http://www.merriam-webster.com/dictionary/tolerance.

8. Michael L. Brown, "The Jesus Manifesto: A Call to Revolution," in *Revolution! The Call to Holy War* (Ventura, CA: Regal Books, 200), 4, accessed April 15, 2011, http://jesuspeopleinfo.org/articles/manifesto.pdf.

9. Ibid.

10. Ibid. 3

11. David G. Myers, "Wanting More in an Age of Plenty," *Christianity Today*, April 24, 2000, 95.

12. Dr. Charles Revis, "Why Church Planting?" American Baptist Churches of the Northwest, accessed April 14, 2011, http://abcnw.org/why-church-planting/.

13. Vision for 21st Century Ministry Design, "A Snapshot of the U.S. Church," *McAlvany Intelligence Report*, November 1998, accessed April 15, 2011, http://www.powerlife.org/Consulting/Vision.html.

14. Ron Luce, *Battle Cry for a Generation: The Fight to Save America's Youth* (Colorado Springs, CO: David C. Cook Publishing, 2005), 21-22.

15. Michael L. Brown, *Revolution! A Call to Holy War* (Ventura, CA: Regal Books, 2000) 95.

16. According to Exodus 12:37-38 AMP, there were 600,000 men plus women and children and a "mixed multitude." Calculating these numbers produces a total people in excess of two million.

17. Research gathered from *The Call of the Wild* by Jack London, my own imagination, and http://www.sparknotes.com/lit/call/summary.html; accessed February 1, 2011.

18. "The Call of the Wild: Themes, Motifs, and Symbols," SparkNotes, The Power of Ancestral Memory and Primitive Instincts, accessed April 15, 2011, http://www.sparknotes.com/lit/call/themes.html.

About Chuck Balsamo

Chuck and Emily's story is truly amazing! From their distinction of character and quality of family, to their business and ministerial success, Pastor Chuck & Emily Balsamo are graced for this hour.

As a teenager, Chuck picked up many of the business principles and work ethic that would carry him into a future of high achievement. His family purchased a campground when he was just twelve years old, and Chuck became their hardest working employee as he handled reservations, store management, grounds and maintenance, and everything else that came with running a business of this size.

Chuck was married to his childhood sweetheart, Emily, on August 11, 1990. At rock bottom from addictions, godlessness, and a teen pregnancy out of wedlock, the two gave their lives to Christ together on a Sunday night, Feb 17th, 1991, at 10:15 pm while having a conversation over the phone with an old high school friend.

This newfound faith gave Chuck and Emily a strong desire to make a large and lasting difference with their lives!

At the age of 23, Chuck went into business as a real estate agent in Staunton, VA. By the end of their second, full year in real estate, Chuck and Emily had already achieved a six digit income, and it didn't stop there.

Through one-on-one coaching with the number-one real estate coach in the nation, they developed one of the most powerful and profitable residential real estate offices in America! By year four, the Balsamo's were reaching the $250K mark. In year five, at the height of their success—when the business was on track to close 160 sales and earn more than $400K—Chuck and Emily took a giant leap of faith out of business into full-time ministry!

The decision proved to be a good one. In (1999) Murfreesboro North Carolina, Chuck's first two-day "revival meeting" extended for 97 days! In a church of 50 people, 171 guests came to Christ and hundreds more were healed of everything imaginable. From this, doors for ministry opened, filling the calendar with 300 meetings per year—for the next three years!

What started in that revival has never stopped. Chuck and Emily have been to India, Uganda, Ukraine, Dominica, Mexico, and many other parts of the world, where ten thousand people have come to know Christ and thousands more have been changed forever at their meetings and festivals! Chuck is proudly affiliated with the Assemblies of God.

They have a son, Coree, and a daughter, Heaven, who both love Jesus more than anything and both have promising futures. Coree and Heaven are loads of fun, wild pranksters, and dreamers. They love to laugh and make others laugh with them!

The Balsamos never claim perfection. They still have their challenges, setbacks, and failures. They strive to be more like Christ in every way, always giving the credit to God for anything good in them.

The Balsamos have three dogs, a Chihuahua named Chica, Pug named Ming Mi, and a Chug named Lucy. They also have four water gardens and 50 koi fish. They love to hike, run, surf, and travel. They love meeting and getting to know new people. They love their hometown!

Today, Chuck and Emily pastor Destiny Family Center, a vibrant, victorious church in Stuarts Draft, VA. In just a short time, Destiny has become a solid force of local and regional influence, impacting hundreds weekly.

Chuck leads and instructs the Destiny Campus of Life Christian University offering accreditation through the Doctorate level, and advanced ministerial impartation! Chuck currently holds his Master's Degree with LCU and graduates for his Doctorate in June of 2012. He has published his first book of many to come, *Make Me a Legend*, nationally released November 15, 2011.

Chuck blogs at www.ChuckBalsamo.com where he provides humor and inspiration to many worldwide. Visit him in person on most Sundays at Destiny Family Center, or visit him at another church event or conference, or visit him in his very powerful social network (Facebook, Twitter, etc.).

I Want A Million Friends

I want to shake hands with a million people before I die. I want to personally relate in love and partnership with one million people worldwide, to inspire your biggest dreams and boldest actions, and make history with you.

Some will argue that getting to know one million people isn't possible, but when I say, *"personally relate,"* I mean that I want to communicate with you in person, on television, or in my social network—until I have your heart and you have mine, and we all have God's bigger heart together. I feel like this can be done.

If you want the inspiration I'm offering to you, find me on the Internet. Also, come meet me in person at Destiny Family Center or at one of my other speaking events, and remember to reach out your hand so I can shake it!

Even if you don't do anything else, just become my friend on Facebook! It's the fastest and easiest way to relate with people besides meeting face to face.

I pray for my friends and partners every morning, before the sun comes up. I hope you always feel the difference!

Here is my contact information:
Chuck Balsamo
36 Rose Ave
Stuarts Draft VA, 24477
Personal Website: http://www.chuckbalsamo.com
Church Website: http://www.destinyfamilycenter.com
Facebook: http://www.facebook.com/chuckbalsamo
Twitter: http://www.twitter.com/chuckbalsamo
Linkedin: http://linkedin/in/chuckbalsamo
YouTube: http://www.youtube.com/user/chuckbalsamo

In the right hands, This Book will Change Lives!

Most of the people who need this message will not be looking for this book. To change their lives, you need to put a copy of this book in their hands.

> *But others (seeds) fell into good ground, and brought forth fruit, some a hundred-fold, some sixty-fold, some thirty-fold* (Matthew 13:8).

Our ministry is constantly seeking methods to find the good ground, the people who need this anointed message to change their lives. Will you help us reach these people?

> *Remember this—a farmer who plants only a few seeds will get a small crop. But the one who plants generously will get a generous crop* (2 Corinthians 9:6).

EXTEND THIS MINISTRY BY SOWING
3 BOOKS, 5 BOOKS, 10 BOOKS, **OR MORE TODAY**,
AND BECOME A LIFE CHANGER!

Thank you,

Don Nori Sr., Founder
Destiny Image
Since 1982